D1383589

China

Options for Reform in the Grain Sector

The World Bank
Washington, D.C.

Copyright © 1991
The International Bank for Reconstruction
and Development/THE WORLD BANK
1818 H Street, N.W.
Washington, D.C. 20433, U.S.A.

All rights reserved
Manufactured in the United States of America
First printing July 1991

World Bank Country Studies are among the many reports originally prepared for internal use as part of the continuing analysis by the Bank of the economic and related conditions of its developing member countries and of its dialogues with the governments. Some of the reports are published in this series with the least possible delay for the use of governments and the academic, business and financial, and development communities. The typescript of this paper therefore has not been prepared in accordance with the procedures appropriate to formal printed texts, and the World Bank accepts no responsibility for errors.

The World Bank does not guarantee the accuracy of the data included in this publication and accepts no responsibility whatsoever for any consequence of their use. Any maps that accompany the text have been prepared solely for the convenience of readers; the designations and presentation of material in them do not imply the expression of any opinion whatsoever on the part of the World Bank, its affiliates, or its Board or member countries concerning the legal status of any country, territory, city, or area or of the authorities thereof or concerning the delimitation of its boundaries or its national affiliation.

The material in this publication is copyrighted. Requests for permission to reproduce portions of it should be sent to Director, Publications Department, at the address shown in the copyright notice above. The World Bank encourages dissemination of its work and will normally give permission promptly and, when the reproduction is for noncommercial purposes, without asking a fee. Permission to photocopy portions for classroom use is not required, though notification of such use having been made will be appreciated.

The complete backlist of publications from the World Bank is shown in the annual *Index of Publications*, which contains an alphabetical title list (with full ordering information) and indexes of subjects, authors, and countries and regions. The latest edition is available free of charge from the Publications Sales Unit, Department F, The World Bank, 1818 H Street, N.W., Washington, D.C. 20433, U.S.A., or from Publications, The World Bank, 66, avenue d'Iéna, 75116 Paris, France.

ISSN: 0253-2123

Library of Congress Cataloging-in-Publication Data

```
China, options for reform in the grain sector.
        p.   cm. -- (A World Bank country study, ISSN 0253-2123)
    Includes bibliographical references.
    ISBN (invalid) 0-8123-1876-4
    1. Grain trade--Government policy--China.   I. International Bank
for Reconstruction and Development.   II. Series.
HD9046.C62C45   1991
338.1'731'0951--dc20
                                                     91-24700
                                                          CIP
```

ACKNOWLEDGEMENTS

This study was prepared by a World Bank sector study mission which visited China for four weeks in September 1989. The mission was staffed by Messrs. Richard Burcroff II (Task Manager and Economist), Alan Piazza (Assistant Task Manager and Economist), Mohinder Mudahar (Economist), Martin Evans (Agricultural Economist), Philip Judd (Agronomist), Thomas Kerr (Economist), and Vinh Le-si (Systems Analyst). Mr. Yao Xianbin (Agricultural Economist) participated in the mission's work in Washington. During the Bank's internal review process, many valuable comments were received from Messrs. Shahid Javed Burki, Joseph R. Goldberg, Gershon Feder and Odin Knudsen, whose advice is gratefully acknowledged.

Responsibility for coordinating the study on the Chinese side was assigned to the Ministry of Agriculture (MOA), which, through its Department of Policy, Reform and Legal Research, coordinated the mission's visit and organized dissemination of the study report within China. In this connection, special mention should be made of the many contributions by Professor Guo Shutian, Director of the Policy, Reform and Legal Research Department; Mr. Zhang Kaiping, Director of the MOA's Office of External Economic Relations; and Mr. Zhao Hong, Division Chief within the Ministry of Finance's World Bank Department.

The study's findings and recommendations were reviewed with the Chinese Government in an international symposium held in Beijing in January 1991. This version of the study report was revised in light of comments made during the symposium.

OFFICIAL EXCHANGE RATE

Currency Unit = Yuan (¥)

Up to December 15, 1989:

US$	=	¥ 3.72
¥	=	US$0.27

Effective December 16, 1989:

US$	=	¥ 4.72
¥	=	US$0.21

Effective November 17, 1990:

US$	=	¥ 5.22
¥	=	US$0.19

CONVERSIONS

1 jin	=	0.50 kg
1 kg	=	2.00 jin
1 mu	=	0.0667 ha (1/15 ha)
1 ha	=	15.00 mu

ACRONYMS

ABC	–	Agricultural Bank of China
ADF	–	Agricultural Development Fund
AIC	–	Agricultural Inputs Corporation
AmBC	–	Ammonium Bicarbonate
AN	–	Ammonium Nitrate
ANRPI	–	CAAS' Agricultural Natural Resources and Planning Institute
ARPC	–	Agricultural Regional Planning Commission
btkm	–	billion ton-kilometers
CAAS	–	Chinese Academy of Agricultural Sciences
CAS	–	Chinese Academy of Sciences
CATEC	–	County-level Agrotechnical Extension Center
CEROILS	–	China National Cereals, Oils and Foodstuffs Import-Export Corporation
CGIAR	–	Consultative Group for International Agricultural Research
CMPh	–	Fused Calcium Magnesium Phosphate
CPFM	–	Bank's Commodity Price Forecasting Model
CSE	–	Consumer Subsidy Equivalent
DAP	–	Diammonium Phosphate
DRC	–	Domestic Resource Cost
EPC	–	Effective Protection Coefficient
FCR	–	feed conversion ratio
FTC	–	National Foreign Trade Corporation
GB	–	provincial or county level Grain Bureau
GGB	–	General Grain Bureau (national level)
GVAO	–	gross value of agricultural output
IAE	–	CAAS' Institute of Agricultural Economics
ICBC	–	Industrial & Commercial Bank of China
IFDC	–	International Fertilizer Development Center
IME	–	Industrialized Market Economy
KCL	–	Potassium Chloride
MCI	–	Ministry of Chemical Industry
MLYR	–	Middle and Lower Reaches of the Yangtze River
MOA	–	Ministry of Agriculture
MOC	–	Ministry of Commerce
MOF	–	Ministry of Finance
MOFERT	–	Ministry of Foreign Economic Relations and Trade
NMP	–	Net Material Product
MWR	–	Ministry of Water Resources
NPC	–	Nominal Protection Coefficient
PAAS	–	Provincial Academy of Agricultural Sciences
PRS	–	Household Production Responsibility System
PSE	–	Producer Subsidy Equivalent
RCC	–	Rural Credit Cooperative
RCRD	–	Research Center for Rural Development
RSAL	–	Rural Sector Adjustment Loan
SAIC	–	State Administration of Industry and Commerce
SFI	–	Soil and Fertilizer Institute, CAAS
SINOCHEM	–	China National Chemicals Import and Export Corporation
SMC	–	Supply and Marketing Cooperatives
SPB	–	State Price Bureau
SPC	–	State Planning Commission
SSB	–	State Statistical Bureau
SSP	–	Single Superphosphate
SWOPSIM	–	USDA's Static World Policy Simulation Model
trade grain	–	grain with paddy rice and whole millet expressed in milled form
T & V	–	Training and Visit System of Agricultural Extension
TSP	–	Triple Superphosphate
TVEs	–	Township and Village Enterprises
VCR	–	Value Cost Ratio

CHINA

OPTIONS FOR REFORM IN THE GRAIN SECTOR

Table of Contents

vi

Tables in Main Report

Box in Main Report

Annexes

EXECUTIVE SUMMARY

(i)   Frustrated by the inability to raise rural living standards substantially after 30 years of socialist revolution, China initiated in late 1978 its well known rural reforms, which advanced the transformation of agriculture from the precepts of central planning to a market-driven system. In response, the real value of gross output in agriculture doubled between 1978-89, and this was accompanied by a considerable diversification in China's agricultural production and food consumption patterns. Owing tc higher per capita incomes and increasingly urbane preferences, the importance of table grains and low-quality vegetables in the Chinese diet diminished and was supplemented with increased meat intake, a diverse array of fruits and higher quality vegetables, and a distinct preference for higher quality table grains that rarely became available through the state commercial system. Equally important from an international perspective, China is now the world's largest grain producer--the output of grains increased by nearly ⅓ over China's pre-reform levels in 1978-89 /a --and after the USSR and Japan, China has become the World's largest net importer, though imports still account for only 5% of total supply. The country has also become a major exporter of grain derived products, such as live animals, meats and some convenience foods.

(ii) China, in 1991, finds itself at a crossroads in agricultural policy-making. While the considerably less regulated activities in the livestock sector and cash and industrial cropping were responsible for the still commendable growth of 3.5-4.5% p.a. that has been realized in agriculture since 1984, performance in the grain sector has been uneven. It is thus the contention of this report that further liberalization in the grains sector should be the centerpiece of future agricultural reforms.

(iii) <u>The Dimensions of Reform</u>. During the 1990s, China's policy makers will have to grapple with a number of challenges. Strategies must be devised which can:

- maintain the growth of grain output at the rate of 1.5-2.0% p.a., to achieve a level of about 480 million tons by the end of the Century, with the mix being altered somewhat to favor feedgrains and wheat for which demand will be rising rapidly;

- reform the pricing, marketing, inter-provincial distribution and foreign trade in grain and modern agricultural inputs;

- intensify grain sector investment programs, within constraints posed by available resources; and

---

/a   The gains in grain production were from an already high base by standards in other LDCs.

- minimize subsidies and the attendant fiscal burden.

(iv) In this connection, China's own target of 500 million tons, although technically feasible, would be difficult to reach, and in any case given the trend in demand, such a level of grain output might not be necessary. Movements in grain output during 1989-1990 have been very encouraging, and if sustained, place annual production of 480 million tons within reach. Though showing remarkable response to the limited liberalization in the first half of the 1980s, grain production stagnated between 1985-1988, but regained its previous (1984) peak of 407 million tons in 1989. In 1990, assisted by extremely favorable agroclimatic conditions and a massive irrigation repair program, an early estimate of grain output is about 425 million tons. China also was able to reduce consumer subsidies through most of the 1980s, but the fiscal burden surged to new highs in 1989 and 1990 following a glut in grains and the collapse of free market prices. Further progress is called for given the budgetary predicament.

(v) China can remain largely self-sufficient in grains, under the less ambitious (but more realistic) performance possibilities suggested in para (iii) above. However, a shift in foreign trade patterns would be needed to service feedgrain demands in the livestock sector and the growing demand for wheat and wheat products. Under more liberalized marketing and foreign trade policies, China would shift from being a net exporter of maize and soybeans to a net importer in order to service domestic demands for feed grains. This would be balanced in part by net exports of rice.

(vi) <u>Priorities in the Grain Sector</u>. If agricultural efficiency (and efficiency in the grain sector) is to be the objective for agricultural reform in the first half of the 1990s, the feasibility of official grain production targets should be revisited, as well as the host of administrative interventions being programmed of late to achieve these targets. The "material balances" approach towards inter-regional grain transfers, the allocation of fertilizers, and the design of grain and fertilizer import programs needs revision. This should be followed by a longer-term but comprehensive program to strengthen the policy, institutional and infrastructural underpinnings needed to allow markets to play a far larger role in the grain sector. The program must encompass both grain and inputs pricing reforms, while in parallel taking the necessary measures (initially, through administrative means) to redirect public expenditures and farmer savings towards quickly gestating investments in agricultural and on-farm infrastructure and, within China's agroindustrial complex, investments to modernize grain handling and distribution capabilities. Equally important, future reforms in the agroindustrial complex should aim for a progressive diminution of monopoly powers inherent in the state-owned commercial system's control and management of the internal marketing and foreign trade in grains and for key inputs such as chemical fertilizers. These proposals are spelled out in greater detail below.

(vii) Perhaps the most important unfinished business in the grain sector concerns the unfinished state of China's **pricing and marketing reforms**. These need to be resumed starting with the reform of official pricing and an expansion of public investment to improve the technical efficiency of the state-owned grain distribution system, followed by price liberalization and measures to promote competition. While adopting this reform, care will have to be taken to insure that the array of official urban sales prices (and by extension, the price of "rural resales") are increased in absolute terms at least by amounts corresponding to the increases in official procurement prices. Otherwise, the net financial outlay needed to deliver subsidized grain to urban ration card recipients will also increase. To prepare for a more complete liberalization perhaps two or three years from now, it is recommended that the Chinese government

- accelerate its potentially far-reaching new program to establish national and provincial wholesale markets for grain, refine pricing mechanisms and broaden participation in these markets; and

- identify institutional, legal, regulatory and other measures needed to break the General Grain Bureau's (GGBs) effective monopoly in grain distribution.

The *modus operandi* of the GGB should also be adjusted, towards that normally associated with grain market regulation: maintaining strategic stockpiles, price stabilization, seasonal procurement and disposal to mitigate regional gluts and shortage, emergency relief and subsidized transfers to chronically poor and remote areas. Meanwhile, enterprises outside of the state commercial system should be permitted to enter the grain trade in order to gain experience. Later, the more successful firms could be invited to participate in divestiture programs, should government decide to withdraw the GGB from its current superordinate position in the internal grain distribution system, and be encouraged to invest in their own marketing capacities.

(viii) A necessary component must be a thorough recasting of the **urban ration sales system**. Since market prices for grain in China's free markets have fallen precipitously due to record production in 1989 and 1990, China should seize the moment to raise urban ration prices and reduce per capita allocations in order to reduce the subsidy burden without causing too much hardship for the urban poor. The large overhang of monetized grain ration coupons must be sterilized and gradually eliminated (by one estimate, these were equivalent in value to 20 million tons of grain in 1988), dates of expiration need to be announced and enforced on newly issued coupons. Doing so would cause minimum hardship to most of the eligible recipients. It should be replaced by a system which will identify and target the urban poor which could be administered through the existing ration shops. The most direct means would be to reduce or eliminate the ration allotment to higher income households. Other possible measures include the closure of ration shops in higher income neighborhoods and the restriction of subsidized sales to inferior grades of rice and wheat, and to less preferred grains (for table use) such as corn.

(ix) Reform of the pricing and distribution of **agricultural inputs** could commence with the phasing out of the fertilizer distribution subsidies (higher grain procurement prices will compensate), the linking of fertilizer distribution with compulsory grain procurement abolished, and China's brief experiment with liberalized fertilizer marketing during the mid-1980s reinstituted (which mainly involved locally manufactured, low analysis fertilizers). A similar effort should be initiated to improve the allocation of higher analysis fertilizers, though unlike grains, the phasing of fertilizer pricing and marketing reforms must accommodate the continuing shortage of high-analysis fertilizers in China and be implemented even more carefully to prevent an erosion of farmers purchasing power. Plan prices for the centrally managed stocks and imports should be increased to achieve some parity with international prices, and the regional allocation criteria simplified in a manner that would tend to make fertilizers more available to crops having high production and income earning potential. In this connection, after geographic allocations have been determined, perhaps the higher analysis fertilizers could be auctioned off to the farming population, which might achieve a kind of "second-best" efficiency, and also augment revenues.

(x) To prepare for a longer-term reform of China's bifurcated and still highly administered fertilizer distribution system, the creation of new channels should be encouraged, perhaps by allowing China's burgeoning rural cooperative enterprise sector and other non-state agricultural marketing concerns to enter the fertilizer trade. Initially, these new channels could be utilized to provide more depth to the existing official network at the retail level, and expanded geographical coverage. Over the longer-term, as the availability of high-analysis fertilizers becomes better aligned with demand (and the need for rationing subsides), these kinds of non-state agents should also be encouraged to enter into the marketing of fertilizers at the wholesale level, lifting product directly from manufacturers and importers for resale to locales and farmers in accord with market pricing signals. /b

(xi) In the realm of seeds policy, urgent attention should be given to research priorities, and to constraints on the marketing of certified seeds, which serve to inhibit the importation, adaptation and dissemination of the superior germ plasm available mainly in the international market place for seeds. /c It is recommended that additional budgetary resources be allocated during the Eighth Five Year Plan period, to upgrade the scientific and technical capabilities of research staff; increase the availability of foreign scientific and technical publications; and finance a substantial increase in the exchange of germ plasm and scientific information with international crop research institutes within the CGIAR network.

(xii) To gain ready access to the high potential germ plasm offered in international markets, China should minimize the regulation of seeds research to only the minimum required to maintain research standards and the purity of new lines and varieties. Enabling legislation and supporting regulations should be introduced, of the kind needed to assure prospective joint venture

---

/b The report also recommends that the Chinese government review its goals to achieve complete self-sufficiency in the production of nitrogenous and phosphatic fertilizers by the Year 2000. The analysis shows that a balance between investment in additional production capacity and increased imports would be a more economic way to service projected consumption requirements.

/c China's research personnel have remained isolated from many of the striking developments in the past two decades, eg. in maize, soybeans and wheat, that could profitably be used to extend the production of these crops in the Central and Southern rice production zones, and thus help realign the commodity composition of domestic grain production with internal demand.

partners that proprietary interests (so-called "breeders rights") will be
honored. /d Plant quarantine regulations should be simplified and recast in a
way which would facilitate the timely release of quality seed imports from
quarantine and reduce the scope for an arbitrary interpretation of the
regulations. Lastly, to underpin the commercial viability of China's seed
industry and potential joint venture arrangements, it will be necessary to
allow some flexibility in the pricing of seeds released by the National and
Provincial Seeds Corporations, and by other (registered) entities which might
become involved in the marketing of superior seeds. Increased seed prices
would be more than compensated for grain procurement prices raised to more
realistic levels.

(xiii)   The state's continued close administration and dominant share in the
interprovincial grain trade perpetuate substantial economic and social costs.
Constraints to interprovincial trade necessitate excessive and expensive
central government grain stocks, which are estimated to have averaged about 87
million tons annually during the 1980s. Inflexible distribution planning in
the context of annual plans, aggravated by transportation constraints, have
driven operating costs markedly upwards. Price distortions depress incentives
in surplus production areas to sell grain to deficit areas, and, in
combination with the fungibility of urban ration coupons and constraints on
the internal transfer of maize and other feed grains from North China, have
encouraged surplus rice producers in the Yangtze basin and South-and-Southwest
China to feed large quantities of high cost rice to swine and poultry.
Additionally, supplying grain to poor and mountainous areas appears to be a
relatively low priority. Key reforms should include the phased elimination of
administrative barriers to interprovincial trade and of transfer pricing, the
reduction of operating costs through a scaling down of excessive central
government stocks and GGB planned trade, and the large scale expansion of
private and collective free market trade. As interprovincial trade moves from
planned trade at administered prices toward market determined flows during the
1990s, the role of the GGB could be shifted to systems programming and
regulation (para xii).

(xiv)   Additional gains could accrue were China to shift from the current
annual planning of **foreign trade in grains** to a longer term but more flexible
horizon. At present, the grain trade is a reserved monopoly for the state's
foreign trade corporations (FTCs), which operate on the basis of annually
established import and export targets. /e Sometimes trade is negotiated
bilaterally, other times the state-owned parastatals lift (or place) grains
directly and oft-times unexpectedly in foreign markets. China's FTCs as an
initial step should be encouraged to sign medium-term contracts or at least
issue letters of intent to selected foreign suppliers for core amounts of
grain imports and exports (else hedge in international commodity markets),
thereby assuring lower expected prices for grain imports and a smoother--
likely higher--progression of f.o.b. prices for its grain exports. Over the

---

/d   The British and Turkish regulations may provide a useful referent.

/e   The targeted amount of grain imports is closely linked to expected movements in China's
overall balance of foreign trade, i.e. to the mandates of foreign exchange rationing rather than in
response to developments in China's comparative advantages.

longer-term, however, the real gains would come from decentralizing the management of China's foreign trade in grains. The FTCs are simply unable to respond quickly enough to changing circumstances, neither passing through gains from exporting to Chinese producers nor adjusting their import and export programs readily to seasonal changes in China's internal grain situation. The analysis also shows that for a given allocation of foreign exchange, it would be more economic for China to import fertilizer than wheat, since the application of fertilizer with value equivalent to one ton of wheat can result in 3.5-6.0 tons of additional wheat output.

(xv) While there is growing acceptance by policy researchers in China that a structural deficit in grain supply is likely to be the long-term trend, the prioritization and programming of **public agricultural investment** has fallen hostage to the devolution of fiscal responsibility. Recent moves to reverse the declining trend in real agricultural investment should be reinforced. By any criteria, both macroeconomic and sectoral, agriculture has a legitimate claim on a higher share of the state's investment budget than the low level to which it had fallen in the late 1980s. Meeting future agricultural and grain sector growth requirements will depend critically on increases in both cropping intensity and in yields on existing cultivated land, and on improvements in the quality of production. The key to realizing these goals will be the rehabilitation and repair of irrigation and drainage networks in the water scarce production zones of North China. (It is estimated that some 10-15 million ha. of cultivated area require drainage facilities to prevent waterlogging, reduce salinization and arrest tendencies towards declining grain yields.) In the early 1980s, the average area actually irrigable fell short of the official total area in one year out of four, due to water shortage. Apart from a crash program in Winter 1989/90 to repair part of the irrigation infrastructure, it is unlikely that much improvement was realized during the second half of the 1980s, thus the economics of major new expansion on existing and reclaimed lands are questionable when compared with simpler rehabilitation and on-farm works.

(xvi) Particular priority should also be given to an expansion of agricultural research activities, the strengthening of agricultural extension to accelerate the transfer of relevant technology to farmers, and reestablishing effective links between agricultural research, extension and education at the national, provincial and county levels. A prime investment priority should thus be to upgrade China's agricultural research complex. At least a doubling of annual expenditures would appear justified, which would bring China's total expenditures on agricultural research in line with nearby Asian countries. Within the technology diffusion nexus, problems in the new extension system (grounded in county-level agrotechnology centers) and its financing have yet to be worked out. So far, less than one third of the counties have established agrotechnical extension centers, and fully 20% are still not served by even a rudimentary extension program.

(xvii) In an effort to augment local resources for the construction of water control and other rural infrastructure, the state in mid-1989 announced the reimposition of mass mobilization policies and additional taxation from irrigated agriculturalists. Since a considerable cess already is levied on farm households in China through compulsory grain procurement, water user

charges in irrigated areas, and the burden of local "extractions" (taxation)
to finance village services, it would seem, rather, that the correct priority
for reasserting administrative means would be in the milieux of investment
programing and its financing: largely by having the state claw-back some of
the authority to set and monitor expenditure priorities, previously devolved,
in order to redirect same towards agricultural investment. /f

(xviii) The disturbing trend towards some recollectivization--implicit in the
new grain policy framework--also is manifested in official frustration with
the slow pace of **private on-farm investment**. A policy option that is currently
being implemented in some of the "grain base" counties calls for the reversion
to county and township government of farmers rights acquired under the PRS.
The aim is to promote land consolidation, larger sized farms (i.e. 20 ha.) and
farm mechanization, and to provide a mechanism for enforcing the state's grain
procurement objectives. The economic rationale for consolidation cum
mechanization is grounded in a belief that grain production is imbued with
scale economies, otherwise denied in smallholder agriculture. That
fragmentation is an issue, having deleterious effects on both investment and
productivity, few would deny. But since the scope of the program could
eventually encompass 20 million ha. of agricultural land (over 20% of the
total), the Government of China would be well advised to first review the
(doubtful) validity of the scale-economies proposition as means for
stimulating grain production, then consider less draconian alternatives such
as those underway in the Meitan, Guizhou and Pingdu, Shandong experimental
zones which have been designed to improve farm structure and stimulate on-
farm investment.

(xix) Related is a growing perception of tenurial insecurity, which recent
studies suggest might be having an adverse impact on farmer investment in
agriculture. Reversing this perception may hold the key for redirecting farm
household savings towards long-term investment in land improvements and on-
farm infrastructure. However, a more flexible and secure system of
agricultural land use rights may have to be introduced first. Again, the
Meitan and Pingdu experiments may offer useful lessons. However, research that
would enlarge the information base would be highly desirable.

(xx) Financial Implications. The state has established a very ambitious
program for the long-term development of the grain sector, which raises
questions about the adequacy and availability of financing. A long-term
planning exercise carried out for the grain sector in 1988 estimated that
average annual expenditures in 1988 prices of some ¥ 250 billion (all sources)
will be required between 1988-2000 to reach the target of 500-520 million tons
of grain by the Year 2000. An average annual expenditure of ¥ 15.0 billion is
projected for water resource and land reclamation investments alone, which
would represent more than a 200% increase over total state agricultural
investment (i.e. investment by the central and provincial governments) in
1988. During the period of the Eighth Five Year Plan period (1991-1995), the

---

/f   In this connection, the central government must somehow forge a political consensus with
provincial and local governmental units about the necessity for allocating additional local (as well
as state) budgetary resources to agricultural programs.

MWR expects that government spending on water resources development can be increased from the current level of ¥ 7 billion annually to ¥ 8 billion (at 1988 prices), which would represent only about half of the annual volume of investment identified in the long-term planning exercise. Investments required to achieve the mission's grain production projections (para iii) also were estimated, using crude incremental capital-output ratios that were constructed from a review of staff appraisal reports for agricultural projects in China, and an assumed gestation period of 5 years. Though derived by an entirely different methodology, the projected annual requirement (equivalent to ¥ 18.7 billion in 1988 prices) is remarkably similar to the annual requirement for water resource infrastructure and land reclamation in the grain sector that was derived in the government's long-term planning exercise. The mission's estimate is associated with projected real growth in grain production of 1.9% p.a. While lower, and grounded in production responses to liberalized pricing, internal marketing and foreign trade, these results are in the neighborhood of the implied official estimates of the growth in grain production of 2.0-2.3% p.a. that will be needed to produce 500-520 million tons by the Year 2000. Thus, the order of magnitude estimated by the government is probably the minimum investment required between 1988-2000 to attain the government's long-term grain production target.

(xxi) The government's planning assumptions give cause for concern, especially on the sourcing side of the ledger. Particularly suspect are the farmer savings estimates, which are projected to provide more than 60% of the total resources needed. The implicit planning assumptions in the above exercise: of a sustained 30% rate of farmer savings; that farmers could earn enough from an increased specialization in low valued cropping (i.e. grains) to sustain these rates; and that agricultural activities writ large will provide attractive alternative opportunities for direct farmer investment in areas where township and village enterprises have taken off; should be reexamined and carefully reconsidered before grain sector development programs and expenditure plans are fixed.

(xxii) A more viable investment strategy would emphasize quickly-gestating investments having a high payback. Such are available in the agricultural sector, in the form of irrigation/drainage systems repair and rehabilitation works, especially in the fertile but water deficient areas of North China. Grain production increases of 15.0-22.5 million tons could be associated with these kinds of investments. Though rehabilitation works typically gestate quickly, often within during the same year that implementation begins, the overall financing requirement will not be small in comparison with present state investment allocations for agricultural development. For example, should only 10 million ha. ultimately be rehabilitated, at a unit cost of say ¥ 1500 per ha. (US$317), a total investment of ¥ 15 billion would be required. However, if implemented during the Eighth Five Year Plan period in lieu of some of the larger projects in the MWR's more capital intensive and longer gestating investment program, the rehabilitation work could be completed within 3-4 years. Equally important, it could be financed well within the resource envelope government has identified for MWR's program, while minimizing the requirement for additional taxes and contributions from the rural population, or resource transfers from the "urban" sectors.

(xxiii) Grain production benefitted from unusually favorable agroclimatic conditions in 1989 and 1990. It is thus of utmost importance that the Chinese government does not permit itself to be lulled by the recent good harvests into further postponing grain sector reform and delaying investment and related revenue raising efforts. If refined and implemented in the near future, we believe the proposed reforms would considerably improve the efficiency of grain production, marketing and foreign trade, while reducing the adverse fiscal consequences imbued in present arrangements. These would also set the stage for the ultimate conversion of both the grain sector and agriculture as a whole to a largely self-financed, market driven sector.

(xxiv) <u>Postscript</u>. Following the review of this report with the Chinese authorities, the Government of China revised its grain production estimates for 1990 upwards again to 435 million tons as more accurate assessments began to flow in from the provinces. On May 1, 1991, the Government announced major upwards adjustments in both the prices of urban ration grain sales, between 50 and 200%, and the pricing of interprovincial transfers. It also prohibited sales in the future of higher quality grains through urban ration shops, took steps to reduce urban per capita ration allotments for the remaining grains, and gave provinces the general authority to restrict or abolish the use of outstanding ration coupons. Several major provinces (eg. Shandong and Guangdong) have already done so. Principles were also enunciated to guide and accelerate the development of regional wholesale markets, which are intended to initially supplement and ultimately replace the system of planned distribution which still predominates in China's grain sector.

(xxv) Genuine political courage was required to adopt these policies as urban ration prices were increased on May 1 for the first time in over two decades. Considerable skill was required to minimize disruption, as the burden is falling largely on China's vocal and politically influential urban population. On both counts, the Government of China deserves very high marks. While implementing these reforms, it has succeeded in convincing ration recipients of the over-riding needs to reduce the burden of consumer subsidies, and, over time, to wean the grain distribution system from State direction and support. The Government has also let it be known that additional price adjustments can be expected in the comparatively near future to allow parallel increases in farmer procurement prices without exacerbating budgetary pressures. It is thus conceivable that by the end of the Eight Five Year Plan period (1995), the role of market mediation in China's all-important and ever-sensitive grain sector may attain a status comparable to the use of market forces in the less regulated, higher-valued, agricultural activities. In doing so, China will have accomplished the transition to market determined distribution for nearly all of its agricultural commodities, leaving behind at last that untenable position, midway between plan and market, where the grain sector has been marooned since the mid-1980s.

I. DEVELOPMENTS IN CHINESE AGRICULTURE SINCE 1979

A. INTRODUCTION.

1.01   The Declining Relative Importance of Agriculture. 1/ For much of the period since the Chinese Revolution economic growth has been reasonably rapid, albeit from a very low base. According to official statistics, national income measured at constant prices rose at an average annual rate of 6.0% between 1952-1978, or at 4.0% p.a. in per capita terms. During the first decade of the economic reforms begun in December 1978, economic growth has been spectacular. Official estimates show real income to have risen in 1978-1984 at 8.3% per year (7.1% per capita), and even faster between 1984-1987 at 10.5% per year. So despite a higher population growth rate in the mid-1980s, real per capita incomes rose by at least 9.0% p.a. This is well above any other large country's performance during that period and more than twice the Bank's estimate for China's per capita income growth before the reforms were introduced.

Table 1.1   China--Sectoral Composition of NMP/GDP, 1949-1989 /a

(Percent share at current prices)

	Agriculture	Industry	Services
1949	68	13	19
1952	58	20	22
1957	47	28	25
1962	48	33	19
1967	47	34	19
1972	38	44	18
1978	33	49	18
1981	38	47	15
1984	40	45	16
1985	35	45	20
1986	34	45	20
1987	34	46	20
1988	32	46	21

/a   Table contains rounding errors. Figures reported for 1949-1972 refer to sectoral shares of Net Material Product (NMP); thereafter to GDP. NMP differs from GDP in that some services are not included in NMP. Also, by Chinese recording convention, agriculture includes some industrial production (sideline activities) by farm households.

Source: World Bank (1990g), Table 11

1.02   As indicated in Table 1.1 the structure of China's economy has been adjusting away from agriculture while its comparative advantages in international trade have moved from primary products towards labor intensive manufactures. Agriculture's contribution to GDP fell from about 2/3 to 1/3 during the first three decades following Liberation, while industry almost

---

1/   Materials in paras 1.01-1.02 are drawn from Anderson (1990).

quadrupled its share of national income from what in 1949 was only one eighth. Beginning in 1979, the share of agriculture was boosted substantially following large increases in producer prices during the early 1980s, introduction of the Household Production Responsibility System (PRS), freeing of rural markets and rapid growth in the supply of chemical fertilizers. But since the mid-1980s the share of agriculture has resumed a downward slide, and now (1988), at 32%, is near what would be observed internationally for the country's per capita income and size. 2/ The extent of the decline in the share of agricultural products in China's exports was even more marked. Prior to the 1970s, more than half of all exports came from agriculture. Since 1970, the composition of exports has changed dramatically. By 1988, agriculture's share was only 21%. The counterpoint to this rapid decline is the relatively fast growth that occurred in industrial and services production and employment, and in non-agricultural exports.

1.03   Self-sufficiency in Foods.   The longer run decline in China's earnings from agricultural exports has not altered the fact that the country remains essentially self-sufficient in staple foods, but it has meant that the self-sufficiency ratios have shown a moderate decline since the 1970s. 3/ Grain self-sufficiency fell from 102% in 1970-74 to 94% in 1985-1986 and has since remained at about that level. Part of the decline has been because of the rapid increase in effective demand for wheat and livestock products. While these comparatively small declines in agricultural self-sufficiency might seem minor, the direction of change is towards more import dependence, a trend exacerbated by rising incomes, China's growing population, and limited land endowment. Because China's shares in world production and consumption have become so large, changes in China's self-sufficiency ratios have had profound effects on international markets, which could become even more profound during the 1990s, a point taken up in Chapter II.

B. FROM PLAN TO MARKET IN AGRICULTURE

-The Legacy of Central Planning

1.04   During 1949, one of the major economic problems faced by the national leaders was to find ways to feed the Chinese population of 540 million. As part of the "socialist transformation" of the agriculture sector initiated in the early-1950s, the Chinese government imposed material balances planning, which encompassed administered producer and consumer prices for most crops and the monopolization of the procurement and distribution of grain, vegetable oil, cotton and other industrial crops. The state-run agricultural procurement and distribution system 4/ quickly replaced private trade and has provided the urban population with the bulk of its staple food requirements at nearly constant prices since the early-1950s.

2/ World Bank (1990g), Table 12.

3/ World Bank (1990g), Table 18.

4/ Also referred to as the "state commercial system" and "state trading system".

1.05 Forty years later in 1989 the population had doubled and the economy has made significant progress in many sectors. Despite spectacular gains in agricultural development, however, one of the major policy concerns continues to be methods for assuring an adequate supply of basic food for the urban population, the rural industrial labor force and cash and commercial crop farmers. In reality, this is an adequacy being measured against a rapidly rising scale, now well above minimum nutritional norms, but accompanied of late by unfamiliar fluctuating prices (in free markets) for the higher quality grains that no longer make their way through the state commercial system. 5/

1.06 The economic reforms started in the late 1970s decollectivized agricultural production and introduced the PRS in place of the old labor-day work payment system. During the first half of the 1980s, agricultural gross output value (GVAO) expanded at more than double the rate of the previous 25 years. Grain production increased in volume on average by 2.1% p.a. (1979-1989), or about 30% faster than before. However, the expansion in the first years of the reform was considerably more rapid than in later years--grain production increased by 4.2% per annum in 1979-84, but stagnated thereafter (with large annual fluctuations) between 1984-1989.

1.07 Until the peak harvest of 1990 (about 425 million tons), 1984 and 1989 were benchmark years for the grain sector 6/ when production reached previous highs of about 407 million tons. As a result of the progressive decollectivization of farming, markedly increased producer prices, and a 130% increase in fertilizer nutrient application since 1979, China found itself in 1984 with surpluses which exceeded the State's storage and distribution capabilities. In 1985, the State procurement system for agricultural products underwent a major change and prices of competing crops were raised substantially or set free. As a result of these policies, grain production fell in 1985 to 371 million tons, and--excepting 1990's harvest, which responded to extraordinarily favorable weather--has fluctuated since then between 391-407 million tons (cf. Table 2.1).

1.08 Although the PRS greatly decentralized agricultural production

---

5/ A long standing objective is to attain and maintain self-sufficiency in grain production. The figure of 450-475 kg/cap/year of unprocessed grain (400 kg or more of milled grain), which is considerably higher than China's peak year consumption of 394 kg/cap in 1984, has become planners' datum for Year 2000, with a longer-term target of 600 kg early in the 21st Century. China has been largely successful in achieving self-sufficiency in most grains and animal products, though with some deterioration in recent years. In the wake of decollectivization, however, there has been a growing imbalance between the commodity composition of grain production, a rapidly increasing demand for feed grains, and a fairly flat demand for table grains, much of which reportedly is being diverted to supplemental feeding of animals.

6/ The definition of grain in China differs from the internationally accepted definition. In China, grain is defined to include wheat, paddy rice, corn, soybean, sorghum, millet, barley, oats and other crops such as beans, peas, other pulses, buckwheat and potatoes. Potatoes are converted to a dry-weight basis by using 5:1 conversion ratio. Paddy rice is converted to milled rice by using 0.7 milling rate conversion factor. All the grain production data in China is reported by including rice in the form of paddy rice. On the other hand, grain consumption is reported as trade grain in which rice is included as milled rice. Lastly, the government estimates of grain used as food are slightly lower than those reported in this paper since the latter also include grain losses, wastage and industrial use.

decisions, the state still intervenes through a host of mechanisms, including (a) procurement policies and marketing arrangements for most staple foods which are preponderantly under state ownership or control, (b) input distribution policies that are tied to grain procurement policies, (c) subsidized grain consumption policies, primarily for urban residents, (d) restrictions on the inter-provincial movement of grains, and (e) state administration and management of China's foreign trade in grains. Market sales have been increasing during the 1980s, but in the grain sector they are limited mainly to rural areas and sales to government at negotiated prices. At present, farmers only sell about 2, 7 and 18% of their food grains, oil crops and pork production on the open market. The economic reforms of the 1980s have promoted the rapid expansion of free market trade in vegetables, fruits, animal and other agricultural products, but the state-run trading system remains by far the most important supplier of wage goods to urban consumers.

-Reform in the 1980s

1.09 _Price Reform_. Apart from the PRS, the most important policy change introduced by the government at the beginning of the reforms was the adjustment of procurement prices for major crops. Before the reform, two distinct prices, quota prices and above-quota prices, existed in the state commercial system. Quota prices applied to crops sold by the collectivized production units in fulfillment of procurement obligations; above-quota prices to crops sold in excess of the obligation. Announced at the end of 1978 and effective in 1979, quota prices were increased 20.9% for grain, 23.9% for oil crops, 17% for cotton, 21.9% for sugar crops and 24.3% for pigs. In addition, the premium paid on the above-quota delivery of grain and oil crops was raised from 30% to 50% of the quota price, and a 30% bonus was instituted for above-quota delivery of cotton. 7/ Thus, the average total increase for the state procurement prices was 22.1%. However, if only the marginal prices, that is the above-quota prices, are considered, the increase in the state procurement prices was 40.7%. 8/

1.10 Corresponding to the increase in procurement prices, the administered sales prices at the retail level were raised 33% for pork, 32% for eggs and 33% for marine and aquatic products in 1979; however, the domestic sale prices of feed grains and the main staple foods--table grains and edible oils--were not changed. To compensate for the increase in retail-level prices of non-staple foods, each registered urban resident received ¥ 5-8 per month. State and municipal outlays for price subsidies increased substantially in the early 1980s when procurement at above-quota prices increased sharply as a share of total procurement. 9/ As a way to reduce the state's financial burden and increase the role of markets, the mandatory quotas for commodities subject to administered procurement were temporarily abolished, for cotton in 1984 and

---

7/ For a detailed chronology of price changes in 1979 and thereafter, see Sicular (1988a).

8/ World Bank (1990g), Table 2.

9/ The financial burden became especially difficult to bear when an unexpected output growth of both staples and non-staples began to emerge in 1982. Consumer price subsidies alone increased from ¥ 9.4 billion in 1978 to ¥ 37 billion in 1984, from 8.4% of the state budget to 24.6%.

grains in 1985, and replaced by procurement contracts (and withdrawal of the state guarantee to purchase above-"contract" deliveries) which were supposed to be negotiated between units of the state's commercial system and farmers. The reference price for contract procurements was a weighted average between the previous quota price and above quota prices. However, contract amounts were to be subject to negotiation. An immediate effect of the change was a 9.2% decline in the price margin paid to farmers. Following the resultant decline in production in 1985 and stagnation thereafter, the "contracts" were made mandatory again in 1986 (Sicular 1988a).

1.11 <u>Market Reforms</u>. Parallel with price reform, a markedly greater role was given to markets, in place of planning, for guiding agricultural production and marketing decisions. This new tolerance for market-guided resource allocation was felt especially and immediately after the reforms were introduced in cash and export crops sectors, but much less so in grains. Because state grain procurement prices had been artificially depressed at even lower levels prior to the reforms than today, the more grain an area exported to other regions in China, the more loss it incurred. Provinces with a comparative advantage in grain production were thus reluctant to raise the level of grain output. On the other hand, local communes were often forced to expand the area sown to grains at the expense of higher-valued cash crops, often resulting in net losses to the communes and member farmers. The loss of regional comparative advantage was especially serious in areas traditionally dependent on the inter-regional trade in grains to facilitate a prior specialization in cash and industrial crops and pasture-based animal husbandry (eg. North China). National self-sufficiency thus had degenerated into regional self-sufficiency by the time the reforms were introduced.

1.12 The inefficiency of this structure of grain production was admitted by the leadership at the inception of the reforms. Subsequent decisions to increase grain imports, reduce procurement quotas, and reduce the number of commodities subject to production targets and administered procurement aimed to rationalize grain production. Restrictions on the inter-regional trade in agricultural products by private traders were also loosened. As a result of these and the procurement price reforms, the production and intensification of both grains and cash crops expanded markedly between 1979-1984, with much of the change in cropping pattern being in accord with regional comparative advantage. 10/ Moreover, the pattern of agricultural production began to diversify in favor of higher-valued non-grains. For example, the area sown to cash and industrial crops increased from 9.6% of total sown hectarage in 1978 to 13.4% in 1984. The climax of the marketing reform was the State Council's declaration after a record grain harvest in 1984, that the state would no longer establish mandatory procurement plans in agriculture, and that mandatory procurement quotas were to be replaced by the aforementioned procurement contracts between the state and farmers for commodities still subject to planned production and distribution. As a result of these adjustments, the value of agricultural output still increased at the respectable rate of 3.4% in 1985. The expansion in animal husbandry and aquatic products was even faster. Nevertheless, the physical output of grains

---

10/ World Bank (1990c, 1990e).

declined by 6.9%, which was the first pronounced decline in this sector since the reforms were introduced.

-Response and Reaction

1.13 The market oriented reforms aroused ideological anxiety from the very beginning. Concerns over loss of control were widely reported after 1978 (Sicular 1988a), but in the face of the unprecedented production increases between 1979-1984, the pro-market segment of the leadership was able to deepen the marketing reforms for most agricultural commodities. However, when the growth rates slowed from the unprecedentedly high levels of the early 1980s, and grain production tapered off in 1985 and thereafter, the government retreated from the near total market liberalization announced earlier. Through Party injunctions to guarantee state procurements of grains from 1986 onwards, the voluntary procurement contract was again made mandatory and administrative intervention in production and in the market has been increasing. Facing stagnation in grain production since 1984 (the 1989 crop was slightly larger than 1984's, but yields were lower in spite of a focussing of the state's agricultural support programs on grain production in 1989), the state's monopoly on foreign trade in grains and the inter-regional distribution of grains and fertilizers was reinstituted in 1989.

1.14   With the remarkable diversification of agricultural and off-farm opportunities made possible by the reforms, the period since 1979 has seen a comparatively rapid decline in the importance of grains as a source of rural income. An even more profound reduction in the significance of table grains in the urban consumption bundle also occurred, which bears directly on premises behind the current perception of crisis. While the official statistics are less than revealing, the State Statistical Bureau's (SSB's) consumer-expenditure surveys, various informal surveys and anecdotal evidence suggest that consumers have substituted high quality produce and meat products for table grains, as these became increasingly available after 1979.

1.15 The events of 1985-1988 were revealing in another way. The Government tried twice, in 1986 and again in 1988, to stimulate grain production and markedly scale down its urban consumption subsidies. The mechanisms used were hikes in producer prices and a combination of official price increases to the food and feed industries and further decontrol of internal grain marketing. Three lessons emerged. The expected supply response to price indeed materialized. But also, that considerably more investment in (a) the repair and rehabilitation of China's irrigation and drainage infrastructure is needed, parts of which have fallen into disrepair since the reforms were introduced and local public expenditure priorities shifted to revenue earning activities, and (b) the development of alternative channels to the State-owned distribution system will be required for the "market" to work as a resource allocation mechanism.

-Areas of Limited Reform

1.16 While the reforms outlined in the preceding paragraphs address impor-tant aspects of the agricultural economy, progress in other policy areas during the 1980s was restricted, thus maintaining a considerable degree of inefficiency. Principal among these are China's interventions in agricultural foreign trade, incomplete liberalization of the land market, constraints on labor mobility and the nonmarket production and allocation of material inputs such as fertilizers.

1.17 Foreign Trade. Excluding changes in stocks, China's grain supply (cf. Table 2.1 of the main report) steadily increased until 1984, then declined. With the exception of 1984 and 1985, however, China has been a net importer of grain. Though quantities have been large relative to total world trade, the contribution of net grain imports to total supply has never exceeded 3.9% (in 1981), which had fallen to 2.0% by 1988.

1.18 During the 1980s, China's agricultural foreign trade continued to be highly administered, showing large real distortions between domestic and border prices for the more important traded commodities 11/. As a result, tremendous economic rents are accruing to the state in the exporting of rice and, possibly, also in corn. Similarly, significant economic subsidies are being absorbed in the importation and marketing of imported wheat and corn. This picture is corroborated by international comparison. While grain consumers in the industrial market economies bear high taxes, urban consumers in China enjoy substantial subsidization. The Chinese pattern is similar to many low income developing countries that subsidize consumers and tax producers, though the magnitudes of taxation and subsidies appear to be much higher in China.

1.19 Factor Markets. The PRS in China provides farmers with a 15 to 30 year land lease. As long as local authorities refrain from tampering with these contracts, farmers will have an adequate sense of tenure security and a fairly long planning horizon for many types of farm investments. However, the land leases are not inheritable, and until recently were not transferable among farmers by sublease or by sale, neither were they mortgageable. The constitution was amended in April 1988 to authorize and legalize the transfer of land use rights. However, implementing policies, regulations and administrative mechanisms to actually facilitate a land market have only been promulgated in May 1990, and not yet been initiated. The inability to conduct land transactions has obvious adverse implications for efficiency. The constraint is especially harmful given the high degree of fragmentation and the extremely small size of farms in many areas of China. A land market would facilitate voluntary consolidation. It will also enable a reallocation of land to those who have higher productivity, or fewer alternatives to agricultural production.

1.20 In the wake of decollectivization and the stunning growth in off-farm employment that ensued, China's "floating population" burgeoned. The traditional destinations of the migratory work force shifted away from China's frontier provinces towards the rapidly growing coastal areas and major metropolitan areas. By some estimates, the migratory work force now includes some 50-60 million people. However, in an effort to limit growth of a

---

11/ The administration of China's foreign grain trade is discussed in Annex 1, para 30. See Annex 2 for a review of China's performance in the international grain trade.

marginalized urban population so characteristic of other developing countries, the Government of China has not formally authorized these movements. The result is that the work force is being channeled into seasonal and temporary work thereby having little real effect on the "mainstream" urban labor markets and perhaps use of more efficient factor proportions, while in parts of rural China where shortages of agricultural labor are appearing (again, in the dynamic coastal provinces and peri-urban environs), local governments are introducing farm mechanization programs since access to agricultural land is constrained by rigid requirements on land leasing and other forms of transfer, in which only local households can legally obtain rights to farm.

1.21   Since the Government is neither willing to authorize these informal migrations, nor has it the power to prevent them from occurring, the immediate effect has been the maintenance of fragmented labor markets in both the urban and rural areas, losses in efficiency and potential growth, and--because the floating population is not eligible to obtain urban residency permits--a denial of access to urban services and food ration coupons, causing them to live in semi-squalor while pursuing a fairly perilous existence. Though still a comparatively small component of the urban population, this could become an increasingly important issue in years to come as the size of the migratory work force increases.

1.22   The major **material inputs** in Chinese agriculture are, by and large, not distributed by market mechanisms. Fertilizer marketing in China is cen-tralized. During 1982-88, certain components of the marketing system were liberalized but China reimposed central control in January 1989. About two-thirds of all fertilizer is allocated in exchange for crop procurement by the state. The Agricultural Inputs Corporations (AIC: at national, provincial and county levels) 12/ are responsible for wholesaling about 90% of all the fertilizer, and the Supply and Marketing Cooperatives are responsible for retailing 85% of AIC fertilizer. Fertilizer losses (both physical and chemical) are high because existing fertilizer storage and transport facili-ties are not adequate. Fertilizer supplies are allocated by the higher authorities on the basis of productivity, procurement targets and remoteness, irrespective of local demand. The mandatory allocation of fertilizer to regions and crops also does not take into account incremental crop response to applied fertilizer. As a result, there is loss in potential crop output. Nutrient/crop price ratios in China are comparable to many other developing countries. However, plan prices are subsidized both directly and indirectly (the financial cost of the fertilizer subsidy in 1988 was about $1.91 billion), 13/ which has generated excess demand for fertilizers. While some free market trading takes place, the "free" markets are fragmented geographically and are not efficient.

1.23   The supply of diesel is centrally allocated through provincial authorities. As diesel serves sectors other than agriculture, these are com-peting claims on the available supply, but these are resolved essentially by

---

12/   Described in Annex 1, Section V.

13/   World Bank (1990d), para 7.16.

bureaucratic rules. Up to 1982, diesel was sold at a unified price which was held constant over several years. An official "high" price was introduced in 1982, primarily for sales to industry. The negotiated price system was introduced in 1986. Diesel supply was linked with contract grain purchase (5 kg diesel/100 kg grain) in 1986. During 1987, the high and negotiated prices were higher than the subsidized price by 60% and 120%, respectively.

1.24 The supply of electricity, like diesel, serves several sectors. Electricity prices are fixed by the government at sector-specific levels, and have remained unchanged for many years. The differentiation in prices across sectors is a source of inefficiency. In addition, the price for both agriculture and industry is subsidized.

1.25 The existing input distribution system has several problems. First, the distribution systems for fertilizer, diesel and electricity are inefficient, rigid and costly to administer. Second, since there is generally a shortage of fertilizers, diesel and electricity, input supply linked with contract grain procurement results in leakage and corruption. Consequently, the intended beneficiaries do not fully benefit from the scheme. Third, market distortions (and many prices) not only confuse the farmer but also result in wastage and misallocation of scarce farm inputs. In the case of fertilizer, farmers do not always get the type of fertilizer they want and in adequate quantities. However, any reform in fertilizer price policy will have to be accompanied by crop price reforms. Moreover, the government's decision to keep inefficient fertilizer plants in operation (Annex 2, para 64), an over-emphasis on nitrogen at the cost of other nutrients, and allocation of fertilizers based on grain procurement rather than productivity considerations probably cause more efficiency losses than those caused by fertilizer subsidies.

-Trends In Agricultural Expenditure

1.26 Structural change on the real side of the grain sector has been accompanied by a change in the structure of agricultural financing and a shift in priorities. This became especially pronounced after the reforms were introduced. In 1984, the year of China's largest grain harvest until last year, total State 14/ spending on agriculture was actually below what it was in the first year of the reforms. In recent years agricultural spending has picked up again, at least in nominal terms, but as a proportion of total state expenditures agriculture's share has followed a declining trend during the last 10 years. In parallel, the prioritization and programming of public expenditures for agricultural development have fallen hostage to the devolution of fiscal responsibility, militating against substantial expenditures on non-revenue earning activities. The locus of agricultural financing thus shifted from budgetary expenditures through the system of finance bureaux to the state-owned and specialized banks, and to various non-bank financial intermediaries. The operation of services expected from these investments probably has also suffered from an excessive fragmentation, which continues to typify public sector support for agricultural programs in China.

14/ Defined by the Chinese as the sum of public expenditures financed by the central and provincial-level governments.

1.27 In the financial sector, the largest institutional source of
agricultural financing is the Agricultural Bank of China and its associated
Rural Credit Cooperatives, which together account for about 25% of the total
assets of the banking system. Thus the priority given to agriculture would
appear to be considerably higher through the financial sector than through the
public expenditure channels. The term structure of agricultural lending
heavily favors production credit, thus the sectoral composition of real
investment sponsored by the financial sector would again appear biased against
agriculture. Also, a sizeable share of the short-term "agricultural" lending
has been directed to crop procurement financing and to rural industrial and
commercial enterprises. Meanwhile, the burden of consumer subsidization
continues to escalate. In 1988, the state's total financial outlay associated
with the provision of subsidized foods (mostly grains) to urban areas through
the state-owned distribution system amounted to about ¥ 38.0 billion (US$ 10.2
billion), representing more than 10% of total state expenditures and nearly
equivalent in value to the average annual increments in GVAO since 1984. Most
of financing appears to be sourced through transfers within the "urban"
sectors. However, a additional amount--in the form of an economic opportunity
cost (i.e. foregone crop revenue)--is borne by the farming population, through
the indirect taxation implicit in mandatory sales at below-market procurement
prices. In 1988, the opportunity cost placed on China's grain farmers was
equivalent to 62% of the amount expended by government in 1988 on supplying
low cost urban foods. 15/ By comparison, annual state investment in
agricultural infrastructure was only ¥ 4.7 billion.

1.28 During the coming years, there will likely be questions of "feasibility"
in the fiscal and financial sectors that correspond to the efficacy of targets
established in the real sector. The financing of an ambitious grain production
program will in any event require the exploitation of previously untapped
savings and budgetary resources for agricultural investment, some reversal of
the devolution of revenue and expenditure authority, perhaps a reordering of
inter-sectoral financing priorities, and a marked reduction in consumer and
grain marketing subsidies.

-Incidence of Poverty

1.29 In spite of the widespread general increase in rural living standards
owing to the reforms, pockets of chronic rural poverty continue to exist in
the less accessible and natural resource deficient regions of China.
Similarly, absolute poverty is found within the lower income strata in urban
areas, composed mainly of the "floating" or migratory rural work force.
Estimates of the incidence of chronic poverty vary, but even the most robust
studies are constrained by information gaps to assessing the incidence of
poverty on the basis of absolute poverty lines. For purposes of this report
the estimated absolute poverty lines in rural and urban areas correspond to
the estimated cost of a subsistence basket of food and nonfood goods to the

---

15/ Rough estimates of the loss of farm revenue alone on mandatory grain sales indicate that
the net economic loss increased from about ¥ 5.2 billion in 1985 to ¥ 23.0 billion in 1988 (Annex
3, para 41). The estimated financial outlays also understate the true costs of the grain bureaux'
operating losses (Annex 3, para 21).

rural and urban populations.

1.30   The food component of the subsistence basket includes modest quantities of vegetable oil and animal fat, vegetables, pork and eggs (supplying 215 Kcal) and a little more than 0.5 kg of grain per day (supplying 1935 Kcal), providing a total of 2150 Kcal of food energy per day. 16/ Expressed in value terms, the minimum food basket translates into the poverty lines and incidence of absolute poverty shown in Table 1.2.

Table 1.2   Estimated Incidence of Absolute Poverty in China

	1978	1985	1989	Percentage Change: 1989/78	Percentage Change: 1989/85
Poverty Line (¥/year)					
-urban	-na-	247	349	--	41%
-rural /a	100	178	219	78%	23%
Incidence of Poverty (million, %)					
Urban Poor	--	2 (1.0%)	2 (0.9%)	--	0%
Rural Poor	272 (33.5%)	82 (9.8%)	65 (7.3%)	-70%	21%
Total	--	84 (8.0%)	67 (6.0%)	--	20%

/a The modest increase in the rural poverty line compared to the urban trend reflects an adjustment to offset the increasingly downward bias in SSB household survey income data.

1.31   The estimates in Table 1.2 indicate that the incidence of absolute poverty in China declined sharply from 270 million poor in 1978 to about 70 million in 1989, or from more than 30% to about 6% of total population. However, the estimates also suggest that nearly all of the decline in poverty occurred during 1978-84.   Pressure on the real income of the rural poor, due to the sharp increase in food prices, appears to have blocked further reductions in poverty in the second half of the 1980s. The slow down of rural enterprise during 1989 and 1990 also reduced off-farm employment opportunities and contributed to a decline in real rural income in 1989.   Most of China's poor are now concentrated in portions of the interior provinces of Northwest and Southwest China, where the meager natural resource base and other constraints impede development.   There is also a residual of households, disadvantaged by high dependency ratios, ill health and other difficulties, scattered in otherwise well-off regions throughout the country.   These families have not fared well in the transition to a more decentralized market-oriented economy   The apparent resurgence of poverty strongly supports anecdotal evidence that large numbers of poor were being pushed below the

16/ Discussed in World Bank (1991). The estimates attempt to correct for the downward bias in the underlying SSB household survey data, which omit some sources of income and value subsistence grain production (i.e., not sold off the farm) at very low planned prices.

poverty line by the increases in basic foodstuffs prices during 1985-88 --in particular, by the two-thirds increase in nongrain food prices--and in some areas, may have suffered from a deterioration of the social safety net.

1.32 Most of the rural poverty zones appear to be located in China's grain deficit provinces, and a component part of the government's food security and grain movement programs is to maintain at least minimal standards of staple food consumption in these areas. Lacking detailed information, it is difficult to determine how effective these interventions have been, though it is striking that famine has disappeared from the Chinese scene since the early 1960s, which suggests that an adequate (albeit not bountiful) level of food security is being realized even in zones of chronic rural poverty.

II. PERFORMANCE & PROSPECTS IN THE GRAIN SECTOR

2.01 From the inception of the reforms in 1979 until 1990, the main sources
of growth in crop agriculture fell in three patterns. Institutional change,
principally the spread of the PRS, dominated the initial years, while price
policies, liberalization in the markets for higher valued commodities, and a
continued expansion of fertilizer consumption (albeit at a slower pace) were
largely responsible for growth that ensued between 1984-1988. In 1989 and
1990, China enjoyed unusually good agroclimatic conditions. In 1989, the
absence of drought and flooding in the grain production zones resulted in
production equivalent to the previous peak of 407 million tons achieved in
1984. In 1990, a new record of 425 million tons was produced, with 2/3 of the
increment coming from China's Northeastern Provinces where weather "not seen
in 20 years" was an important factor, supported by a fairly massive rural
works program that was organized in the Winter months of 1989/90 to
rehabilitate irrigation and drainage works throughout China. 1/ Because of
these investments and the increased availability of chemical fertilizers,
China's grain production possibilities frontier under normal weather
conditions *within the constraints posed by current production and marketing
incentives* has probably been shifted outward to perhaps 415 million tons.
During the coming years, the **technological** basis for growth in crop production
will largely depend on the continuing diffusion of yield enhancing
improvements associated with fertilizer responsive plant varieties, improved
water control and fertilizer use. This generalization applies both to grains
and to non-grains. In view of the importance of chemical nutrients in this
schema, prospects in the fertilizer sector are reviewed below corollary to
performance in the grain sector.

A. SOURCES OF GROWTH

2.02 Several attempts have been made to empirically identify factors
contributing to the astounding performance of agriculture between 1978-1984,
and reasons for the slowdown that followed. The most comprehensive recent
studies include Lin (1989a), McMillan *et al.* (1989) and Wen (1989). Lin found
that in 1965-1987, 40.8% of the realized growth in agricultural **productivity**
can be attributed to input growth (of which nearly two-thirds can be
attributed to an expansion of chemical fertilizers), 43.6% to institutional
change associated with decollectivization. Meanwhile, the contributions of
disembodied technological change and price effects on total factor
productivity appear to have been minimal, about 1.1%. Using a standard
Dennison-Solow type growth accounting approach, McMillan *et al.* suggest that
2/3 of the observed increase in total factor productivity since 1979 can be
attributed to farming institutional reform, and 22% to price rises. Wen found
that adoption of the PRS contributed 51% of the growth in **total production**
observed between 1979-1987, with improvement in the agricultural/manufacturing

---

1/ This program involved 4.8 billion cubic meters of earthwork, using 4.2 billion labor-days,
to improve about 30% of the area under irrigation. Grain production in 1990 was also stimulated by
the production, importation and earmarking of an additional two million tons of fertilizers.

terms of trade in rural areas, and negative residual effects accounting for the remainder.

2.03 Since 1984, neither the dramatic gains from institutional change nor the rapid growth in inputs were available to further stimulate output. By 1984, the PRS had effectively diffused throughout rural China, annual cropping had reached its "X-efficiency" frontier and the sources of growth became the more traditional ones (Lin-1989a): inputs (about 1/3) and changing crop composition and market price effects (about 2/3). Meanwhile, the growth rate of fertilizer input dropped from 8.9% p.a. in 1978-84 to only 3.7% in 1984-87.

2.04 Technology. During the 1950s, 1960s and early 1970s, China developed a remarkably effective research and extension network, grounded in the people's communes and enjoying considerable state support. This system both developed and adapted new grain production technologies, fostered a rapid diffusion to the farm level, and organized massive investments in rural infrastructure (e.g. irrigation). As a result of this legacy from the first three decades after Liberation, grain crop yields in China are now quite high by international standards--though somewhat overstated due to underestimated crop area, and are exceeded only by those of Japan and Korea in the Asia Region. And if improved germ plasm and higher quality fertilizers with a better nutrient mix were more widely available in China, the gap between Chinese yields and those of the more land-productive countries would be even smaller (Stone-1986b).

2.05 The characteristics of technological change that has occurred at the farm level since introduction of the PRS were identified in a companion study by Lin (1989b). His results show that Chinese farmers' application of non-marketed factors (land and labor) tended to equilibrate marginal productivity with regional factor scarcities. However, the effects of employing more efficient input combinations were offset by negative shifts in overall demand for improved grain production technology, which tended to cancel out gains at the farm level once gains attendant to spread of the PRS had fully accrued. This implies that the costs to farmers of adopting embodied technology, previously diffused by the communes and the state, had increased substantially after the PRS was introduced, which--in the absence of effective, alternative, technical support services organized in the public sector--resulted in the negation of total factor productivity growth in agriculture after 1984. 2/

B. TRENDS IN THE GRAIN SECTOR

2.06 Within the grain sector, and in contrast to the wealth of official data for grain production, official estimates of grain utilization are incomplete and inconsistent. Available official and unofficial estimates of grain supply and utilization are summarized in Table 2.1 for the period 1970-89. The

---

2/ Lin's findings support the impression that future technical change will have to be embodied in new technologies, that in particular the inventory of existing and readily available grain production technologies have already been diffused within China's agricultural sector, and that the public sector's involvement in agricultural research, extension and education needs to be strengthened.

figures for total supply are the sum of the SSB's estimates of total grain production 3/ plus net trade in grain. Stocks are excluded from these estimates. Official figures for grain utilization are not available, and the estimates of direct consumption of table grain (as food), indirect consumption as animal feed, and seed requirements shown in Table 2.1 have been calculated from a variety of sources. 4/ Other forms of disappearance and utilization, including storage losses, waste and use in food and non-food manufacturing, are not shown.

2.07 These figures indicate that the strong expansion of grain production, augmented by a surge in net grain imports in the early-1980s, increased total grain supply by 70% from 243 million tons in 1970 to 414 million tons in 1984. Grain production stagnated during 1985-88, and total supply dipped to an annual average of 395 million tons, then recovered to 418 million tons in 1989. Population growth has been moderate-- total population increased by one-third during 1970-89, at an average annual rate of 1.6%--and total per capita grain supply increased by 35% from 297 kg in 1970 to 401 kg in 1984 before declining by about 6% to 378 kg in 1989.

2.08 Corresponding to a 26% increase in total population and a 33% increase in per capita consumption, estimated direct consumption of table grain increased by 68% from 158 million tons in 1970 to 265 million tons in 1984.

Table 2.1 Supply and Utilization of Whole Grain /a

Year	Midyear Population	Grain Supply				Grain Utilization				
		Grain Production	Net Imports	Total Supply	Per Capita Supply	Food /b	Feed	Seed	Food /b	Feed
	-(million)-	-----(million tons)-----			-(kg/cap)-	---(million tons)---			--(kg/capita)--	
1970	818.3	240.0	2.9	242.8	297	158.1	23.1	14.3	193	28
1975	916.4	284.5	0.4	285.0	311	180.2	31.6	14.8	197	35
1980	981.2	320.6	11.5	332.0	338	238.8	46.2	14.2	243	47
1981	993.9	325.0	13.3	338.3	340	247.9	48.1	14.0	249	48
1982	1008.3	354.5	15.2	369.7	367	254.4	52.2	14.1	252	52
1983	1021.8	387.3	12.2	399.5	391	257.4	55.8	14.2	252	55
1984	1033.2	407.3	6.9	414.2	401	265.1	64.1	13.9	257	62
1985	1044.6	379.1	-3.6	375.5	359	257.0	78.3	13.9	246	75
1986	1057.9	391.5	-2.0	389.5	368	262.8	87.1	13.9	248	82
1987	1073.0	404.7	8.6	413.3	385	265.3	92.1	13.9	247	86
1988	1092.9	393.8	7.9	401.7	368	271.9	104.3	14.0	249	95
1989	1104.0	407.5	10.0	417.5	378	274.9	112.0	14.0	249	101

Source: World Bank (1990a), Table 1, and SSB (1990).

/a Includes rice in paddy (whole grain) equivalent.
/b Total direct consumption of table grain.

3/ Which detail total production by major grain and by province for each year 1979 to 1988.

4/ cf. World Bank (1990a), paras 1.06-1.11.

Reflecting a moderate decline in per capita consumption, direct consumption of table grain is estimated to have increased only marginally in subsequent years, reaching 275 million tons in 1989. However, the relative shares of different grains has been changing. The increase in wheat consumption over time, especially during the post-reform period has been spectacular. Total wheat consumption more than doubled during the post-reform period from 46 million tons in 1978 to 98 million tons in 1988. The relative share of wheat in food grain consumption increased from 16.5% in 1960 to 22% in 1978 and 38% in 1988. In the case of rice, however, the relative share declined from 36% in 1960 to 34% in 1978 and then increased to 38% in 1988. Thus, during 1988, wheat became as important as rice for direct food consumption. The relative share of potatoes, coarse grains, other grains and soybeans in food grain consumption declined over time; the relative share of corn increased from 10% in 1960 to 20% in 1978 and then declined again to 10% in 1988.

2.09 Driven by the tremendous expansion of livestock production over the last two decades, estimated utilization of grain as animal feed increased steadily by almost 400% from 23 million tons in 1970 to 112 million tons in 1989. Seed requirements, by comparison, have remained roughly constant at about 14 million tons over the last two decades. Together, estimated utilization of grain as food, feed and seed increased from 196 million tons in 1970 to 401 million tons in 1989, or from 239 kg per capita to 363 kg per capita.

2.10 The differences in total grain supply and the sum of these three forms of grain utilization averaged 51 million tons during 1980-84 but then declined to an average 26 million tons annually during 1985-88. **5/** The difference was sufficient to cover other forms of grain utilization and allow for a substantial build up of stocks during 1970-84, but necessitated a draw down of stocks during 1985-88. USDA (1988) estimates indicate that year-end grain stocks increased by 75 million tons from 37 million tons in 1970 to 111 million tons in 1984, and then declined by 45 million tons during 1985-88. **6/**

C. PERFORMANCE PROSPECTS

2.11 Performance projections under various policy assumptions were analyzed to show the effects on the level and composition of future demand and supply of food and feedgrains, other agricultural commodities and on movements in pricing. Estimates also were prepared of the future technical possibilities in grain production on the basis of agroecological considerations and technical production parameters, and of China's prospects in the international grain trade. Lastly, a crude estimation was made of investment and agricultural financing requirements, and of the trade-off between fertilizer self-sufficiency and a more import-based strategy.

5/ World Bank (1990a), Figures 1 and 2.

6/ The USDA grain stock figures are in trade grain equivalent (i.e., with rice in milled form). The government does not release grain stock data, but the decline in stocks during the second half of the 1980s indicated by the USDA estimates is roughly corroborated by the reported decline of 20 million tons -- from 98 million in 1984 to 78 million tons in 1986 -- in central government stocks held by the Ministry of Commerce's General Grain Bureau.

2.12   The core of these projections were made using an agricultural sector simulation model (referred to below as the "MAT-1 model") 7/ that was developed to show "real sector" effects in agriculture which could result from manipulation of China's bifurcated internal grain markets, its foreign trade policies for grains, assumed productivity improvements and general macro-economic growth. Performance during the base period (1985-87) and summary indicators of projected sectoral performance are detailed in Annex 4 and shown in Table 2.2. Being elasticity driven, the model's results are subject to the usual estimation errors, which are probably magnified for an agricultural sector as large and diverse as China's. 8/ For these reasons, the projections in the following discussion that were derived from the MAT-1 model extend only until 1995.

Table 2.2 Grains and Livestock Products: Projected Trends In Real Indicators to 1995

(base year = 1986)

	Grain Production /a		Consumption				
	Rate of Growth	Total Productn	Total /a Grain	of which: Feeds	Grain (Direct)/b urban	Per Capita rural	Livestock Products
	(% p.a.)	--(mil. tons)--				--------(kg/cap)--------	
Base Period (1986) /c	--	391.7	406.2	71.5	179.7	235.8	28.9
Projection Scenarios (1995)							
1. Base Run: /d	1.87	462.8	471.1	101.0	181.5	240.7	39.3
2. Grain Ration and Contract Procurement Prices Doubled: /e	1.88	463.1	470.8	100.7	181.4	240.9	39.2
3. Prolonged Agricultural Recession: /f	1.53	449.0	446.9	84.4	179.5	234.2	30.6
4. Sustained Agricultural Recovery: /g	2.11	472.8	484.3	111.1	182.5	243.6	44.8

Source: Annex 4 (MAT-1 Model Projection Runs)

Notes: **1. Productivity Growth Assumptions**   **2. Assumed Growth in Real Per Capita Incomes**

	crop yields	feed conversion efficiencies			urban	rural
	(% p.a., 1986-1995)				(% p.a., 1986-1995)	
low =	1.0	.9		base run =	3.6	3.0
moderate =	1.5	1.0		recession =	2.5	2.1
high =	1.75	1.05		recovery: 3(a) =	5.1	4.3
				3(b) =	6.4	5.4

/a based on Chinese definition: includes fine and coarse grains, some tubers and soybeans at unmilled weights.
/b milled equivalents
/c 1985-87 (= "1986").
/d The base run features moderate productivity increases and the "base run" per capita income growth assumptions shown above in the notes to this table, a complete liberalization of domestic grain pricing and marketing with the exception of amounts currently procured at below market contract prices and sold at urban ration prices, and a switch to an essentially free trade regime in grains and other agricultural products.
/e other assumptions same as base run.
/f devaluation, but with restricted grain imports, low productivity growth and recession assumptions.
/g high productivity growth, income growth assumptions: "recovery 3(a)", others as in base run.

7/   The model and its formulation are described in Annex 4. The detailed structure of an earlier version is presented in World Bank (1988a).

8/   The elasticities of demand and supply employed in the MAT-1 model are enumerated in the Appendix to Annex 4.

D. DOMESTIC CONSUMPTION PROSPECTS

-Demand Determinants

2.13 <u>Factors Influencing Per Capita Trends</u>. Household income and expenditure data from large scale SSB surveys indicate that the decline in urban **direct** per capita consumption of grain has been sustained and pronounced, having fallen a total of 20% from 167 kg (in trade grain equivalent) in 1957 to 145 kg in 1981 to 134 kg in 1989 according to the SSB data (Annex 2, Table 1). Rural direct consumption appears to have increased by 8% from 248 kg per capita (unprocessed grain equivalent) in 1978 to a peak of 267 kg in 1984 and then declined by 3% to 262 kg in 1989. <u>9/</u> Regression analyses indicates that trends in the retail price of grain explain very little of the decline in urban direct per capita grain consumption, with the estimated income elasticity of -0.6 accounting for most of the decline. In rural areas as well, the results of the mission's regression analyses suggest that the pervasive influence of administered pricing and procurement has vitiated the influence of retail price variations on direct grain consumption. **Indirect** consumption of grain as animal feed is estimated to have more than tripled from 28 kg per capita in 1970 to 101 kg per capita in 1989 (Table 2.1). In sharp contrast to the expected continued decline in direct per capita consumption of grain, expected strong demand for animal products will continue to push up indirect per capita demand for feed grain.

2.14 <u>Factors Influencing Total Demand</u>. State imposed restrictions affect the smooth functioning of the price mechanism, and it is difficult to predict the impact of price changes and reforms with certainty. In the rural sector, more than half of the grain procured by the government is purchased at below market planned prices. <u>10/</u> The government's intervention in rural sales of grain is, by comparison, moderate. Sicular's analysis (1988; pp. 285-286) suggests that future changes in the rural free market price of grain and reforms of the volume and price of planned grain procurement will affect rural grain supply and demand both directly, since the market price in rural free markets is the effective marginal price for most surplus grain producers and most rural consumers, and indirectly, since the government planned procurement price affects rural income and, hence, on-farm investment and consumption (as a function of the income elasticity of demand). Further, since the urban free market retail price is the effective marginal price to urban consumers, only changes to the free market price will directly affect urban demand for grain. Reform of the urban ration price of grain will affect urban demand only indirectly, through consequent changes in real income. <u>11/</u> However, in both the rural and urban sectors, changes in prices of animal products and other

---

<u>9/</u> As shown in World Bank (1990a), Appendix 2, the decline in direct per capita grain consumption has been more pronounced and has extended over a longer period of time in higher income rural areas relative to less well-off areas.

<u>10/</u> cf. Annex 2, para 33 and World Bank (1990g), Appendix 1, Table.

<u>11/</u> Urban household income and expenditure survey data from Guangdong and Fujian for 1987 and 1988 strongly support the hypotheses that the subsidy element of grain ration coupons is now fully monetized and that substantial increases in ration prices (particularly when offset with compensating income transfers) will have negligible effects on grain consumption (cf. World Bank [1990b]).

nongrain foods will affect the supply and demand of grain through cross price elasticities of demand and through demand for animal feed.

-Projected Total Consumption of Grain

2.15 The MAT-1 simulation model projects total demand for grain from the base period of 1985/87 to 1995 as a function of expected growth in per capita income (up 42%) and population (up 11%), expected changes in the urban and rural distribution of total population (from 28% urban and 72% rural in the base period to 35% urban and 65% rural in 1995), estimated price and income elasticities of demand and feed conversion ratios (FCRs), and endogenous real price movements. The base run assumes moderate growth in agricultural productivity and per capita incomes (as indicated in the notes to Table 2.2), essentially free international trade in non-grain products, a partial liberalization of China's foreign trade in grains, and maintenance of China's bifurcated internal grain markets with prices for contract procurement and rationed sales (the administered segment of these markets) maintained at their real 1986 levels. The other scenarios are based on several modifications to base run assumptions as indicated in the footnotes to Table 2.2. At constant 1986 prices, the model's base run solution projects total demand to increase by 19% to 482 million tons in 1995 (not shown in Table 2.2). After equilibrating supply and demand of grain through a combination of international trade and price changes, total consumption of unprocessed grain in the base run of the model is projected to be 471 million tons, including a 16% increase in direct demand for table grain and a 41% increase in indirect demand as animal feed.

-Per Capita Direct Consumption and Nutrition

2.16 Several variants were run to estimate the effects of different configurations in sectoral policy and general economic performance on per capita consumption balances. The results are shown in Annex 4, Table 3. The most striking result is the generally projected decline in the direct per capita consumption of rice and coarse grains once more rational pricing policies are introduced, and the stimulus given to consumption of wheat and animal products. This occurs in both the rural areas, where the direct consumption of grains continues to be higher than in urban areas, and in urban areas (where consumption of meats and fish continues to be higher). A doubling of the administered prices for grains in the absence of other policy changes would have strikingly little effect on performance in the "real sector" (though it has fairly profound income distributive implications--para 2.48 below), no doubt because the marginal prices are market prices or negotiated price equivalents, while about only one eighth of total grain produced and consumed in China passes through the official channels at the ration sales and contract procurement prices.

2.17 The projected decline in the direct per capita consumption of rice remains basically invariant to the policy and technical assumptions made. This confirms the findings reported in Annex 2, that as a result of China's already successful production policies, China's consumers have become awash in rice, and if given an opportunity, would simply reduce their overall intake. Under all scenarios, further improvements in China's already remarkable standards of nutrition could be expected to occur, with the least improvement being associated with a prolonged agricultural recession (Annex 4, Table 4). 12/

E.   GRAIN PRODUCTION AND SUPPLY SCENARIOS

2.18   Projected grain consumption would be met from three sources: domestic production, net imports and stocks. China will have to depend on all three sources but their relative importance will be dictated by economic conditions in China and on the world grain markets, and by the political and food security concerns of national leaders. 13/   Based on projected consumption of 471 million tons in 1995 and current (1989) production of about 407 million tons, China would have to expand grain production by about 65 million tons between 1990 and 1995 to fully meet the projected consumption requirement from domestic production. Considering the volume of investment and expenditure required, this doesn't appear feasible, although on strictly technical grounds, it could possibly be achieved by the Year 2000.

-Production Possibilities

2.19   Production Plan to the Year 2000.   The driving objective behind the State's grain production program is self-sufficiency, both nationally and-- where feasible--at the regional level, though it is acknowledged that grain shortage in the longer term is inevitable and deficits of 5-10 million tons can be anticipated from time to time due to fluctuations in production. A second general objective is to keep total imports below 15-16 million tons in any one year (about 3.5% of current production), due to limitations posed by the availability of foreign exchange, limited port handling capabilities and inadequate internal transportation and storage facilities. The minimum target for the Year 2000 is 500 million tons with direct consumption and animal feed making up 85% of the total. Losses in handling, distribution and storage should not exceed about 3% but in practice are running at about 15%. Savings of 10% in this area during the next decade would represent 10-15 million tons of grain per year.

2.20   The Ministry of Agriculture (MOA) has been working on grain production planning to the Year 2000 since the mid-1980s with most of the work carried out by the Chinese Academy of Agricultural Sciences' (CAAS) Institute of Agricultural Economics (IAE), assisted by the Agricultural Natural Resources and Planning Institute (ANPRI) and technical institutes of CAAS with inputs from the provinces. A draft study was released for publication in October 1989, but it is understood that the planning process is still underway. Key

---

12/ Mapping present (1986) patterns, the urban diet would be better furnished with proteins and fats than would diets of rural people, whereas the latter would continue to consume more calories per capita than urban residents. This no doubt is a reflection of higher per capita incomes in urban areas and the workings of China's income elasticities of demand for agricultural products.

13/ Grain stocks were rather low in 1986-88 by Chinese standards (though quite high by international standards (World Bank [1990a]), but the procurement and storage system reportedly has again been overwhelmed by record harvests in 1989 and 1990, with a considerable volume of surplus grain being kept on-farm in makeshift stores as it was after the previous record harvest in 1984.

points from the draft plan are summarized below. 14/

2.21 Production projections in the draft plan are based on production areas, rates of potential yield increase and modelling for the period 1986-2000. It has been assumed that production areas will remain constant on the basis that new land development will off-set land lost to infrastructure development. Data presented by the IAE imply that the major increases in production are expected in the Northern production region, with significant increases in the Middle and Lower Reaches of the Yangtze River (MLYR), Northeast and Northwest. Rice is projected to contribute almost 50% to incremental production. But since total grain production in the main rice regions (S, SW and MLYR) is projected to increase by only 24 million tons, this implies that more than half of the incremental rice production would be located in the water deficient areas of North China, which is an unlikely scenario. There also are doubts that planted area will remain constant.

2.22 The main interventions proposed by CAAS's Institutes to increase grain production are essentially technical ones:

(a) Upgrade irrigation and drainage facilities and expand irrigated area along the lines proposed by the Ministry of Water Resources (MWR); 15/

(b) Increase the total use of organic and chemical fertilizer from about 80 million tons to 150 million tons. Change the organic:chemical fertilizer ratio from it present ratio of less than 42:58 to 50:50 to achieve an N:P:K ratio of 1.0:0.6:0.2 with 66% of phosphate and 90% of potassium contributed from organic manure;

(c) Improve seed production and distribution and expand the area of hybrid rice. It is anticipated that substantial yield increases will be achieved by at least two releases of improved varieties within the next decade;

(d) Increase cropping intensity from 151 to 161% and thus increase planted area;

(e) Increase mechanization to reduce turnaround time between crops and hence increase cropping intensity;

(f) Upgrade extension services to increase the rate of application of known technology;

14/ cf. World Bank (1990c), Sections IX-X for details.

15/ Detailed in World Bank (1990c), Appendix 1.

(g)   Reduce crop losses via restructuring the production of
        insecticide, fungicide, and herbicide to introduce
        higher potency-lower toxicity chemicals; and

(h)   Pay closer attention to increasing yields on the
        extensive medium to low yield production area which
        represents over 60% of planted area.

2.23   These proposals are technically sound and identify many of the main
priorities. However, the effective internal demand for large additional
volumes of low-quality hybrid rice appears to be quite limited, not to mention
export prospects, 16/ thus throwing into question the essential marketability
of significantly increased rice production. In addition, sound estimates of
fertilizer requirements are difficult to make in the absence of good basic
data on the use and value of organic manure and the incremental nutrient
required from chemical fertilizer by crop and zone to achieve high economic
yield.   It is doubtful that cropping intensity can be increased to 161%
(compare with Table 2.3 below). Much of the planned irrigation development is
in single crop zones e.g. the Northeast which will tend to lower the overall
multiple cropping index. Lacking some form of joint production system within
the framework of the PRS (or a system of custom machinery services), there are
practical difficulties in increasing mechanization among small farmers with
scattered plots. Emphasis needs to be placed on improving the supplies of
fertilizer and agrochemicals so that they are readily available in the field
when required. Breeding of improved disease and pest resistance into the
major grain crops should receive priority along with the promotion of
integrated pest management in rice fields. Since loss reduction is equally
important as production gain, measures should be introduced to reduce the
substantial handling and storage losses occurring between farmer and consumer. 17/

2.24   Water Resource Constraints.   China's total effective irrigated area in
1988 was 44.4 million ha., about 46% of the total cultivated area. About 64%
of the irrigated area is in the Northern and MLYR Production Regions (map),
where much of the good agricultural land also is located. Irrigated areas
presently account for about 2/3 of overall farm output. In the early 1980s,
the average area actually irrigable fell short of the official total area in
one year out of four, due to water shortage. It is unlikely that much
improvement was realized before 1989, though various reports which could not
be confirmed by the mission suggest that in some provinces and counties,
increased attention has been given in 1989 and 1990 to improving the
irrigation and drainage infrastructure. The priority given to water resource

---

16/ Demand for low quality rice (i.e. hybrid rice and other high yielding varieties) may have
peaked (World Bank [1990a]), while export prospects for low quality rice are not good.

17/ In this connection, some Chinese experts believe that China may not be able to produce more
than 90 million tons of incremental grain by the Year 2000 under the best of circumstances, which
would include policy and institutional reforms to provide appropriate incentives, to stimulate
agricultural innovation and an expanded use of modern inputs, to improve rural infrastructure and
measurably augment investment. If this proves to be correct, it is likely that China will have to
increase net imports substantially in order to meet projected grain demand, or else curtail
consumption through pricing and administrative means.

development by CAAS's Institutes stems from the fact that the share of China's total sown area planted in grains, though declining since 1980, was still high in 1988 (76.4%), thus grain production also occupied much of the effective irrigated area.

2.25 New developments are both time consuming (5-10 years gestation) and costly--particularly when associated with land reclamation schemes. In view of the projected continuation of only moderate growth in grain production during the 1990s (para 2.32), and the likely continued fall-off in the per capita consumption of table grains (para 2.17), the economics of major investment in new irrigation and drainage projects for the sake of expanding grain production are questionable when compared with simpler, quickly gestating rehabilitation and on-farm works. It is estimated that some 10-15 million ha. of cultivated area require rehabilitation of irrigation and drainage facilities to prevent waterlogging and reduce salinization. Experience with the Bank-assisted North China Plain Project and the proposed Irrigated Agriculture Intensification Project (also located in North China) show that the progressive deterioration of the massive developments undertaken in the 1970s are beginning to affect yields, and would have resulted in declines of grain yields by 1-2 tons per ha. under "without project" conditions due to progressive water shortage and deteriorating soil chemistry. Since similar conditions exist throughout North China, it is reasonable to expect that large areas of agricultural land are similarly threatened.

2.26 Among the MWR's large portfolio of irrigation and land reclamation projects, 18/ priorities should be focussed on rehabilitation, repair and systems completion work in the water scarce areas of North China. New developments should receive, at best, very low priority. These kinds of investments, and their location would serve mainly to maintain current grain production aggregates in the wheat and feed grain areas.

2.27 The Seed Technology Gap. Omitted from the CAAS' recommendations is the cost reducing potential associated with (a) the importation of short-duration wheat varieties capable of higher yields in the warmer and more humid climes of Central and South China, (b) the cold tolerant and moisture tolerant but input intensive hybrid maize varieties that have shown impressive performance in other developing countries, and (c) soybean varieties having greater meal and oil content, thus improving both yields and usefulness as animal feed. The centers of wheat, corn and soybean production are located in Northern and Eastern China, 19/ and (for wheat and corn) in the inland province of Sichuan. Though wheat yields are high, the use of high yielding semi-dwarf varieties has not spread to Central and South China to any large extent (even though the urban demand for wheat products in these traditionally rice producing regions has been strong and growing), largely because the available varieties do not fit easily into the existing rice-based rotations due to their still prolonged (125 day) growing period and susceptibility to the *fusarium* wilt fungus. Meanwhile, corn and soybean yields remain substandard, largely because

---

18/ Annex 1, para 4 and World Bank (1990c), Appendix 1, Table 2.

19/ cf. World Bank (1990c), Map 2.

budgetary constraints and research policies have inhibited the free exchange
of staff, information and germ plasm between China's agricultural research
establishment, international research centers and the research laboratories of
international seed companies. In this connection, it is noteworthy that recent
testing in the north (Shandong) and in Central China (Hubei) of single hybrid
corn by a private international seed company gave significantly better yields
(by 30-50%) than China's best maize varieties. 20/

2.28   International plant breeders have noted the limitations of existing
wheat, maize and soybean varieties being promoted by China's research
establishment, and have recommended that plant quarantine regulations and
restrictions on seed testing be relaxed to permit the importation and
adaptation of superior international varieties. During the process of "opening
up", the attitude of senior members in China's research establishment—being
justifiably proud of past advances made in the absence of foreign input, but
lately a bit hegemonious—will have to be changed to permit a fruitful
adaptation of the superior varieties now available. Much of the readily
adaptable germ plasm, however—in the form of "breeder", "original" and
"foundation" seeds—has been developed by and remains the property of
international seed concerns. Though anecdotal, the stories of failed efforts
to establish joint venture seed grain enterprises in China have become legion,
being characterized by obstruction from the research establishment, the
related use of quarantine procedures to inhibit dissemination of breeder and
foundation seeds, and an unwillingness to acknowledge the proprietary
interests of international seeds companies in the seed technology being
offered. Thus to facilitate transfers, it will be essential for China over
the longer term to enact laws and transparently enforceable regulations
pertaining to breeders rights, in order to encourage the formation of the
mutually profitable joint-venture arrangements under which the international
seed companies prefer to operate. In this regard, the British and Turkish
codes may provide useful examples.

2.29   Production Incentives. In addition to technical constraints on the
uptake of cost reducing innovations in grain production, producer incentives
remain distorted and weak. Although comprehensive cost of production and farm
gate pricing data were not made available for this report (either in time
series or cross-section), piecemeal evidence suggests that farm gate pricing
policies in the latter half of the 1980s placed a levy of large magnitude on
grain farmer incentives *vis-a-vis* pricing at international parities. This
appears to have been especially prevalent in the official procurement prices
offered to wheat and rice producers. 21/ When evaluated at international farm

---

20/ The germ plasm for China's maize was imported mainly from American and European sources more
than 20 years ago. Reflecting conditions in the countries of origin, China's maize varieties have
been improved and refined over the years to perform reasonably well under the cooler and drier
conditions in Northern China and Sichuan. Even under these agroclimatic conditions, however, China's
maize breeders have reached the limit on yield potential with this older germ plasm, while its
adaptability to the warmer and moist climes of Central and Southern China has proved to be very
limited.

21/ For farmers located close to grain depots, the pricing disincentive has been partially offset
by their ability to purchase fine grains at subsidized prices (the General Grain Bureau's so-called
"rural resales") to feed swine and poultry.

gate parities for rice and chemical fertilizers, the array of net revenue/operating cost ratios in 4 of China's 6 agricultural production regions showed the following pattern:

Region:	N	MLYR	NE	NW
Wheat	2.6	3.4	1.6	2.4
Rice	3.8	4.9	4.0	4.1
Corn	1.7	1.1	1.6	1.2
Soybean	4.6	3.6	13.1	8.1

Though the rice estimates are undoubtedly biased upwards, perhaps half-again (a quality discount was not applied in the above estimates when computing farm-gate parities), the magnitudes for all crops but corn suggest that an expansion of production could be induced through the use of less distorting pricing policies. For the Northern Region, a comparison was made with net revenue/operating cost ratios computed at financial prices (Annex 2, para 18), which showed that prices actually faced by farmers led uniformly to lower ratios, again with the exception of corn, and again demonstrating the loss of income at the farm gate associated with China's grain sector pricing policies.

2.30 On the other hand, being founded in border price parities, these generalized estimates overlook the reality of inputs shortages in China, particularly fertilizers. The "3-linkages Program" (Annex 3, para 28) and the "Grain Base Development Program", aiming to promote intensified grain production on 20 million hectares (about 1/5th of China's total cultivated area) by the Year 2000, serve to channel subsidized inputs into grain production at artificially low prices. Were it possible to assign true shadow values for, say, fertilizer inputs, to reflect actual scarcities at the regional level--such scarcities being induced both by administered regional allocations and by inland transportation and distribution problems--the "true" ratios in 1989 economic prices would likely have proved lower than the estimates presented above, thus reducing the strength of the implied incentives foregone. Still, the differences in the net revenue/operating cost ratios at the "true" scarcity and actual prices in 1989 would have remained positive, since the cost of chemical fertilizers on average account for only 18.4% of total operating costs. 22/ Thus a doubling of the border price of fertilizers to reflect actual scarcity at the regional level and potential alternative on higher-valued non-grain crops, would have reduced the ratios by about only 10% from the estimates shown in para 2.29.

-Aggregate Supply Prospects

2.31 An analysis of technical production possibilities provides an important dimension to analysis of the supply problem, but does not address opportunity costs and therefore can't address issues of economic feasibility and sustainability. Runs of the MAT-1 model are therefore employed for this

---

22/ World Bank (1990c), Appendix 8 Tables 8-11.

purpose. The array of production projections corresponding with various policy scenarios are set forth in Table 2.3. In all but the recession scenarios, a considerable expansion of grain production is projected. Indeed, under the most optimistic of the "recovery" scenarios, grain production is projected to reach 472.8 million tons (perhaps because the MAT-1 framework is not resource constrained.) In all of the scenarios, however, the results appear to be driven about equally by demand and the assumed productivity increases. 23/

2.32 The scenarios most closely resembling conditions during the base period are the "recession" scenarios in Table 2.3, especially the second one: "general agricultural recession". This scenario features productivity growth that is marginally lower than the average of the past two decades, a moderate devaluation (which occurred de facto after 60 or so regional exchange adjustment centers were established in 1986-88), but maintenance of import restrictions. Here, total grain production by Chinese reckoning of 449.0 million tons represents an annual growth in grain production of "only" 1.53% p.a. between 1986-95, which admittedly compares well with international trends, but is considerably less than the 5.0% p.a. average annual increases realized by China during the first half of the 1980s, or the implied average annual increase of 2.43% from 1989 that will be needed to reach 500-520 million tons by the Year 2000. There could occur, however, an expansion of vegetable production by almost 20 million tons, partially in response to foreign demand, but mainly in response to the assumed growth in per capita incomes (even under the "low" growth assumption in this scenario), whose production would be availed by an increase in the multiple cropping index from 146 in 1986 to 154 in 1995.

2.33 The implications of this comparison are sobering. Were China to maintain basically current restrictions on grain marketing and foreign trade in grains, the likely result will be a continued diversion of fine grains into animal feeds, and frustration of its longer-term grain and livestock sectoral production objectives. To the extent that yield increases at the farm level also reflect market forces, through the link between the uptake of superior technologies and "revealed" profitability, the productivity growth assumptions in this scenario may not be too far off the mark under the current policy environment. Further, as shown below in Section G, these disappointing results would likely occur in an environment of escalating market prices. Implications from the "recovery" scenarios are equally sobering: being essentially "market" or demand driven, it will not be enough for China's agricultural sector to produce only what can be (and is being) produced. For example, the expansion of rice exports and comparatively limited importation of other agricultural commodities to satisfy an increasingly powerful internal market, will require upgrades in quality across the rice producing zones. 24/

23/ This is shown by referring to the similar results of the two "recovery/trade reform" scenarios, where the first one assumes higher productivity growth than the second, while the latter contains higher income growth, devaluation and unrestricted free trade in agricultural products.

24/ In rice, for example, China has proved its ability to secure very high yields, but the bulk of production is low quality, a result of breeding deficiencies (especially hybrids) and poor post-harvest care. In the face of strong competition from the USA, Thailand, most recently from Vietnam and quite likely from Burma in the future, it may prove very difficult for China to regain entry in
(continued...)

Table 2.3 Projected Changes in the Composition of Agricultural Production (1985-1995)

(million metric tons)

| | TOTAL GRAINS /a | TABLE GRAINS | | | | | ANIMAL FEEDS | |
		Rice	Wheat	Coarse Grains	Soybean	Tubers	Grains /b	Tubers
Base Period (1985-1987)	391.7	171.7	87.9	37.5	11.4	13.3	56.7	13.3
Projection Scenarios (1995)								
1. Base Run /c	462.8	193.5	111.4	42.7	12.9	13.8	73.9	14.6
2. Ration and Contract Prices Doubled: /d	463.1	193.6	111.4	42.7	12.9	13.8	74.0	14.7
3. Recession Scenarios:								
-low productivity growth /e	446.2	190.2	106.0	40.6	12.4	13.7	69.1	14.1
-general agric. recession /f	449.0	190.8	107.9	40.2	12.3	13.4	70.0	14.4
4. Recovery/Trade Reform Scenarios:								
-agricultural "recovery" /g	472.8	194.4	115.5	42.8	13.3	13.6	78.1	15.2
-recovery and trade policy reform /h	472.7	200.2	112.8	43.0	13.3	13.5	75.0	15.0

| | OTHER OILS/INDUSTRIAL CROPS | | | HORTICULTURE | | MULTIPLE CROPPING INDEX |
	Oilseeds	Cotton	Sugar	Fruits	Vegetables	
Base Period (1985-1987)	15.3	4.0	4.9	14.1	167.9	146
Projection Scenarios (1995)						
1. Base Run /c	19.0	5.1	7.5	18.1	189.3	151
2. Ration and Contract Prices Doubled: /d	19.0	5.1	7.4	18.1	189.4	151
3. Recession Scenarios:						
-low productivity growth /e	18.3	4.8	6.9	16.9	187.3	153
-general agricultural recession /f	18.0	4.7	7.4	16.7	186.4	154
4. Recovery/Trade Reform Scenarios:						
-general agric. "recovery" /g	20.2	5.3	8.0	19.1	192.0	151
-recovery and trade policy reform /h	20.2	5.3	7.7	18.0	192.1	154

Source: MAT-1 Model Projection Runs

Notes: (see notes to Table 2.2)

/a based on Chinese definition: includes fine and coarse grains, some tubers and soybeans at unmilled weights.
/b mainly coarse grains.
/c the base run features moderate productivity increases and the "base run" per capita income growth assumptions shown above in the notes to this table, a complete liberalization of domestic grain pricing and marketing with the exception of amounts currently procured at below market contract prices and sold at urban ration
/d other assumptions same as base run.
/e low productivity growth plus base run assumptions.
/f devaluation, but with restricted grain imports, low productivity growth and recession assumptions.
/g high productivity growth, income growth assumptions: "recovery 3(a)", others as in base run.
/h moderate productivity growth, "recovery 3(b)" assumptions, devaluation and free trade in agricultural products.

F. INTERNATIONAL TRADE & PRICES

2.34 China, like many developing countries, continues to pursue extractive policies towards agriculture to support industrialization and non-agricultural development. In the foreign trade sector, this should appear as an anti-trade bias, induced by the trade regime, patterns of subsidization and taxation,

---

24/(...continued)
international rice markets on a broad scale using its current varieties, post-harvest and grading procedures.

exchange rate policies and the foreign exchange allocation system. Indeed, even for grains, the anti-trade bias appears rather severe, in spite of China's importance in the international grains trade.

2.35 On the basis of information available for 1988, "spot" estimates of nominal and effective protection and of domestic resource costs were computed for the four major grains 25/ to show the disincentives posed by denied foreign trade (and import substitution) opportunities near points of grain importation and exporting in China. 26/ When valued at the prevailing official exchange rate in 1988, the anti-trade bias on rice and soybeans was strong in 1988. 27/ At a shadow exchange rate, however, all four commodities (wheat, rice, corn and soybeans) appear to have been severely disprotected. Clearly, in 1988, China's foreign trade corporations (FTCs) and the state-owned commercial system were enjoying substantial economic rents at the expense of producers located near the shipment centers. 28/

-China's Revealed Comparative Advantage in Grains.

2.36 Owing to the country's vast size, underdeveloped marketing and over-stretched transportation system, an effective price transmission for agricultural products across regions and inland from the coastal provinces and other border points is severely constrained. Since an improvement in rapidity of price transmission will require major new investments, involving long development periods, an interim of several years could pass before China can become equipped with the necessary infrastructure to permit changes in the prices of tradeables to markedly influence domestic prices much beyond China's points of entry. For predicting gains from export specialization under these conditions, Balassa's (1965) index of revealed comparative advantage is utilized, 29/ which is the ratio of China's sectoral share of agricultural exports to world agriculture's share of the value of the total international trade. Estimates are shown in Table 2.4. The decline in China's revealed comparative advantage in grain products, vegetable oil and for agriculture as a whole, with occasional fluctuations, has been steady: between the early 1970s and 1987 the index declined more than fifteen-fold in the case of rice, declined to very low levels in the case of wheat, and was about halved for vegetable oil and agriculture.

25/ World Bank (1990g), Tables 19-20.

26/ Where border price transmission effects in this continental-sized nation might not otherwise be diluted by transportation constraints between inland production centers and port facilities, official procurement and distribution policies, and the simple inefficiency of state-owned parastatals responsible for China's internal and foreign trade in grains.

27/ Again with the caveat that China's low quality rice was being compared without discounting with the higher quality rices being traded internationally.

28/ While heavily subsidizing grain imports to encourage consumption.

29/ Estimates of theoretical comparative advantage are shown in World Bank (1990g), Tables 19-20.

2.37 Reference to the net imports of individual commodities during the 1980s 30/ suggests why: net exports of maize have plateaued, net imports of wheat continue to expand, while China's previously large net exports in the international rice trade have virtually disappeared.

Table 2.4 China's Revealed Comparative Advantage /a in Grains, Agriculture & Other Sectors, 1955-1987

	Agriculture				Other Primary Products	Textiles	Other Manufactures
	rice	wheat	veg oil	total			
1955-59	-na-	-na-	-na-	-na-	-na-	2.1	-na-
1965-69	-na-	-na-	-na-	2.1	0.30	3.3	0.44
1970-74	36.33	0.25	2.40	2.3	0.30	3.4	0.48
1975-77	30.30	0.26	1.45	2.2	0.70	3.9	0.46
1978-80	-na-	-na-	-na-	1.9	0.80	4.6	0.48
1981-83	-na-	-na-	-na-	1.6	1.00	5.0	0.47
1984-86	4.05	0.17	1.23	1.4	1.10	5.1	0.47
1987	2.25	0.20	1.02	1.3	0.70	6.5	0.49

/a Share of an economy's exports due to these commodities relative to the share of these commodities in total world exports, following Balassa (1965). Following Anderson, agriculture is defined as SITC sections 0,1,2 (excluding 27,28) and 4; Other primary products (minerals and metals) as SITC section 3 and divisions 27, 28 and 68; textiles (and clothing) as SITC divisions 65 and 84; and other manufactures as SITC sections 5-9 (excluding 65, 68 and 84).

Sources: (1) Rice, wheat vegetable oils--Yeats (1990)
(2) All others--Anderson (1989), Table 3.8, p. 41

-Foreign Trade Scenarios

2.38 Current projections of Chinese import requirements, export possibilities and international and domestic price movements are available from a variety of sources. 31/ The sometimes contradictory results of recent projection exercises are a reflection of the numerous, tenuous assumptions made in the absence of more assured planning criteria, but they all point to a common conclusion: that China's future interventions in the international grain trade, and the manner in which this is managed, could cause dramatic changes in the level and structure of international prices, and therefore in the volume of foreign exchange which China will have to remit annually to finance its purchases of foreign grains. The results of the USDA's Static World Policy Simulation Model (SWOPSIM) are summarized below, including foreign trade scenarios and the likely impact on the structure of international grain prices.

2.39 The SWOPSIM is designed to detect separately or conjointly the influence of trade policy changes and domestic market liberalization in exporting and importing countries. A base run on the impact of trade and internal liberalization by China was carried out by Dixit and Webb (1989). 32/ This run was based on the assumption of a complete unilateral liberalization of China's foreign agricultural trade regime and demonopolization of the administration of foreign trade (i.e. a price transmission coefficient of 1.0 was assumed), highly negative producer subsidy equivalents (PSEs) (about 80% for rice and

30/ Annex 2, paras 41-44 and World Bank (1990g), Table 15.

31/ World Bank (1990g), para 4.17.

32/ Results are summarized in World Bank (1990g), Table 24.

pork) **33/** and strongly positive consumer subsidy equivalents (CSEs). The official exchange rate was utilized.

2.40   The base run scenario suggests that were China to abandon its policy of taxing agriculture and subsidizing consumers, China's production would expand and consumption would contract. With no offsetting adjustments by other participants in the international grain markets, world commodity prices would be even more depressed than in recent years. **34/** The international prices of rice and pork, for example, could decline by as much as 15%, and though wheat and coarse grain prices would fall by lesser amounts, China's policies would none-the-less continue to influence world wheat and coarse grains prices more than the policies of any other country except for the USA and EEC.

2.41   World trade volumes could expand considerably if China unilaterally liberalized its policies. The expansion of China's exports could be especially large in the rice and pork trade. **35/** In corn, China switches from a net exporter to a net importer, expanding net imports of corn by 3.3 million tons to feed its rapidly expanding pork industry. Global trade in wheat remains virtually unchanged, and China's net imports decline slightly. There would also be interesting distributive effects: all in China's favor. From a unilateral liberalization, China's trade balance could improve by $9 billion and its producer incomes by $19 billion. The big losers would be the USA, EEC and the other developing countries.

2.42   To isolate the influence of the various policy assumptions employed by Dixit and Webb, several variants of the model were tested. The effects of unilateral policy change were re-examined by first halving the PSEs and CSEs assumed for grains in China, which the mission feels is a more realistic representation of observed domestic/border price ratios. Then, by freeing up the sector on the basis of the revised subsidy equivalents, tests were run on more restrictive (and probably more realistic) price transmission coefficients. These tests were repeated under an assumed devaluation of the real exchange rate with PSEs and CSEs reset at their original levels. Lastly, the results of earlier runs to examine the effects of liberalization by the Industrialized Market Economies (IMEs) are presented, to compare possible outcomes of the Uruguay Round and perhaps a countervailing action to China's own liberalization. **36/**

33/ When computed with reference to border price equivalents (SWOPSIM solutions are generated essentially by setting China's PSEs and CSEs at zero).

34/ In a separate paper, Roningen and Dixit (1989) show that the USA's policies on average depress world agricultural prices 6 per cent. The SWOPSIM analysis thus suggests that by pursuing a policy that taxes the agricultural sector, China has effectively neutralized the price depressing effects of U.S. agricultural policies.

35/ Even were China able to regain a dominating position in the shallow international rice trade, the total export volume would be small (1.6-2.0 million tons), which would hardly affect the above conclusion (para 2.21) concerning the inadvisable program to foster a substantial increase in rice production.

36/ The results also are summarized in World Bank (1990g), Table 24.

2.43   In all of the scenarios representing unilateral reform by China of its policy framework for grain sector pricing and marketing, the projections of world commodity prices, global trade volumes and the distribution of gains and losses internationally would be in the same direction as in the base run. Though the movements in international prices, trade volumes and gains to the Chinese economy in the trade liberalization and devaluation run exceed the base run results. A comparison of the international price effects from unilateral reform by China with scenarios of agricultural trade liberalization by the IMEs shows rather starkly the strong potential influence which China could have on the international grain trade. Though liberalization in the context of the GATT framework by IMEs of their international rice, wheat and corn trade would tend to offset the depressing influence on international prices stemming from a unilateral liberalization by China, the Chinese influence would generally carry in pork markets, and would reinforce a downward trend in the price of oilseeds that would also result from a freeing of the IMEs' agricultural trading policies. 37/

G. DOMESTIC PRICE PROJECTIONS

2.44   Projections of domestic agricultural prices were made by using the MAT-1 model. Summary trends under various policy scenarios, in constant 1986 prices, are shown on the left hand side of Table 2.5. A comparison of these trends with projected movements in international prices is shown on the right hand side of the table for the base run. Not surprisingly, the projections mirror the results of the volumetric projections discussed above, for consumption, production and China's foreign grain trade.

Table 2.5 Projected Free Market Price Trends to 1995 Grains and Livestock Products

(base year = 1986)

Scenario	Domestic Price Trends							Domestic/International Price Ratios (constant 1985 prices, 1986=100)			
	All Crops /a	Rice /b	Wheat	Coarse Grains	Soybeans	Livestock Products		Rice	Wheat	Maize	Soybeans
	-----(total % change: 1986-95)-----										
1. Base Run /c	0.1	-6.9	3.4	11.3	-6.7	15.6	Year				
2. Grain Ration and Contract Procurement Prices Doubled: /d	0.1	-6.8	3.3	10.9	-6.0	15.3	1986-	100	100	100	100
							1995-	99	137	129	92
3. Recession Scenarios:											
-low productivity growth /e	6.0	-1.3	11.4	18.5	-6.1	20.6					
-general agric. recession /f	8.0	-0.5	17.4	28.9	-8.1	30.5					
4. Recovery/Trade Reform Scenarios:											
-general agric. "recovery" /g	0.5	-10.4	4.0	13.8	-4.7	18.9					
-recovery and trade policy reform /h	5.0	-0.6	6.0	26.8	0.0	23.9					

Source: MAT-1 Projections

Notes and Footnotes /a - /h: (see bottom of Table 2.3)

37/ To realize these gains, however, China would have to permit competition among Chinese enterprises in the foreign grain trade, firstly by relaxing licensing requirements and the effective monopoly reserved for the China National Cereals, Oils and Foodstuffs Import-Export Corporation, and secondly by improving price transmission to China's grain producers. The results also assume that China would be producing and exporting rice to international quality standards, and could rapidly expand the production of corn and soybeans. Again, it will be necessary for China to firstly improve the quality of its rice exports, and second to import superior germ plasm to improve the yield potential and agroclimatic adaptability of its maize and possibly also of soybeans.

2.45   In all of the scenarios, the domestic prices of wheat and coarse grain prices, and especially the prices of livestock products are projected to increase in real terms. Domestic rice prices, on the other hand, are projected to decline under all scenarios, a reflection of the currently saturated rice market in China and limited export opportunities for China's low quality rice. The results also show that if constrained growth in trend prices is an important objective of grain sector policy, the least disruptive scenario would be to raise contract procurement and urban ration prices (scenario 2) without further adjustments to the trade regime for grains and the real exchange rate. 38/ Though there would be an opportunity cost: about 9.6 million tons annually in foregone grain production, more than 20 million tons in foregone consumption, and 5.8 million tons/year in foregone intake of livestock products (not shown). All of the projections suggest, however, that it is the consumption of animal products which will drive both the prices of feed and food grains in the coming years, since the volumes of urban and rural per capita direct consumption are basically invariant across scenarios (Annex 4, Table 3) while the consumption of animal products and feedgrains are quite volatile. Further, the level of increased animal products consumption will largely determine (together with productivity growth) the size and composition of future increments in Chinese grain production.

2.46   The indices of projected trends in domestic wholesale prices relative to the Bank's international price projections again show that only marginal gains in the export market could be expected should China continue to stimulate the production of low quality rice. These indices also reinforce the conclusion drawn above that China would be ill-advised to concentrate in the future as it has in the past on maize exportation as a policy objective, rather than using domestically produced maize to satisfy the growing internal demand for feedgrains, while meeting unfulfilled demand through lower cost imports. The comparisons also imply that the same holds for soybeans should domestic prices begin to stiffen.

H. THE OPPORTUNITY COST OF SUBSIDIZED GRAIN

2.47   As opposed to the financial outlays required of government to sustain the existing, state-run distribution system for grains and fertilizers, the net economic subsidy resulting from China's urban consumption policies is measured with reference to market prices and/or border prices. The total value of hidden consumer subsidies in 1985/87 ("1986"), measured with reference to domestic free market prices, is estimated to have been ¥ 40.7 billion, nearly ¼ of the total value of agricultural output in that year (Annex 4, Table 7). This was partially offset by the indirect producer tax, implicit in the low contract procurement prices, which was estimated to be ¥ 19 billion or nearly ½ the value of hidden subsidies. The economic opportunity cost of the subsidies in 1986, computed with reference to product price differentials only, made up the difference between the hidden subsidies and the indirect

---

38/ Assuming that the moderate trends in agricultural productivity can be maintained and that growth of urban and rural per capita incomes won't diverge much from recent levels.

tax. **39/**

2.48 Real values of both the hidden subsidies and producer taxes decline considerably when projections are made under the MAT-1 policy assumptions, as does the estimated economic opportunity cost. Not surprisingly, the biggest reduction occurs through the simple expedient of doubling the administered prices associated with grain procurement and ration sales (though not the largest projected increase in GVAO). Even under the other scenarios, the projected economic loss declines somewhat, while the farming population would be the main beneficiaries--who respond to higher real incomes by increasing production, and urban consumers would be the main losers--due mainly to reduced subsidization and shifts in the commodity composition of consumption towards unsubsidized, higher valued products.

I. EVIDENCE FROM TAIWAN 40/

2.49 Food balance sheets for Taiwan between 1952-87 provide a capstone referent for projecting future trends in China's grain sector. **41/** The data indicate that, with the strong sustained increase in per capita GNP, total per capita grain utilization increased by two-thirds from 254 kg in 1952 to 426 kg in 1987. More than 95% of the increase in total per capita grain utilization occurred during the two decades 1952 to 1972 (total grain utilization reached 411 kg per capita in 1972 and then increased by only 4% over the next one-and-one-half decades to 426 kg per capita in 1987). Adding in losses through waste and utilization of grain as seed and in manufacturing, total per capita utilization of grain in Taiwan in 1987 was about 445 kg per capita. Simple regression analysis indicates that the income elasticity of total demand for grain in Taiwan is 0.26. **42/** Comparing per capita consumption of grain and animal products, current levels of consumption in China approximate those of Taiwan in the early-1970s.

-Direct Consumption

2.50 Total direct per capita consumption of table grain increased by 19% from 224 kg in 1952 to a peak of 267 kg in 1969 and then declined by 31% to 183 kg in 1987. This trend strongly suggests that direct per capita grain consumption in China (a) did truly peak in 1984 at 257 kg, and (b) can be expected to decline by a large margin provided future increases in the supply

---

39/ Technically, producer subsidies associated with price distortions in the delivery of inputs (e.g. fertilizers) should also be accounted for in the computation of subsidies. However an array of reference prices (free-market prices, border price parities, or some estimation of the shadow value of productive inputs) is not available. Since the economic value of the inputs subsidies is likely to be small in any event when compared with the hidden consumer subsidy and the indirect producer tax, omission of this item would not alter orders of magnitude.

40/ All references to Taiwan in this report refer to "Taiwan, Province of China".

41/ Annual per capita GNP and grain consumption and utilization in Taiwan during 1952-87 are reported in World Bank (1990a), Table 6.

42/ World Bank (1990a), Appendix 3.

of animal products and other preferred foods are sufficient to allow
significant changes in the composition of average diet. Rice is by far the
most important table grain in Taiwan, and the trend in direct per capita
consumption of rice from 188 kg in 1952 to a peak of 211 kg in 1967 followed
by a decline of 45% to 117 kg in 1987 has driven the overall trend in total
direct per capita consumption. Direct per capita consumption of wheat and
pulses (mostly soybeans), in contrast, increased steadily from 15.4 kg and 7.3
kg in 1952 to 38.2 kg and 23.4 kg in 1987 respectively. Direct per capita
consumption of tubers declined sharply from more than 10 kg in the 1950s to
about 1 kg in mid-1980s. Direct per capita consumption of corn and other
coarse grains increased from less than 1 kg in 1952 to a peak of 13 kg in 1979
and then declined to about 4 kg in 1987. Regression analysis of the Taiwan
per capita GNP and consumption data indicates income elasticities of direct
demand for grain, rice, wheat, corn (and other coarse grains), tubers and
pulses are in the expected range and comparable to similar estimates for the
Chinese Mainland. 43/

-Indirect Consumption

2.51 Contrasting the decline in direct consumption of grain of nearly 80 kg
per capita during 1972-87, indirect per capita consumption of grain as animal
feed quintupled from 30 kg in 1952 to 148 kg in 1972 and then increased
another 64% to 243 kg in 1987. The 95 kg per capita increase in indirect
consumption of grain during 1972-87 was in large part offset by the decline in
direct consumption over the same period. As a result, total per capita
utilization of grain in Taiwan increased only marginally during 1972-87 and
indirect consumption of grain surpassed direct consumption beginning in 1983.
Corn's share of total animal feed increased from 1% in 1952 to 77% in 1987.
Regression analysis indicates that the income elasticity of indirect demand
for grain as animal feed in Taiwan is 1.19, again, comparable to China's.

2.52 The strong growth in indirect demand for grain as animal feed has been
sustained by large increases in the consumption of pork and, in particular, of
poultry and eggs (from 15.1, 1.4 and 1.6 kg per capita in 1952 to 34.8, 20.4
and 11.5 kg per capita in 1987 respectively). Regression analysis indicates
strongly positive income elasticities of demand for pork, poultry, other
meats, and eggs of 0.43, 1.47, 0.91 and 1.08 respectively. Note, finally, that
these figures indicate that in 1987, at levels of total per capita utilization
of grain (445 kg) only 19% greater than average annual domestic per capita
supply of grain in China (374 kg during 1986-88), the per capita supply of
pork and eggs was about double and the per capita supply of poultry about ten
times greater in Taiwan as in China.

J. PROJECTED INVESTMENT, GRAIN DISTRIBUTION EXPENDITURES AND FINANCING

2.53 In 1989, China introduced an austerity program which led to a credit
squeeze at all levels, including in agriculture. In general, the cutback
demonstrated what had been becoming clear earlier in the 1980s, that there is

---

43/ cf. Appendices 2 and 3 to World Bank (1990a).

a need to look for new sources of government revenue, a need to increase the buoyancy of existing revenue sources, and to program a more efficient allocation of government expenditures among sectoral development programs. In this connection, there is also a need to emphasize that more of the revenues generated in the agricultural sector (both transparent and hidden) should be invested for the benefit of the agricultural sector. Though this contribution has been declining of late, revenues foregone in agriculture to limit state outlays for the sake of subsidized urban sales need to be reduced considerably more (Annex 3) to provide farmers with appropriate incentives for achieving the projected grain production targets. Finally, government should provide needed incentives to individual farmers to finance investments from their own savings and borrowing in rural financial markets. In this context, government must also make sure that timely allocations of inputs and credit for agriculture are available in adequate amounts to all farmers without excessive administrative requirements but at real positive rates of interest.

-Investment Requirements

2.54 The state has established a very ambitious program for the long-term development of the grain sector, which raises questions about the adequacy and availability of financing. According to the Ministry of Finance (MOF) and the Chinese Investment & Trust Corporation for Agricultural Development, a long-term planning exercise carried out for the grain sector in 1988 estimated that average annual expenditures in 1988 prices of some ¥ 250 billion (all sources) will be required between 1988-2000 to reach the target of 500-520 million tons of grain by the Year 2000. An average annual expenditure of ¥ 26.7 billion is projected for the investment items, an amount that is 40% higher than total state expenditures on agriculture in 1987, and roughly a six-fold nominal increase over realized expenditures on capital construction in 1987. 44/

2.55 The largest share of annual investments would be earmarked for irrigation and drainage development, reclamation schemes on arable lands and land consolidation projects (56% of the total), to be distributed as indicated in Table 2.6. During the period of the Eighth Five Year Plan period (1991-1995), the MWR expects that government spending on water resources development can be increased from the current level of ¥ 7 billion annually to ¥ 8 billion (at 1988 prices), which would represent only about half of the annual investment needed to satisfy the level of annual investment identified in the long-term planning exercise.

2.56 Average annual investment requirements to achieve the mission's grain sector production projections (Table 2.3 above) also were estimated, using crude incremental capital-output ratios that were constructed from a review of staff appraisal reports for agricultural projects in China, and an assumed gestation period of 5 years. The estimates are shown in the right-hand side of Annex 4, Table 7. There are two striking features in these estimates. First, though derived by an entirely different methodology, the projected annual requirement associated with the base projection run (¥ 16.1 billion at 1986

44/ Reviewed in World Bank (1990h), Section V.

prices, equivalent to ¥ 18.7 billion in 1988 prices) 45/ is remarkably similar to the annual requirement for the grain sector that was derived in the MOF's long-term planning exercise (Table 2.6). Second, the estimate from the MAT-1 model's base projection run is associated with projected real growth in grain production of 1.87% p.a. (projected production of 463 million tons). While lower, and grounded in production responses to liberalized pricing, internal marketing and foreign trade, these results are in the neighborhood of the implied official estimates of the growth in grain production of 2.0-2.3% p.a. that will be needed to produce 500-520 million tons by the Year 2000. Thus, orders of magnitude reported in Table 2.6 are probably the minimum representation of the average annual investment between 1988-2000 required to attain the government's long-term grain production targets.

Table 2.6 Government Projections: Annual Investment Expenditure On Grain Sector Development Programs (1988-2000)

Program	Average Annual Investment
	(1988 ¥ billions)
Irrigation/Drainage Development /a	5.8
Land Reclamation Works /b	6.7
Land Consolidation Program /c	2.5
Total	15.0

Source: World Bank (1990h), Section V

/a   Development of new areas.
/b   Mainly on low-medium yield grain areas and coastal lands.
       Includes some irrigation/drainage rehabilitation works, aiming
       to increase grain yields by 3/4 to 1¼ tons/ha.
/c   To promote "scale farming" in grains some 20 million ha.
       Includes irrigation/drainage investments at the farm level.

2.57   The planning assumptions behind the long-term projections give cause for concern, especially on the sourcing side of the ledger. Particularly suspect are the farmer savings estimates, which are projected to provide more than 60% of the total resources needed--quite apart from farmers additional contributions under corvée. (Financing sourced through the State budget would account for only 10% of the requirement.) Both the volume of savings and the assumptions that farmers would be willing to allocate their savings to the grain sector (or that the financial sector could continue to bear the costs of funds associated with high deposit rates of interest for on-lending to low return activities) are suspect. Firstly, though farmer savings are high by any standard, the savings rates have proved unstable in recent years, dipping from 38% in 1987 to a figure below 20% by the end of 1988, before recovering

---

45/ Computed by applying the Bank's GDP price deflators for gross domestic investment in China (1987 = 5.7%, 1988 = 9.7%).

somewhat in 1989 and 1990. **46/** The implicit planning assumption in the above exercise of a sustained 30% rate of savings may need to be examined in considerably more detail before grain sector development programs and expenditure plans are fixed. Second, the assumption that farmers could earn enough from an increased specialization in low valued cropping (i.e. grains) to sustain these rates is equally questionable, and likely quite sensitive to the grain pricing assumptions employed. Third, recent surveys have suggested that constraints associated with administration of the PRS, particularly the maintenance of existing restrictions on land transfers and the constant threat of bureaucratic interference at the local level, have contributed to perceptions of tenurial insecurity. **47/** If generally true throughout China, the findings of these surveys imply that farmers will continue to be reluctant to invest in land improvements and other durable farm assets, regardless of improvements in pricing, marketing and inputs policies. Fourth, it is unlikely that agricultural activities writ large will provide attractive alternative opportunities for direct farmer investment in areas where township and village enterprises (TVEs) have taken off, areas which encompass about 40% of China's rural population and some of the most productive agricultural land. Thus the Government could be forced to adopt a counter-productive degree of rural coercion were it and the financial sector to seriously attempt to obtain farmer savings for investment in grain production of the magnitude foreseen in Table 2.6.

2.58   A more viable investment strategy would emphasize quickly-gestating investments having a high payback. Such are available in the agricultural sector, in the form of irrigation/drainage systems repair and rehabilitation works. It is estimated that some 10-15 million ha of cultivated area, mostly located in the fertile but water deficient areas of North China, require rehabilitation of irrigation and drainage facilities to prevent waterlogging and reduce salinization. Grain production increases of 15.0-22.5 million tons could be associated with these kinds of investments. Though rehabilitation works typically gestate quickly, often within during the same year that implementation begins, the overall financing requirement will not be small in comparison with present state (i.e. central and provincial governments') investment allocations for agricultural development. For example, should only 10 million ha. ultimately be rehabilitated, at a unit cost of say ¥ 1500 per ha. (US$317), the total investment requirement of ¥ 15 billion would be equivalent to nearly four times the entire state financial expenditure on capital construction in agriculture during 1987, and would equal in value the annual requirement for the entirety of grain sector investment foreseen in the long-term planning exercise. However, if implemented during the Eighth Five Year Plan period in lieu of the MWR's more modest investment program (para 2.55), the rehabilitation work could be completed within 3-4 years. Equally important, it could be financed well within the resource envelope government

---

46/ Estimates for 1987 and 1988 provided by the former Research Center for Rural Development of the State Council. Recent press reports suggest that farmer savings have again increased, as manifested in an unusually large increase in farm household savings deposits with the Agricultural Bank of China. This probably represents an extension to the rural sector of the general weakness in consumer demand that appeared in 1989 and 1990.

47/ cf. Feder et al (1990) and Prosterman et al (1990).

has identified for MWR's program, while minimizing the requirement for additional taxes and contributions from the rural population, or resource transfers from the "urban" sectors. 48/

-Expenditure on Subsidized Food Programs

2.59 In addition to investment expenditures, governments at various levels recover only a small portion of the farm inputs subsidies (mainly associated with fertilizer distribution), of differences between the sales price of urban rations (mainly grains) and the higher (though still below-market) official procurement prices, and the differences between c.i.f. import prices and the price of urban ration sales. The government also "reimburses" the financial sector for advances made to cover the General Grain Bureau's (GGB's) annual

Table 2.7 Estimated State Expenditures On Provision of Urban Food Rations, 1988

	¥ billion
Farm Inputs	1.0 /a
Consumer Food Price Differentials	26.4
Grain Import Subsidy	1.1 /b
GGB's Operating Losses	9.5 /b
Total	38.0

Source: World Bank (1990b), Section III

/a Subsidy at retail level only. Excludes manufacturing and import subsidies, and subsidies incurred at the wholesale level for transportation, price differentials and other operating losses (cf. para 1.22 and Annex 3, para 50).
/b Mission estimate.

operating losses in grain distribution. Referred to conjointly as the "grain subsidy" in China, the government in 1988 had to extend approximately ¥ 38.0 billion to finance these uncovered expenditures, equivalent to 14.6% of total state revenues, almost 3% of GDP, and fully 8.4% of agricultural GDP (Table 2.7). So long as the state remains responsible for financing price differentials and shortfalls in the official procurement and distribution system, however, there are few short-term options available for reducing government's total financial expenditure on consumer food "subsidies" (Chinese definition) short of markedly increasing urban ration prices towards the level

---

48/ Under the Eighth Plan, the annual financing of the MWR's program would be structured as follows:

- ¥ 2.5-3.00 billion from Provincial and County Governments for capital construction;
- ¥ 2.5 billion from Provincial and County Governments for small-scale irrigation and on-farm works;
- ¥ 1.5 billion for large-scale flood control and irrigation projects financed by the central Government; and
- ¥ 1.25 billion from various revolving funds.

Additional funds would be sought from foreign sources, of which the series of Irrigated Agriculture Intensification Loans, proposed for financing by the Bank, would constitute the major foreign financial input.

of the higher contract procurement prices and/or reducing the amounts of grain distributed at ration sales prices (approximately 65 million tons in 1987-- more recent figures are not available). For example, to have completely eliminated the consumer food price differential in 1987---which is the largest contributor to the state's food expenditure outlays--the median ration sales prices would have had to be increased by 65%, 49/ and the amounts distributed at "planned" (ration sales) prices reduced by 8.3 million tons. 50/ Since 1987, the differential between planned procurement and sales has widened, while the amounts distributed under planned prices may also have increased. Thus an even larger price increase and the associated cut back in ration sales would be needed to eliminate the price differential today.

2.60 Minor additional savings could be realized by phasing out the "3-linkage" farm inputs program, to which most of the inputs subsidies shown above can be attributed, and the grain import subsidies. There are also minimal subsidies on fertilizer imports (not shown). Reducing cover for the GGB's operating losses, however, will require investments to improve the GGB's technical handling and storage capabilities, institutional strengthening and staffing reforms, and--over the longer term--more exposure to market forces and competition, and possibly some divestiture.

2.61 If the above reservations are valid, the prospects for grain fundamentalism are not very encouraging. In addition to possible agrotechnical and purely economic constraints on achieving self-sufficiency in grains by the Year 2000, China will face binding constraints on the financial resource mobilization side--that can only be relaxed at the expense of realizing her higher-priority non-agricultural development objectives. What is basically required is a hard nosed comprehensive flow of funds analysis for the entire agricultural sector, domestic and external, and centered on grains to realistically establish the financial feasibility of its questionable plans for grain production. The outcome could prove sobering, and would certainly improve the state's ability to forecast developments in the real sector and to influence these through perhaps more viable policy interventions.

K. PROJECTED DEVELOPMENTS IN THE FERTILIZER SECTOR

2.62 Plans and Prospects. Fertilizer production capacity has been added almost every year and major additions occurred during the 1970s. However, additions to capacity tapered off after 1979. 51/ Several new fertilizer plants are now under construction and are expected to come on-stream in the early 1990s. Actual and projected consumption, production and imports for nitrogen, phosphate and potash fertilizers in China is shown in Table 2.8. Fertilizer production growth is expected to be much higher for phosphate and

---

49/ Computed from World Bank (1990g), Table 4.

50/ Computed with reference to World Bank (1990f), Appendix 1, Table 1. In the 1980s, sales at rationed prices have exceeded procurement at the planned contract price. In 1987, the difference (8.3 million tons) was supplied from procurement at the near-market level negotiated procurement prices.

51/ World Bank (1990d), Figure 6.

potash than for nitrogen production. Based on current government investment programs, it appears that the government is targeting investments to attain self-sufficiency in domestic nitrogen and phosphate production by the Year 2000. However, China may not have a comparative advantage in nitrogen and phosphate production over imports, at least at the scales envisaged.

Table 2.8 Consumption, Production and Imports of Chemical Fertilizers, 1980-1988

Year	Consumption				Production				Imports			
	N	P_2O_5	K_2O	Total	N	P_2O_5	K_2O	Total	N	P_2O_5	K_2O	Total
	----------------------(million tons)------------------------											
1980	10.2	2.4	0.1	12.7	10.0	2.3	0.02	12.3	1.5	0.4	0.1	2.0
1985	13.5	3.5	0.9	17.9	11.4	1.8	0.02	13.2	2.0	0.9	0.4	3.3
1986	13.7	4.5	1.1	19.3	11.6	2.3	0.02	13.9	1.7	0.6	0.6	2.9
1987	13.9	4.9	1.2	20.0	13.4	3.2	0.04	16.7	-na-	-na-	-na-	5.4
1988 /a	14.9	5.2	1.4	21.4	13.6	3.7	0.05	17.4	-na-	-na-	-na-	7.3

Source: World Bank (1990d), Tables 3, 12 and 18.

/a Estimated.

2.63 Self-Sufficiency vs Imports. On the basis of projected fertilizer consumption and actual fertilizer production in 1988, incremental nutrient consumption projections to the Year 2000 could be as follows:

	N	P_2O_5	K_2O	Total
	----(million tons)----			
1990	2.26	2.10	1.60	5.96
1995	4.80	3.52	2.30	10.62
2000	7.22	4.87	2.95	15.04

According to the Ministry of Chemical Industry (MCI), the investment costs for fertilizer production in China during 1989 averaged between ¥ 3,500-4,000 per nutrient ton or at least about $850/ton of nutrients at the present exchange rate (¥ 4.72/US$). Assuming that all incremental nitrogen and phosphate fertilizer consumption to the Year 2000 will be locally produced (and that all potash will continue to be imported), the estimated total investment and import costs in constant 1989 prices from 1988 to 2000 would be $10.3 billion and 5.9 billion, respectively, 52/ averaging $0.86 billion per year on investment items and $0.48 billion annually on potash imports.

2.64 When compared with the 1988 level of consumption, an additional 11.02 million tons of nutrient (23.1 million product tons) would need to be distributed from the factories and ports in the Year 2000 to retail points. At present, the existing fertilizer marketing infrastructure in China is neither adequate nor in good working order. Hence, sizeable downstream investments in marketing would need to be associated particularly with an expansion of domestic manufacturing capacity. As a rule-of-thumb, the international fertilizer industry allocates at least another dollar in marketing facilities for every dollar to be invested in production facilities. 53/ According to

52/ World Bank (1990d), para 9.03.

53/ Kreuser and Sheldrick (1988).

this general rule, additional investments totalling some $9.4 billion in fertilizer marketing infrastructure could be required by the Year 2000, averaging $0.78 billion per year in 1988 prices. The above investments do not include variable marketing costs. Typical average fertilizer marketing costs in Asia are about $40/product ton. **54/** As a result, the annual average marketing costs needed to finance the **average** annual additional distribution between 1988-2000 (12.55 million product tons) **55/** could be in the neighborhood of $0.5 billion. Alternatively, were all of the incremental fertilizer consumption to be met through imports, annual imports by the Year 2000 could amount to 31.2 million product tons, costing US$ 5.1 billion per year in constant 1989 international prices.

2.65 _A Balanced Approach._ Being grounded in limited information, the cost estimates given above are necessarily crude. However, a simplified comparison of annual outlays--were China to pursue its self-sufficiency strategy (except potash)--with an import strategy to satisfy incremental consumption requirements, is summarized below:

| | Average Annual Outlays | |
Category	Pure Import Strategy	Investment-Cum-Import Strategy
	----------(billion $)-------------	
NPK Imports	3.36	-
NP Investment in Production	-	0.86
K Imports	-	0.48
NP Production Costs	-	2.28
NPK Investment in Marketing	0.78	0.78
NPK Marketing Costs	0.50	0.50
Total	4.64	4.90

Source: World Bank (1990d), para 9.07

2.66 The annual outlays under an investment-cum-import strategy are estimated to be about $4.90 billion/year, which is slightly higher than projected outlays under a fertilizer import strategy. However, there are risks associated with either approach which argue in favor of a lesser degree of self-sufficiency than is currently being planned. An investment strategy is likely to encounter cost overruns since Chinese unit investment cost estimates tend to be on the low side, and often understate contingencies. Furthermore, an investment strategy--to an extent China would increase its presence in international markets for fertilizer raw materials--might also induce unpleasant price increases since these markets are even more concentrated on the supply side than the fertilizer product trade. On the other hand, an import strategy could place added price pressure in the oligopolized international fertilizers markets, possibly inducing significant price

---

54/ Mudahar and Kapusta (1987).

55/ The annual increment is projected to be lower in the early years, expanding to 23.1 million product tons by the Year 2000.

increases. Use of longer-term contracts may partially offset these pressures, which the industry would likely avail to China in view of the China National Chemicals Import and Export Corporation's (SINOCHEM) international reputation as a reliable and responsible customer. It is thus preferable that a balance be struck, one which could minimize the risks inherent in either approach while constraining annual outlays to manageable levels.

III. STRATEGIC & POLICY IMPLICATIONS FOR THE GRAIN SECTOR

3.01 In the 1980s, free market prices for grain in China have shown cycles of collapse (1984 and 1985), wild seasonal swings around an upwards trend (1986-1988), and another abrupt collapse (late-1989 and 1990), generally mirroring cycles in grain production and importation. During periods of price escalation, the gap between free market and contract procurement prices widened, making it very difficult for the government to finance extra procurements in periods of comparative shortage. During periods of relative surplus, the GGB was unable physically to store and move sufficient grains through the state's commercial system to maintain price floors. Foreign trade could have been used to dampen some of the grain price fluctuations near ports and major cities, and in the animal feed industry. But the cumbersome administration of foreign trade led to unnecessarily lagged response to domestic supply gaps, and to peak importations during years of peak production, frequently unsynchronized with domestic production and consumption balances.

3.02 The Government's objectives for the grain sector are vague, both in respect to details and policy instruments. Wedded to a targeting that doesn't discriminate amongst product quality or nutritional content in the increasingly diverse Chinese diet, national planners and policy makers are extremely concerned about a flattening out of grain production that has occurred since 1984, but the current government strategy does not appear to provide an appropriate long-term approach to the grain problem. Virtually the only agreed operational objectives for the sector are a desire by the Year 2000 to (a) attain self-sufficiency at unnecessarily (and unrealistically) high levels of consumption (450/475 kg/capita of unprocessed grain) and thus production in excess of 500 million tons per year), with the stimulation of rice production as a key element in the production strategy, and (b) to measurably reduce the burden of consumer food subsidies on state finances.

3.03 This lack of articulation, or perhaps an inability to set firm priorities, no doubt represents in part the continuing lack of consensus among China's top leadership concerning both the importance of the grain problem to the future development of the agricultural sector and the economy at large, and also the appropriate direction and pace of reforms to strengthen grain sector performance and its policy environment. Thus, current programs--reflected mainly in annual plans for the grain sector--remain the "hardest" single statement of government objectives and priorities, though these have an extremely short-term outlook.

3.04 The main conclusions of this report concerning the potential future performance of China's grain sector in the area of production and supply are the following:

- Government's lower-bound production target of 500 million tons of grain per year by the Year 2000 appears to be technically feasible, but its attainment will likely require the continued, costly diversion of agricultural lands, production inputs and

financial resources into grain production by administrative means. 1/
Such diversion would entail a major reversal of the reform program
in agriculture, including major restrictions on farmers' rights
acquired under the PRS. However, the technical feasibility of
targeting 50% of the production increment to increased rice
production is very questionable (para 2.21).

- With fundamental changes in policy, additional and still
  substantial gains in grain production might become financially and
  economically sustainable, perhaps in the neighborhood of 480
  million tons per year. However, grain cropping patterns will
  change, with the largest shares of incremental production accruing
  to an expansion of feedgrains (51% of the increment) and wheat
  production (32%), and much less prominently to increased rice
  production (17%). To achieve this level, however

  (a) a major reform of China's pricing and marketing
  regulations will have to be introduced, both for the
  procurement and sale of grains and fertilizers, aiming
  initially to provide more flexibility for the GGB and
  AIC enterprises whose operations are governed by the
  mandates of the state's commercial system, then later
  to promote a substantial involvement in the management
  of internal trade by non-state entities;

  (b) a more commercial orientation of China's
  international trade in grains and production inputs
  (eg. fertilizers and superior seeds) will have to be
  introduced to permit importing and exporting in accord
  with China's international comparative advantages,
  rather than governance by sectorally determined
  foreign exchange balances. Concurrently,
  responsibilities for foreign marketing and importing
  should be broadened to encourage competition among
  state-owned marketing enterprises and the
  participation of independent, more financially
  responsible entities;

  (c) the emphasis in the government's public investment
  priorities given to the implementation of low-cost and
  quickly gestating irrigation/drainage rehabilitation
  works should be increased, especially in areas where

1/ The main issue here concerns how projections and targets might be used when setting and
adjusting the future policy framework. In the context of attempting to move towards increased
reliance on market forces in the grain sector, projections and associated targets should be employed
only to indicate performance possibilities. If in doing so, China also is able to achieve its
current projections, so much the better. But should actual performance in the 1990s appear to be falling
short of pre-ordained targets, the temptation to reimpose administrative means to achieve these
targets should be assiduously avoided. To do otherwise would be inconsistent with the reforms
recently initiated, extensions to deepen these reforms which are proposed in the following
paragraphs, and would also prove quite destructive of farmer confidence and measures introduced in
1990 to shift the grain trading network towards a more commercial orientation.

it is possible to stimulate the incremental production of feedgrains and wheat (eg. the North China Plain). Meanwhile, the priorities assigned to the financing of expensive new irrigation development and land reclamation schemes, especially to projects aiming to stimulate rice production, should be carefully reconsidered; and

(d) to facilitate an economically efficient expansion of grain production, modalities must be identified which can mobilize additional investible resources through China's decentralized public investment system.

3.05   Concerning <u>demand and consumption</u>, the report's analysis shows that

- The total consumption of unprocessed grain can be expected to increase in response to population pressures and the draw on feedgrains from increased per capita consumption of animal products (itself being induced by continued growth in per capita incomes), perhaps to a level of 485-490 million tons per year.

- On a per capita basis, however, the MOA's long-term grain consumption target of 450/475 kg/cap/year of unmilled grain is not realistic and should be re-estimated using more robust techniques. The economic forces which influence consumer preference--stemming from the interactions between higher incomes and the likely adjustment of market prices to more responsive pricing and marketing arrangements--would sustain per capita demands for grain (both for direct consumption, and indirectly through the medium of animal feeds) in the neighborhood of only 380-410 kg/cap/year, equivalent to about 350 kg of milled grain. Thus, short of policy induced shortages in the supply of non-grain agricultural commodities aiming to stimulate additional grain consumption (hopefully, an unlikely event), the workings of consumer preference can be expected to constrain per capita grain consumption well below the government's long-run planning target.

3.06   Provided that the structure of incremental grain production can be shifted to favor feed grains and wheat, China--with appropriate pricing, marketing and foreign trade policies--can remain largely self-sufficient in grains, even under the less ambitious (but more realistic) performance possibilities suggested above. However, a shift in <u>foreign trade</u> patterns would have to be permitted to occur to service feedgrain demands in the livestock sector and the growing demand for wheat products.

- Firstly, the central government and provincial governments in the maize and soybean producing regions will have to recognize that China needs to shift from being a net exporter of these commodities to a net importer in order to service domestic demands for feed grains, then rectify the distorting incentives provided to producers and the FTCs by the current pricing, foreign trade and foreign exchange allocation policies.

- Second, to the extent possible within its internal transportation
  constraints, China should endeavor to substitute the importation
  of chemical fertilizers in lieu of wheat imports, both to conserve
  outlays of foreign exchange and to stimulate domestic wheat and
  feed grains production.

- Thirdly, China should encourage the importation of superior wheat,
  maize and soybean varieties, which--after testing--could
  facilitate the extension of wheat production to the environs of
  emerging centers of demand, and markedly improve corn and soybean
  yields.

3.07 The policy and institutional reforms needed to achieve even the more
modest performance scenarios suggested by this report are comprehensive, while
financing the associated investments will require a hard look at intersectoral
public expenditure priorities. Several national grain policy issues have
emerged of late. Some are genuine issues of economics, technology and finance,
others derive from the leadership's bias towards grain production targets as a
symbol of national success or security, rather than as rationally determined
requirements of economic development. As such, they are non-issues in reality,
but will continue to distort grain sector (and agricultural) policies so long
as they retain their hold on government leaders. Over the longer term,
however, China will have to face the basic question of whether self-
sufficiency in grain production is a viable food security strategy. The costs
of maintaining the current, highly subsidized system have been noted above. If
China is also nearing its effective grain production frontier, there is also
the likelihood that further gains in production will entail major and costly
infrastructure investments (eg. to expand irrigation and drainage facilities,
which would divert water away from higher valued municipal and industrial
uses), a further expansion of cultivation onto reclaimed and marginal lands,
and the substitution of lower valued grain production for higher value
agricultural activities. Import ιinancing would be (and is) a concern, though
additional exports of raw and processed agricultural products remain a
distinct possibility, which could help relieve the burden from the rest of the
economy of financing grain imports. On the other hand, a very rapid
deterioration occurred in China's import positions for wheat and fertilizers
in 1986-1989, caused by essentially stagnant wheat production and growing
demand for chemical fertilizers. 2/ An import based food security strategy
would have to carefully consider the trade-offs between incremental fertilizer
imports, which could be used to stimulate domestic grain production, and
imports of whole grain. It would also have to be managed very carefully to
avoid placing avoidable pressure on world market prices for these commodities.

2/ Having attained the status of the world's largest net importer of fertilizers, China in
1988, also became the world's largest wheat importer, about 16 million tons. However, following
record harvests in 1989 and 1990, wheat imports have begun to abate slightly, to about 15.1 million
tons in the 1989 marketing year, and an estimated 12-13 million tons in 1990.

A. PERSPECTIVES ON THE GRAIN PROBLEM

3.08 A complex set of factors were responsible for the plateauing of grain production in the second half of the 1980s, which have marooned the grain sector and its policy milieux in that unfamiliar territory between plan and market. With the expected return of normal weather in 1991, stagnation could return in the early 1990s, although owing to the irrigation rehabilitation work carried out in the Winter of 1989/90 (and increased availability of chemical fertilizers), production may fluctuate around a level higher than was achieved in the late 1980s. The root causes appear to reflect mutually unobtainable objectives in grain policy. From a **quantity perspective**, consumers--in response to increased per capita income--have been showing a distinct preference for meats and other feedgrain derived products, but fewer table grains. Meanwhile, government wants to stimulate feed grain exports and reduce net grain imports irrespective of China's comparative advantages. From a **pricing perspective**, the maintenance of low grain procurement prices, even lower ration sales prices, and the growing burden of grain related subsidization has served to frustrate producer incentives, stimulate some over-consumption **3/** and frustrate government's desire to reduce its large grain subsidies (given mainly to China's restive urban population). From the standpoint of **investment priorities**, the inherent conflicts between (a) the "federalization" of public expenditures and the need to expand investments in grain production and marketing infrastructure, and (b) the diversion of farmer savings to housing and higher-return non-agricultural investment, need somehow to be resolved short of a wholesale return to administrative means.

3.09 <u>The Dimensions of Reform</u>. The resolution of the "contradictions" inherent in these conflicting objectives will require a broad-based approach to grain sector reform, encompassing:

- weaknesses in China's grain sector management associated with unrealistic targeting while ignoring resource costs,

- an inappropriate production strategy which emphasizes fine grains when demand is shifting strongly in favor of coarse grains and other animal feeds,

- the partial opening of product markets in the agricultural and grain sectors while also opening markets for production factors, especially for fertilizers, high quality seeds and the transfer of land use rights, to encourage an efficient adjustment in the allocation of productive resources, and

- the need to address policy reforms, institutional restructuring and investment requirements in some key areas, including price distortions, the grain distribution system and management of inputs supplies, China's apparatus for technology transfer in

---

3/ With pricing policies that were aligned with relative abundance and scarcities, the shift away from table grains (especially rice) would have been measurably enhanced, and reliance on subsidized rural resales to furnish fine grains for animal feeds would have been reduced.

agriculture, the administration of China's foreign trade in grains, the need to reform the urban grain rationing system, and the government's unrealistic projections for mobilizing the required financing.

The projections made in Chapter II are sobering. It will prove difficult, but by no means impossible, for China's agriculture sector to move from its current low growth state as typified in the "Prolonged Agricultural Recession" scenario to one of "Sustained Agricultural Recovery". It is the contention of this report, however, that steps must first be taken to introduce broad adjustments to current grain sector policies. The specific recommendations for reform in the following Sections are made on the assumption that growth and efficiency will continue to be China's over-riding performance objectives, and that these would be applied as consistently to grain sector policies and interventions as they are to the rest of the economy.

3.10   Priorities and Sequencing.   The recent literature on socialist economic reform sheds doubt on the theoretical validity of trying to identify a finely-sequenced ordering of reforms at the sectoral level. Rather, the sequencing should generally be confined to a reorganization of the apparatus for macroeconomic regulation. On the other hand, supporting policies to improve performance at the sectoral level should be approached across a broad front according to what is feasible and implementable given current sectoral knowledge.   Hence, only priorities are proposed below: involving policy adjustments whose implementation could and should be addressed immediately, and adjustments which can only begin after preparatory work has been completed, but which none-the-less deserve equally urgent priority.

B. AN UNFINISHED AGENDA: PRIORITIES IN THE GRAIN SECTOR

-Pricing and Marketing Policies

3.11   Grain Pricing and Marketing.   Perhaps the most important unfinished business in China's agricultural reform concerns the halfway state of current pricing and marketing reform. In a sense, the "easy" steps have been completed, though a mix of central planning and limited role for the market continues to hinder performance and efficiency in the all-important grain sector.

3.12   Conceptually, the completion of China's grain pricing and marketing reforms would seem rather easy: mere elimination of "two-track" pricing and the assignation of full responsibility to market forces for the allocation of China's grain supplies. However, a number of important institutional issues will have to be served first, not the least of which is a phasing out of the near complete monopoly of the state commercial system in the realm of both grain and inputs distribution, the poor state of much of China's storage and handling infrastructure, continued long distance transportation constraints, and the ubiquitous urban grain ration system—which in the face of political sensitivities and lacking a targeting apparatus to provide a safety net for the urban poor—may elude quick reform. All of these militate against the quick fix approach. All require substantial investments to improve the distribution and transportation infrastructure. It is thus probably naive to assume that inter-regional markets could be created and begin to function efficiently overnight through the simple expedient of price liberalization. On the other hand, the government recognizes that it simply can't afford the escalating costs, financial and economic, that are associated with the existing system.

3.13 Under these circumstances, the reinitiation of grain sector reform should be progressive but phased: **starting first by raising the administered grain procurement and urban ration prices for grains, and reducing the amount of grain sold at subsidized prices.** While adopting this reform, care will have to be taken to insure that the array of official urban sales prices (and by extension, the price of "rural resales") are increased in absolute terms at least by amounts corresponding to the increases in official procurement prices. **4/** Recently announced plans to reduce the annual base ration allotment from 15 kg/cap to 12 kg/cap, and reduce the volume of urban ration sales from about 65 million to 50 million tons—equivalent to the volume of contract procurements—are important initial steps. The reiteration in the Eighth Plan documents of government's intention to phase out over a three year period the administered price differentials on compulsory procurements and ration sales, if implemented, would constitute an even more significant step.

3.14 There is also an option to improve domestic grain availability (and therefore food security) through the reduction of post-harvest losses, which are considerable. Current drying, storage and handling losses are estimated to be as high as 15 million tons per year, equivalent to 15% of annual grain marketings and about 4% of annual production. (Additional losses occur on-farm.) Losses in the distribution system reportedly occur as a result of antiquated facilities and equipment, exacerbated by China's inadequate transportation system which requires that excessive regional stores be maintained. A storage construction program has been approved for financing under the Eighth Five Year Plan (1991-85), involving minimal expansion of storage capacity by 5 million tons/year. Much more is needed (however the ownership and management of China's grain distribution system might ultimately be organized), and it is recommended that **a major investment program be initiated, to augment and rehabilitate China's grain storage and distribution system, including the gradual expansion of bulk handling capabilities where justified. 5/** Before a program of sufficient magnitude can be implemented, however, it is likely to be necessary that responsibility for these kinds of investments should also be reassumed by the state and made a state-investment priority. In parallel, to prepare for a more complete liberalization perhaps two or three years from now, **it is recommended that the Chinese government review the role of the grain bureau system, and identify institutional, legal, regulatory and other measures needed to break its effective monopoly in grain distribution, and consider measures to convert the modus operandi of state entities towards that normally associated with grain market regulation** *viz.*

4/ Otherwise, the net financial outlay needed to deliver subsidized grain to urban ration card recipients will also increase (para 2.59).

5/ A storage rehabilitation and investment program of 10-15 million tons per year would be well within present needs.

maintaining strategic stockpiles, price stabilization, seasonal procurements and disposals to mitigate local gluts or shortage, emergency relief and subsidized transfers to chronically poor and remote areas. Meanwhile, **enterprises outside of the state commercial system should be encouraged to enter the grain trade in order to gain experience,** perhaps initially by renting stores and facilities from the grain bureaux' enterprises, being allocated space on the state railway system, and given access to distribution financing credits through the state banking system. **6/ Later, the more successful firms could be invited to participate in divestiture programs after the GGB withdraws from its current dominant position in the internal grain distribution system, and be encouraged to invest in their own marketing capacities.**

3.15 _Urban Ration Sales._ A necessary component of any attempt to reform pricing and the mechanism for price determination will be a thorough recasting of the urban ration sales system. A menu of proposed options is shown over-page. Since market prices for grain have fallen below the "negotiated" price levels (which constitute the higher of China's two-tiered administrative pricing structure) due to record production in 1990, the current very low market prices for grains provide an ideal opportunity to increase prices in the organized segment of China's markets. Chinese policy makers are presently considering this option, and has noted that the window of opportunity may quickly pass, as reduced production is expected in 1991 due to farmer reluctance to continue planting grains in the current glut. It is therefore strongly recommended that **China seize the moment to raise urban ration prices and scale back volumes distributed under ration sales in order to reduce the subsidy burden.** Fearing a backlash among urban residents, however, Government seems to be following a lengthy, phased approach, involving steps to:

- gradually reduce the annual per capita entitlement represented by each coupon and the total amount of grain to be made available each year under rationed sales;

- slowly demonetize the outstanding coupons by raising the urban ration sales price in several steps towards negotiated/free market levels; but

- continue to tolerate the considerable existing fungibility (leakage) in the use of coupons--whether remitted by registered households or by purchasers in informal secondary markets--and gradually sop-up the outstanding issue as and when these are remitted.

3.16 This approach towards demonetizing the stock of outstanding coupons could, over time, reduce some of the embodied liquidity, provided the state and local governments can resist pressures from registered recipients to

---

6/ In this connection, investment by entities outside of the state commercial system will not occur until prices are free to vary across time (seasonally, and between years), and in transport until prices can vary across space.

A Menu of Options for Consumer Price Reform and the Phased Reduction of Consumer Food Subsidies

Volume: Without Providing Fully Offsetting Cash Transfers

-Immediate elimination of all ration price sales to industry (agroprocessing, animal feed, etc.).
-Phased elimination of **variable** ration sales (i.e., ration sales in excess of the 15 kg/month **base** allotment).
-Phased reduction in **base** ration allotment from 15 to 10 kg/month or less (perhaps through annual reductions of 2.5 kg/month phased in over 2 or 3 years).

Price: Without Providing Fully Offsetting Cash Transfers

-Phased modest increase in ration sale prices (perhaps a real annual increase of 50% for four years).

Quality: -Restrict ration price sales to lower quality grades of rice, wheat, corn, soybeans, and vegetable oil. Sales of high quality grades could continue, but only at variable free market prices.

Coupon Dating: -Newly issued ration coupons to include expiration date (either month or year of issue).

Coupon Overhang: -Sterilize coupon overhang, perhaps by requiring holders to deposit coupons into special accounts in State banks. Depositors would be allowed to withdraw from these accounts in a phased manner over subsequent years (perhaps in equal blocks over a five year period). After a preannounced date, the remaining overhang of coupons would be invalidated.

Other Targeting: -Restrict ration sales to low income urban recipients (a variety of approaches, e.g., work units would select a given percentage of staff for entitlement to coupons, could be tested).
-Provide ration coupons to low income unregistered urban households (i.e., to poor urban residents not currently entitled to receive ration coupons).
-Close selected urban ration shops located in high income urban neighborhoods.

Fiscal
Contracting: -Central to local government transfers in support of grain subsidies to be fixed initially at some portion (less than 100%) of 1989 or 1990 levels, then phased down.
-Localities to retain any additional reductions in subsidies.

This proposal, would: (a) take advantage of the existence of urban ration shops by reducing, but not eliminating, ration price sales; (b) gradually force a greater share of household purchase of grain and vegetable oil onto the free market, necessitating a substantial buildup of free market trade in these products; (c) facilitate the increase of planned mandatory and negotiated farm-gate procurement prices to free market levels; and, (d) reduce subsidy outlays, economic distortions, and social inequalities while minimizing any decline in the welfare of the urban poor. Modest reforms of ration volume and price, in connection with the recommended changes changes to coupon dating and measures to sterilize the coupon overhang could be implemented immediately at the national level. Sharper reductions in ration sale volume and increases in the ration price, restrictions on grain quality, and other forms of targeting could first be experimented with in pilot regional reforms prior to implementation at the national level.

retain this source of income supplementation. But there are dangers in an extremely gradualist approach, however, that China should seek to avoid. Presently, the outstanding coupons represent entitlement to about 20 million tons of grain, almost one-third of the amount distributed annually through the ration sales system, and equivalent to about ¥ 6 billion when valued at the current array of ration sales prices. 7/ Should consumer confidence again fail and a run on the ration shops occur, as happened in August 1988, the disruption in the grain distribution system would be considerable. It could also place additional pressure on China's monetary aggregates, since outlays for financing procurements, moving an equivalent amount of grain to replenish draw-down in a short period of time, and cover the associated operating losses in the grain bureaux system must be met by China's treasury and banking system. 8/

3.17 It is acknowledged in China that the ration coupons--monetized and transferrable to the floating population and other temporary residents--serve mainly as an unearned income supplement to registered urban households, who otherwise have little desire to increase their direct consumption of grains. Since the outstanding coupons represent a store of value that can not be regulated easily within PBC's framework for monetary control, **it is recommended that the Government take immediate action to sterilize the threat posed by the outstanding issue, perhaps by requiring deposit in "blocked" accounts in the state-owned banks, with annual ceilings on the amounts which can be withdrawn, accompanied by an announcement that price retroactivity on outstanding issues will not be honored once urban ration sales prices have been increased.**

3.18 **In parallel, dates of expiration should be announced (and enforced) on newly issued coupons.** Doing so would cause no extreme hardship to most of the eligible recipients, since their revealed preference in recent years has shifted decidedly away from the direct per capita consumption of table grains, and particularly away from the low quality grains distributed by the grain bureaux. Ideally, dates of expiry should be announced for outstanding coupons and enforced. However, this is probably not possible since the outstanding coupons have the appearance of China's paper currency, can be traded freely by the holder at ration shops and other state outlets for a variety of commodities, and have no issue date attached. Rather, it is recommended that

- the total volume of contract procurements and urban ration sales be completely phased out during the Eighth Plan period, with the exception of allotments for the urban poor. For these latter amounts, explicit budgetary subsidies should be allocated to the responsible state and local agencies, but delinked from the

---

7/ and considerably more, if valued at negotiated and market prices.

8/ If the incremental credit requirement were, say, only ¥ 10 billion, this could increase the stock of money and quasi-money in China by as much as ¥ 26 billion, once the money multiplier has worked its way through the financial system. While some of the increased liquidity might be sopped up within 6-8 months of issue -- when the grain bureau enterprises repay their short term loans using the proceeds of sales -- the resultant increase in China's monetary aggregates from such a run on the state grain shops could have an immediate inflationary impact whose effects may linger due to a rekindling of inflationary expectations.

mechanism of below-market procurement pricing, which should be abolished; and

- ration pricing in the future be restricted only to the lower quality grades of rice, wheat, maize, soybeans and vegetable oil. Sales of high quality grains would have to continue through the state commercial system until commercial distributors have been able to organize, but at variable free market prices.

It is also recommended that the target for aligning ration sales prices with compulsory procurement prices <u>not</u> be established at the current contract procurement prices, but rather with reference to market or border prices. This would encourage increased efficiency in the grain sector (by realigning price relatives) as well as reduce subsidization.

3.19 Urban subsidy reform should also be supported by fiscal contracting, in which central to local government transfers in support of grain subsidies would initially be fixed at some portion (less than 100%) of the 1989 or 1990 levels. Over time, the transfers would be phased down while ration sales prices are increased and the ration grain allowances are reduced. 9/ To prepare the groundwork for further reform, an alternative system should be designed which will identify and target the urban poor, only (more on this below), to later replace the existing system once the necessary background investigations have been carried out, including a precise identification of the urban poor, the setting of eligibility criteria, plans and procedures for phasing in the new system, and training programs to help the responsible agencies shift their orientation. During the transition, it will probably be necessary to offer income supplements to all of the existing beneficiaries. However, these should only consist of a once and for all supplementation. Otherwise the subsidy burden will continue to grow, albeit in new clothing, thus defeating the purpose of the reform. 10/

3.20 Reductions of the value of subsidies to the nonagricultural population could, of course, be easily achieved through an uncompensated decrease in the ration allotment or increase in the ration price. Phased over several years, such reductions would have a negligible impact on the income of the average nonagricultural resident (Annex 3, para 44). The obstacle is fear of a significant decline in the real income of low income recipients and consequent decrease in physical welfare. International experience indicates, however, that a program which targets benefits to low-income recipients could achieve a phased reduction of the total value of food subsidies without an unacceptable decline of real income or nutritional status of low income urban residents.

9/ While state-mandated ration sales are being phased down, localities should be allowed to retain any additional reductions in subsidies achieved by phasing out the multifarious subnational subsidy supplementation programs.

10/ It must be recognized that, since the nonagricultural population captures (a) the majority of the government's expenditure on food subsidies and (b) implicitly, the equivalent of about two-thirds of the income lost by farmers on mandatory procurement at below market prices, it will not be possible to significantly reduce the fiscal losses and regressive impact of the food distribution system without reducing the value of subsidies to the nonagricultural population.

3.21 The most realistic mechanism for targeting benefits to low income recipients in China might be to reduce the leakage of benefits to high income recipients through the existing urban ration shop system. Since the urban food distribution system is well established, this would require little or no incremental investment or operating costs. **The most direct means of reducing leakage would be to reduce or eliminate the ration allotment for high income households.** Restricting access to only low income recipients would likely prove more practical and less costly in China than in most other countries, since ration coupons are only issued to registered nonagricultural households, and most urban district committees and work units can accurately and readily assess the income of such households. **Other possible measures, which would indirectly reduce high income residents' incentive to make use of the urban ration shops without explicit disentitlement, include (a) closing ration shops located in high income neighborhoods and (b) restricting subsidized sales to inferior grades of rice and wheat and to less preferred grains such as corn.** Lastly, should planned surveys of the welfare of China's unregistered urban residents (i.e., the "floating population") indicate a serious need, **the government should consider an extension of welfare assistance (perhaps through the urban ration system once the mechanics of targeting have been determined), to include demonstrably poor nonregistered urban residents.**

3.22 <u>Inputs Pricing and Distribution.</u> On the production inputs side, **the fertilizer distribution subsidies should be phased out (higher grain procurement prices would compensate), the linking of fertilizer distribution with compulsory grain procurement abolished, and China's brief experiment with liberalized fertilizer marketing during the mid-1980s be reinstituted** (which mainly involved locally produced, low analysis fertilizers manufactured in local small fertilizer factories). <u>11</u>/ A similar effort should be initiated to improve the allocation of high-analysis fertilizers, though the implementation of this kind of approach must accommodate the continuing shortage of high-analysis fertilizers in China and be implemented even more carefully to prevent a measured erosion of farmers' purchasing power. **Plan prices for the high analysis centrally managed stocks and imports should be increased and the regional allocation criteria simplified in a manner that would tend to make fertilizers more available to crops having high production <u>and income earning</u> potential.** In this connection, after geographic allocations have been determined, **perhaps the higher analysis fertilizers could be auctioned off to the farming population,** which might achieve a kind of "second-best" efficiency, and incidentally would also augment revenues to cover current losses in the distribution system.

3.23 To prepare for a longer-term reform of China's bifurcated and still highly administered fertilizer distribution system, the creation of new channels should be allowed and encouraged, perhaps including (in addition to the AICs' present network) fertilizer marketing organizations set-up by China's burgeoning rural cooperative enterprise sector and other non-state agricultural marketing concerns. Initially, these new distribution channels could be utilized to provide more depth to the existing official network at

---

<u>11</u>/ Annex 3, paras 31-35.

the retail level, and expanded geographical coverage. Later, as the availability of high-analysis fertilizers becomes better aligned with demand (and the need for rationing subsides), **these kinds of non-state agents should also be encouraged to enter into the marketing of fertilizers at the wholesale level, lifting product directly from manufacturers and importers for resale to locales and farmers in accord with market pricing signals. 12/**

3.24   Comprehensive experimental programs are underway at the regional level, in the North China wheat belt (Xinxiang, Henan) and in the South China rice belt (Yulin City, Guangxi), which are testing some aspects of the above recommendations.   The initial results were encouraging, and key features of these experiments might serve as a model for more comprehensive nationwide reform.

3.25   In the realm of **seeds** policy, **it is recommended that urgent attention be given to the administration of seeds research, research priorities, and to constraints on the marketing of certified seeds.** All of these factors serve to inhibit the importation, adaptation and dissemination of the superior germ plasm available mainly in the international market place for seeds (para 2.28). Several steps are required to provide China's research establishment with smooth and regular access to this germ plasm.

3.26   First, there appears to be an "awareness" problem amongst the hierarchy of plant geneticists and plant breeders in China, stemming from the cessation of contacts with the international research community during the Cultural Revolution, and the lack of budget since then to finance information exchanges on the needed scale, foreign study visits, refresher training, and overseas degree studies in the related scientific and agrotechnical disciplines. 13/ **It is therefore recommended that additional budgetary resources be allocated during the Eighth Five Year Plan period, to finance these kinds of expenditures, and to facilitate a substantial increase in the exchange of germ plasm and scientific information with international crop research institutes within the CGIAR (Consultative Group for International Agricultural Research) network.**   Since the above items would be inherently non-revenue generating, the requisite budgetary resources--whether sourced locally or financed with assistance--should be remitted on a grant basis (in lieu of normal "charge-back" procedures) to MOA's research directorates, various central crop research institutes and university faculties by MOF and the concerned bureaux of finance at the provincial level.

3.27   Second, it must be recognized that much of the readily available germ plasm in the international sphere is the property of international seed companies, whose own research establishments have expended considerable sums on the development and testing of their breeder and foundation seed stocks. To

---

12/ See Section C below for additional proposals for the fertilizer sector.

13/ All of these factors have served to isolate China's research personnel from many of the striking developments in the past two decades, eg. in maize, soybeans and wheat, that could profitably be used in China to extend the production of these crops in the MLYR and Southern rice production zones, and thus help realign the commodity composition of domestic grain production with internal demand.

protect legitimate proprietary interests in these stocks, the international companies prefer to operate only in countries where cost-recovery can be assured and patent-type protection is available for so-called "breeders rights". To ensure proper management of testing, adaptation and seed multiplication, the international companies also prefer to operate under joint-venture arrangements or within the framework of extended and tightly organized management contracts with local counterparts, since their hard-earned reputation as reliable partners is closely linked to the performance of the germ plasm being introduced. During the 1980s, attempts to set-up joint venture seed production enterprises in China failed to materialize, largely due to the absence of sufficient protection for breeders rights and the seemingly arbitrary application of China's multifarious regulations governing agricultural research. A perhaps unfounded, but widely held impression was created that Chinese researchers were mainly interested in obtaining superior germ plasm more or less free of charge. **To gain ready access to the high potential germ plasm offered in international markets, China would do well to constrain the excessive regulation of seeds research to only the minimum required to maintain research standards and the "purity" of new lines and varieties that are released for distribution to farmers. In parallel, enabling legislation and supporting regulations should be introduced, of the kind needed to assure prospective joint venture partners that proprietary interests will be honored.**

3.28   The revision and simplification of China's plant quarantine regulations and procedures constitutes a third component of a seeds policy package. As these now stand, China's plant quarantine regulations can be and have been utilized to prevent the importation of most any germ plasm, irrespective of the supplier's reputation or the desire of the importing agency to test and perhaps utilize imported germ plasm in their seed development programs. **To undo this unnecessarily restrictive practice (and, ultimately, to benefit China's farmers), the regulations should be recast in a way which would facilitate the timely release of quality seed imports from quarantine and reduce the scope for an arbitrary interpretation of the regulations.**

3.29   Lastly, to underpin the commercial viability of China's seed industry and potential joint venture arrangements, **it will be necessary to allow some flexibility in the pricing of seeds released by the National and Provincial Seeds Corporations, and by other (registered) entities which might become involved in the marketing of superior seeds.** Though the price differential over existing varieties might appear large—perhaps necessitating a 5 to 10-fold price increase in order to capture research and development and other expenditures—the share of seed expenses would remain an extremely small component in total farm production costs, and could be more than compensated for were grain procurement prices raised to more realistic levels.

-Policy Implications For Domestic Grain Transfers

3.30   Despite the improvements brought about by the reforms and partial deregulation of the 1980s, the central government's continued close administration and dominant share of interprovincial grain trade perpetuate substantial economic and social costs. Constraints to interprovincial trade necessitate excessive and expensive central government grain stocks, which are

estimated to have averaged about 87 million tons annually during the 1980s.
14/ Poor planning and transport shortages are known to drive up operating
costs. Price distortions depress incentives in surplus production areas,
which--in combination with low official prices on rural resales (and the
fungibility of urban ration coupons) and with constraints on imports of corn
and other feed grains from North China--encourage surplus rice producers in
MLYR and South-and-Southwest China to feed large quantities of relatively high
cost rice to pigs. Additionally, supplying grain to poor and mountainous
areas appears to be a relatively low priority for the government (Annex 3,
para 4).

3.31 These shortcomings in the planning of internal transfers have been
recognized in China, and several recent steps have been taken which, if
articulated further, could provide the basis for a thorough recasting of the
internal grain distribution system. Firstly, pricing reforms have been
announced so that henceforth the grain exporting provinces will receive the
(higher) prevailing negotiated price for grain sales to deficit provinces
rather than contract procurement prices.

3.32 A second recent development is perhaps the most significant one:
implementation of China's long-debated program to establish national and
regional wholesale grain markets was placed in effect in 1990. A national
cash-forward market for wheat was set-up in Zhengzhou, Henan in 1990, open to
any registered grain enterprise within the GGB system, and provincial markets
were established in Anhui and Jiangxi Provinces for rice and in Heilongjiang
for soybeans. Preparations are being made to open national markets in 1991 for
the other main grains, including markets in Hunan or Hubei Province (rice),
Heilongjiang (maize and sorghum), and Jilin (oils) and additional provincial
markets. In parallel, MOC established a grain reserve of 20 million tons to
be used for market regulation. This reserve is to be acquired over a period
of 5 years, largely from existing stocks, and will be managed independently of
the GGB's administered distributions. However, the future orientation of the
GGB while these markets develop strength has not yet been articulated.

3.33 The establishment of national and provincial wholesale markets in
several of the grain producing locales and trading centers, and the creation
of a strategic grain reserve for stabilizing the new wholesale and retail
markets, could provide the basis for the establishment of detailed regulations
and procedures to govern the transition to a market-based distribution system,
and the institutional capabilities to carry this out. 15/

3.34 A third development has been the remarkable and spontaneous spread of
grain pricing and marketing reforms that occurred in 1990. Following a hiatus
of one year, local decisions were made in the Xinxiang, Henan and Yulin,
Guangxi experimental zones for grain system reform under State Council

---

14/ Grain stocks also are discussed in World Bank (1990e) and (1990f).

15/ The fact that the state-run storage and distribution system was again overwhelmed in 1989
and 1990 by record harvests has given renewed life to the view that efficient storage and
distribution programs can not be managed effectively within existing financing and institutional
arrangements.

jurisdiction to move the experiments forward into their most critical phase: reform of the urban ration sales system and the revision of central-local responsibilities for financing reduced subsidies. In late 1989 and 1990, entities associated with the State Council also invited representatives from other parts of China to visit the Xinxiang and Yulin experimental zones, and made grain system reform a central topic in the 1990 Annual Work Conference on Rural Reform. Subsequently, a number of provinces (Guangdong, Fujian, Shanxi and Liaoning), the provincial-level municipality of Tianjin, and numerous smaller cities and localities introduced their own programs to reduce the subsidization of grains and oils.

3.35 To support these initiatives, it is the recommendation of this report that the process of reform and the deregulation of interprovincial trade be accelerated.   Key steps would include:

- the phased elimination of administrative and fiscal barriers to interprovincial trade by non-state entities;

- a broadened substitution of negotiated for contract prices to reimburse grain transfers from surplus provinces and the setting of negotiated prices at near-market levels uniformly throughout China, 16/ then later (after the marketing infrastructure has been developed to the point where commercial forces can become the predominant influence on price determination), a basic shift in policy to encourage reliance in-the-main on market prices;

- the reduction of operating costs through a scaling down of excessive central government stocks and GGB planned trade; and, later,

- the large scale expansion of free market trade by collective, cooperative and privately-owned distributors.

To support deregulation, regional wholesale markets and markets for grain futures should be quickly established in all eight of the areas proposed by the Ministry of Commerce (MOC). As interprovincial trade moves from planned trade at administered prices toward market determined flows and prices during the 1990s, **the role of the GGB could be shifted to systems programming and regulation.** Key activities of the GGB would include the management of strategic stocks and oversight monitoring of operations in the national and provincial wholesale markets; the assembly, analysis and dissemination of market and price information; guaranteeing the provision of grain to poor areas at stable prices through periodic market supplementation; and the regulation of and enforcement of national standards for all free market trade.

16/ A subsidiary objective of the pricing of inter-regional transfers is poverty alleviation in the grain deficit provinces, which tend to be poorer than the grain surplus provinces. However, poverty alleviation is an inappropriate and very distortion objective for pricing policy. A more sustainable approach to poverty alleviation would be the stimulation of new investment in income generating activities in lower income areas, eg. through budgetary mechanisms and an augmentation of the resources and investment incentives being administered by the state's Office for Economic Development of Poor Areas.

-Foreign Trade Policies

3.36 Grain imports are carried out under an annual program of importation volumes and foreign exchange allocations. Typically, these are determined by "beginning year" estimates, long before hard estimates of production (which is still heavily influenced by weather), consumption and regional price patterns become available. The result has been unaccountably large grain imports during years of good harvests, followed by import shortfalls when production has been tapering off. On the exports side, China's potential has been hampered by the low quality of most of its rice, a traditional export; periodic loss of a competitive exchange rate; and again the programming of exports according to annual plans and foreign exchange earning targets, which are likely to be rendered obsolete once the year's crop volume becomes known.

3.37 Additional gains could accrue were China to **shift from the current annual planning of foreign trade in grains to a longer term program and** *were China to make its grain import intentions known*. At present, Chinese grain importers and exporters operate largely in the "current" markets to fulfill the annual import and export targets, which are considered to be state secrets. Sometimes trade is negotiated bilaterally, other times the State trading corporations lift (or place) grains directly and oft-times unexpectedly in foreign markets. Needless-to-say, this system on the import side allows China to "enjoy" prices more resembling spot prices, though occasionally with export enhancement subsidies. Shifting to a longer-term approach, however, would also require supporting policy adjustments within China's grain system, including more careful and considered management of its commodity stockpiles (which also has a very short-term orientation), and **the programming by the State of longer-term financing or the provision of requisite budgetary set-asides for the China National Cereals, Oils and Foodstuffs Import-Export Corporation (CEROILS) and other National FTCs involved in the grain trade. Were it politically convenient for China to do so, these corporations could even sign medium-term contracts or at least issue letters of intent to selected foreign suppliers for core amounts of grain imports and exports (else hedge in international commodity markets),** thereby assuring lower expected prices for grain imports and a smoother--likely higher--progression of f.o.b. prices for its grain exports.

3.38 Over the longer-term, however, **the real gains would come from decentralizing the management of foreign trade and the internal procurement and marketing of grains. China's parastatals responsible for these operations simply are not efficient or able to respond quickly enough to changing circumstances.** Moreover, as detailed in Annex 3, they haven't been able to constrain costs. In 1989, fully one third of China's grain subsidy was allocated to offset the grain bureaux' operating losses, while it is reported that the equivalent of at least $350 million was allocated to finance grain import subsidies. Equally important, the agencies responsible for China's foreign trade in grains neither pass through gains from exporting to Chinese traders and producers nor do they respond readily to market signals and changes in China's internal grain situation. Thus during 1984, which was a peak year in domestic grain production, China imported over 12 million tons of grain, an almost four-fold increase over imports in 1983 which was a previous

year of record grain production. The "stop go" behavior manifested by the
agencies responsible for international trade and grain movements within China
--largely in response to administrative orders--and the losses due to the
predominance of state-owned monopolies in China's international and domestic
marketings, will likely continue to inhibit the country's ability to respond
quickly to changing configurations and trading positions in the world's grain
markets and pass the incentive signals onwards with due alacrity to its farmer
producers and grain consumers.

-Recommended Investment Priorities.

3.39 **Public Investment.** While there is growing acceptance that a structural
deficit in grain supply is likely to be the long-term trend, the
prioritization and programming of public agricultural investment has fallen
hostage to the devolution of fiscal responsibility. **Recent moves to reverse
the declining trend in real agricultural investment should be reinforced.** By
any criteria, both macroeconomic and sectoral, agriculture has a legitimate
claim on a higher share of the state's investment budget than the low level to
which it had fallen in 1988. China's cultivated area will remain essentially
unchanged, the arable land frontier having been effectively closed during the
past decade or two. Consequently, meeting future agricultural and grain sector
growth possibilities will depend critically on increases in both cropping
intensity and in yields on existing cultivated land, and on improvements in
the quality of production. Key to realizing these goals will be an expansion
of agricultural research activities, increased use of quality seeds and modern
inputs, the strengthening of agricultural extension to accelerate the transfer
of relevant technology to farmers, and reestablishing effective links between
agricultural research, extension and education at the national, provincial and
county levels. **A prime investment priority should be the upgrading of China's
agricultural research complex. At least a doubling of annual expenditures
would appeared justified, which would bring China's total expenditures on
agricultural research in line with nearby Asian countries (Annex 1, para 21).**
Within the technology diffusion nexus, problems in the new extension system
(grounded in county-level agrotechnology centers) and its financing have yet
to be worked out. To reach China's 200 million farm households, the Government
plans eventually to establish a center in each of China's 2,300 counties. So
far, less than one third of the counties have established agrotechnical
extension centers, and fully 20% are still not served by even a rudimentary
extension program. **Priority should also be given to investments in extension
training and facilities, starting with completion of the complex of
agrotechnology centers. On a trial basis, the government may wish to impose
the discipline availed through the training and visit (T & V) approach to
extension on the farmer outreach programs of selected agrotechnology centers.**
In doing so, however, care should be taken to compare the effectiveness of
T & V with results achieved through China's current multi-channel approach
(mass media, demonstrations and advice directed towards lead farmers and
specialized producers), and the likely additional costs associated with the T
& V system (especially personnel costs).

3.40 **Particular priority should be given to the rehabilitation and completion
of China's vast irrigation and drainage network.** In view of the projected
limited growth in grain production during the 1990s, and the likely continued

fall-off in the per capita consumption of table grains, it is questionable whether an expansion of investments in new irrigation and drainage developments can be justified. **Thus this report proposes that irrigation development in China be refocussed on rehabilitation, repair and systems completion work in the water scarce areas of North China.** New developments should receive, at best, very low priority. The kinds of investments proposed by this study, and their location would serve mainly to maintain current grain production aggregates in the wheat and feed grain production zones. Such investments would also be central to the recommendation that China give greater emphasis to the production of coarse grains (i.e. maize and soybeans) while de-emphasizing fine grains. By way of contrast, China faces over-production in rice. Thus **any investment in the water surplus rice growing areas of the South should be given much lower priority, except when a shift to the production of higher-valued irrigated crops is foreseen.**

3.41 In an effort to augment local resources for the construction of water control and other rural infrastructure, the state in mid-1989 announced the reimposition of mass mobilization policies and additional taxation from irrigated agriculturalists. Press clippings indicate that the program is being implemented by a number of provinces. While it can be argued that farmer beneficiaries should assume a larger share of the costs of irrigation development than other, indirect beneficiaries, a considerable cess already is levied on farm households in China through compulsory grain procurement, water user charges in irrigated areas, and the burden of local "extractions" (taxation) to finance village services. It is also questionable whether reimposition of the rural corvée is consistent with the spirit of the reforms, or even necessarily a most effective way to mobilize labor for arduous construction tasks. **It would seem, rather, that the correct priority for reasserting administrative means would be in the milieux of investment programing and its financing: largely by having the state claw-back some of the authority to set and monitor expenditure priorities, previously devolved, in order to redirect same towards agricultural investment.**

3.42 On-farm Investment. The disturbing trend towards some recollectivization--implicit in the new grain policy framework--also is manifested in official frustration with the slow pace of private on-farm investment. A policy option that is currently being implemented in some of the "grain base" counties calls for the reversion to county and township government of farmers' rights acquired under the PRS. The aim is to promote land consolidation, larger sized farms (i.e. 20 ha.) and farm mechanization, and to provide a mechanism for enforcing the state's grain procurement objectives. Related is the State's program to replace 160,000 medium/large tractors during under the coming (Eighth) five-year plan. The economic rationale for consolidation cum mechanization is grounded in a belief that grain production is imbued with scale economies, otherwise denied in smallholder agriculture, and that the source of these economies is linked to investments in larger farm machinery. While it can be argued that the extreme fragmentation in China has denied the production economies that might be associated with consolidated plots, little evidence has been found that economies of farm size are available to labor-intensive, land constrained farming systems including China's, even in grain production. Thus with little apparent benefit in sight, the costs of reimposing collectively organized farming could be rather high and would in any event require continuing operating subsidies to maintain the viability of larger farming units. That fragmentation is an issue, having deleterious effects on both investment and productivity, few would deny. Indeed, experimental programs in China are proving to be fairly effective vehicles for inducing a voluntary consolidation of land while maintaining the spirit of the PRS. **The Government of China would therefore be well advised to first review the validity of the scale-economies proposition as means for stimulating grain production, then consider more market-oriented alternatives such as those underway in the Meitan, Guizhou and Pingdu, Shandong experimental zones which have been designed to improve farm structure and stimulate on-farm investment.**

3.43 If recent reports about tenurial insecurity are accurate (para 2.57), **the introduction of a more flexible and secure system of agricultural land use rights** may hold the key for reducing this perception and for redirecting farm household savings towards long-term investment in land improvements and on-farm infrastructure. One option may be to introduced a market-based system in land use rights, wherein the voluntary transfer of use rights among willing farmers would be sanctioned; the rights to compensation and the assignment of taxation responsibilities would be clarified, made more systematic, then enforced; and--consequent to the establishment of a formal system of land records--the use of title deeds in "land use rights" could be introduced, to serve as security when borrowing funds for on-farm investment in rural financial markets.

3.44 Such a system would have to be designed carefully, however, since it would entail a fundamental change in the relationship between farmers and local officials, thus a recasting of the political environment within which the PRS has been operating. Again, the Meitan and Pingdu experiments may offer useful lessons. However, access to a broader information base would be desirable. To this end, the completion of the UNDP sponsored, Bank executed survey-based study of land issues would fill important informational gaps concerning regional variations in the local administration of farm household rights under the PRS, and thus furnish a needed building block for reform of the agricultural land use system. **It is therefore recommended that arrangements for this study be finalized quickly, to avail a timely review of its findings and conclusions.**

-Agricultural Financing

3.45 Last year China introduced an austerity program which led to a credit squeeze at all levels, including agriculture. This presented a setback for agriculture. Clearly, there is a need to look for new sources of government revenue, efficient collection of existing revenue sources, and efficient allocation of government revenue. There is also a need to emphasize that the revenue generated in the agricultural sector should be invested for the benefit of the agricultural sector. A judicious tax policy for TVEs can provide a good source of revenue. The agricultural tax needs to be made more transparent, buoyant and equitable. Local "extractions" from farmers need to be identified and rationalized. Revenue from land conversion tax should be used to develop new land. **Lastly, very serious consideration should be given** to MOF's desire to amalgamate the various off-budget funds for agriculture under the umbrella of the Agricultural Development Fund (ADF), which if nothing else could measurably simplify the programming and management of budgetary support for agricultural investment.

3.46 Agriculture has made a generous contribution to industry for decades, through net resource transfers until the late-1970s and, in the 1980s, by providing wage goods at low official prices. To enable a sustainable grain production strategy to be put in place, it will be necessary to curtail some of the opportunity costs borne by farmers under the existing urban food system. **Expenditure on consumer subsidies needs to be substantially reduced and a major part of this could be used to finance investment in agriculture.** Finally, government should provide needed incentives to individual farmers to finance investments from their own savings and borrowing from agricultural banks. In this context, **government must also make sure that timely credit for agriculture is available in adequate amounts to all farmers without excessive administrative requirements but at real positive rates of interest.**

3.47 While the leadership should not be lulled by good harvests in 1989 and 1990 17/ into delaying investment and revenue raising efforts, **it is strongly recommended that the investment planning exercise for grain production development to the Year 2000 (paras 2.54-2.58) be reviewed and redone.** With reference to recent developments, it is recommended that comprehensive flow-of-funds projections be made for agricultural expenditures from all of the likely sources of agricultural financing. These projections should be revisited in the context of a more likely array of grain production and foreign trade alternatives, using realistic assumptions about the State's ability to channel budgetary and credit resources into grain development programs, and the practicality of mobilizing farm labor and diverting farmer savings into agricultural investments for the sake of stimulating grain production under current pricing policies.

C. PRIORITIES IN THE FERTILIZER SECTOR

3.48 There is a need to improve the overall operational and economic efficiency of fertilizer production. In this area, the fertilizer industry must produce nutrients and products which are economic to produce and which will improve nutrient efficiency and the nutrient balance in fertilizer use. The small scale fertilizer plants are an important component of the fertilizer sector. The overall efficiency of these plants needs to be improved by closing the inefficient ones and renovating or converting the relatively less efficient plants to produce high grade fertilizers. Many fertilizer plants have low utilization rates due to lack of raw material or other problems. Since most fertilizer plants are highly capital intensive and there is excess fertilizer demand, full utilization of existing fertilizer plants is essential to minimize potentially large economic losses. Further, the quality of fertilizer products and packaging must be improved further to reduce physical losses which are estimated to be over 5% but could be as high as 20% for

---

17/ Whose achievement was aided by unusually good weather.

ammonium bicarbonate which accounts for 60% of total nitrogen production.

3.49 The domestic fertilizer industry will not be able to meet China's projected fertilizer requirements. SINOCHEM, the agency responsible for all fertilizer imports, has done rather well by negotiating favorable terms, but China can economize further by importing large shipments of compound fertilizers, in bulk and during off-season. Preliminary results indicate that, on the margin, China can reduce its import bill by importing large quantities of fertilizer to increase domestic grain production and by reducing grain imports. The analysis shows that for a given amount of foreign exchange it is more economic to import fertilizer than wheat since the application of fertilizer with value equivalent to one ton of imported wheat can result in 3.5-6.0 tons of additional wheat output. China imposed an import moratorium on fertilizer during 1985 and 1986, but whenever fertilizer demand exceeds supply, any import moratoria on fertilizer can result in substantial loss in potential agricultural output. Furthermore, China can benefit from long-term contracts with major fertilizer exporters. Such a strategy can reduce uncertainty with respect to fertilizer price and supply. In addition to SINOCHEM, provincial trading companies should also be encouraged to import fertilizer.

3.50 To these ends, it is recommended that the State Planning Commission (SPC) and MOF commission a careful and realistic review of these options, to be completed prior to inception of the Eighth Five Year Plan. Such a review should focus on the structure and costs in international markets for importing nitrogenous and phosphatic fertilizers, feedstocks, intermediates, and manufacturing equipment, and likely developments in order to assess the likely foreign costs and associated price and technical risks under different combinations of import- and investment-based fertilizer supply strategy. On the domestic side, the review should realistically estimate incremental investment and operating costs accruing to expansion of marketing and transportation infrastructure associated with the supply options, and--under the domestic production option--associated with civil works and plant operation. It is likely that the outcome of the review will suggest a lesser degree of self-sufficiency in nitrogen and phosphate production by the Year 2000 than currently intended, though sufficient to prevent overexposure to the vagaries of international fertilizer markets. Based on the outcome of the review, the indicative investment and fertilizer import targets in the Eighth Five Year Plan should then be modified accordingly, the portfolio of state and provincial investment proposals and import priorities adjusted, and annual plans mobilized.

3.51 Fertilizer use has been an important reason for the spectacular performance of China's agricultural sector since 1978. Any strategy designed to improve the level and efficiency of fertilizer use should aim to improve the economics of fertilizer use, including the provision of:

- an adequate and timely supply of fertilizer at the farm level;

- the implementation of technical policies described in paras 2.22-2.28, which would inter alia improve fertilizer response;

- a rationalization of fertilizer and crop prices;

- reduction in risk on returns to fertilizer use, e.g. through technical and marketing policies which lower yield and price risk; and

- the timely provision of adequate, not necessarily subsidized, credit to purchase fertilizer.

Farmers anywhere in the world, including China, are rational decision-makers and given the options and constraints within which they operate, tend to make rational decisions regarding fertilizer use.

3.52 Fertilizer marketing provides a link between fertilizer production/imports and fertilizer use by farmers under a wide range of agro-economic and agro-ecological conditions. So far the fertilizer marketing system has performed rather well but many problems have begun to emerge. Fertilizer consumption is projected to increase from 89 million product tons in 1988 to 130 million product tons in the Year 2000. To handle this large increment under current constrained conditions, there is a need to further develop the marketing system infrastructure, improve its efficiency and generate necessary information on different aspects of the marketing system. In this connection steps should be taken to:

- improve the design and enforcement of fertilizer quality control systems;

- determine carefully fertilizer demand and adequate supply arrangements;

- increase the nutrient content of fertilizers being distributed in China to constrain the increase in transport requirements;

- increase fertilizer storage capacity and transport facilities;

- provide adequate and timely credit and technical assistance to farmers and marketing agencies; and

- gradually introduce competition in fertilizer purchase and sales, including an expanded role for non-governmental enterprises.

As a guiding principle for the longer term, the state should not be in the business of selling fertilizer.

3.53 There is a need to simplify the complex fertilizer pricing system. Various policy-induced distortions, which result in misallocation of fertilizer use to less-efficient areas and crops, need to be gradually eliminated. Fertilizer subsidies need to be reduced since a large share of subsidies is given to cover losses due to inefficient fertilizer production and marketing. Fertilizer subsidies do transfer some resources to the agricultural sector in order to compensate for the high implicit tax on farmers in the form of compulsory crop deliveries at below market prices, but this is an inefficient and inequitable way to compensate for crop price distortions, also imposed by government policy. However, there may be a need for subsidization of transportation costs for remote areas, subsidization of nutrients which are deficient in soils but are not popular with farmers, or subsidization of fertilizers in areas where fertilizer use is low and the potential response is high. **Where required, such subsidies should be given only for a particular purpose, finite time-frame and with an upper limit on the total cost. The 3-linkage policy needs to be abolished gradually since it serves no useful purpose other than forcing farmers to remain engaged in crops with relatively low productivity and profitability.** Any reform in fertilizer price policy must be accompanied by crop price reforms. However, government decisions to keep inefficient fertilizer plants in operation, an over-emphasis on nitrogen at the cost of other nutrients, and allocation of fertilizers based on grain procurement rather than productivity considerations probably reduce the efficiency of the fertilizer sector more than that of fertilizer subsidies.

D. THE PACE OF REFORM

3.54   The above recommendations are made in the expectation that China's food pricing and distribution system can not and should not be expected to absorb an immediate and profound shock, if for no other reason than that considerable additional investments in marketing and transportation infrastructure will be required to enable free markets to operate. There are social considerations as well. Though per capita incomes have increased dramatically since the rural reforms were introduced, these remain low by international standards, while the safety nets outside of the urban enterprise sector are rudimentary at best. Perhaps equally important (and equally rife with implications for longer term agricultural development), the essential legal and regulatory underpinnings of a market-driven grain economy in China are not yet available.

3.55   On the other hand, it is possible for China to move further towards a market solution while constructing its safety nets and marketing infrastructure. Pointers are already available from China's experimentation with grain sector reform in the 1980s, the experience of Taiwan (as noted in Chapter II), and the performance of agriculture under policies adopted by other developing countries. This report's recommendations were distilled from the essence of China's own experimentation and pointers from abroad, taking account of both the positive aspects and some of the unexpected destabilizing consequences. If refined and implemented in the near future, we believe the proposed reforms would considerably improve the efficiency of grain production, marketing and foreign trade, while reducing the adverse fiscal consequences imbued in present arrangements. These would also set the stage for the ultimate conversion of both the grain sector and agriculture as a whole to a largely self-financed, market driven sector.

REFERENCES

Anderson, Kym (1990): <u>Changing Comparative Advantages In China: Effects on Food, Feed and Fibre Markets</u>, OECD Development Centre Study, Paris

Balassa, B (1965): "Trade Liberalization and 'Revealed' Comparative Advantage", <u>Manchester School of Economic and Social Studies</u>, 33(2): 99-124, May 1965

CAAS (1989): <u>Research on China's Grain</u> (Beijing: CAAS Publishing House, 1989)

Dixit, Praveen M. and Shwu-eng Webb (1989): "Government Support to Agriculture in China: Effects on World Markets", paper presented to the Association of Comparative Economic Studies meetings, Atlanta, December 28-30, 1989

Feder, Gershon, Lawrence Lau, Justin Lin and Luo Xiaopeng (1990), "The Determinants of Farm Investment and Residential Construction in Post Reform China", p. 12, Table 3 (AGRAP prepublication manuscript-March 1990)

Feder, Gershon, Lawrence Lau, Justin Lin and Luo Xiaopeng (1989), "Agricultural Credit and Farm Performance in China", <u>Journal of Comparative Economics</u>, 13, 508-526 (1989)

Fujian Statistical Bureau. <u>Fujian Statistical Yearbook, 1989</u> (Fuzhou: Fujian Statistical Bureau, 1989).

Gansu Statistical Bureau. <u>Gansu Statistical Yearbook, 1985</u> (Lanzhou: Gansu Statistical Bureau, 1987).

Guangdong Statistical Bureau. <u>Guangdong Statistical Yearbook, 1989</u> (Guangzhou: Guangdong Statistical Bureau, 1989).

Guangxi Statistical Bureau. <u>Guangxi Statistical Yearbook, 1989</u> (Guangxi: Guangxi Statistical Bureau, 1989).

Kreuser, J. and W. Sheldrick (1988): "China Phosphate Industry: The Development of a Mathematical Programming Model for Investment Planning", World Bank, Washington, D.C., Mimeo

Lardy, Nicholas (1989): "China's Interprovincial Grain Marketing and Import Demand." (mimeo: University of Washington, February 1989)

Lin, Justin Yifu (1989a): "Rural Reforms and Agricultural Productivity Growth in China", mimeograph, Beijing: Development Institute of the Research Center for Rural Development

Lin, Justin Yifu (1989b): "Inhibition of Factor Markets, Institutional Reform and Induced Technological Choice in Chinese Agriculture: Theory and Empirical Evidence," UCLA Working Paper No. 575, December 1989

McMillan, John, J. Whalley and Li Jing Zhu (1989): "The Impact of China's Economic and Induced Technological Choice in Chinese Agriculture: Theory and Empirical Evidence," UCLA Working Paper No. 575, December 1989

Mudahar, M.S. (1978): "Needed Information and Economic Analysis for Fertilizer Policy Formulation", <u>Indian Journal of Agricultural Economics</u>, Vol. 33 (3), pp. 40-67

Mudahar, M.S. and E.C. Kapusta (1987): Fertilizer Marketing Systems and Policies in the Developing World, Technical Bulletin IFDC-T-33, IFDC, Muscle Shoals, Alabama, April 1987

Prosterman, Roy L. and T. N. Hanstead (1990): "China: A Fieldwork Appraisal of the Household Responsibility System", in Prosterman, Roy L., M.N. Temple and T. M. Hanstad, eds. Agrarian Reform and Grassroots Development: Ten Case Studies (Boulder: Lynne Rienner Publishers, 1990)

Roningen, Vernon O. and P. Dixit (1989): Economic Implications of Agricultural Policy Reforms in Industrial Market Economies, USDA Economic Research Service, Agriculture and Trade Analysis Division, Staff Report No. AGES 89-36

Sicular, Terry (1988a): "Agricultural Planning and Pricing in the Post- Mao Period" China Quarterly 116 (December, 1988): 671-705

Sicular, Terry (1988b): "Plan and Market in China's Agricultural Commerce" Journal of Political Economy vol. 96, no. 2 (1988): 283-307

SSB (1990): Chinese Statistical Yearbook, 1990 (Beijing: SSB, 1990 and earlier years)

SSB (1987). Survey of the National Economy and Social Development in Beijing Municipality during 1981-1985 (Beijing: SSB, 1987).

Stone, B. (1986a): "Systemic and Policy Adjustment in the Administration of Chinese Fertilizer Development", a paper prepared for the World Bank, Washington, D.C., June 12, 1986

Stone, B. (1986b): "Chinese Fertilizer Application in the 1980s and 1990s: Issues of Growth, Balance, Allocation, Efficiency and Response", in U.S. Congress Joint Economic Committee, (ed.), China's Economy Looks Toward the Year 2000, Vol. 1 (The Four Modernizations), Washington, D.C.: U.S. Government Printing Office

USDA (1988): "China: Agriculture and Trade Report" ERS RS-84-4 (Washington, D.C.: USGPO, 1988)

Van der Gaag, Jacques (1984). "Private Household Consumption in China", World Bank Working Paper No. 701 (Washington, D.C.: World Bank, 1984).

Walker, Kenneth R. (1984): Food Grain Procurement and Consumption in China. (Cambridge: Cambridge University Press, 1984)

Walker, Kenneth R. (1989): "40 Years On: Provincial Contrasts in China's Rural Economic Development", The China Quarterly, Vol. 119, pp. 448-480, Sept. 1989

Watanatada, Thawat (1988): "The Transport Bottleneck Problem in China" (mimeo: World Bank, September 1988)

Webb, Shwu-eng H. (1989): "Agricultural Commodity Policies in China: Estimates of PSEs and CSEs, 1982-87", reported in USDA's China Agricultural Trade and Outlook Report--Situation and Outlook Series, USDA Economic Research Service Report No. RS-89-5, November 1989

Wen, Guangzhong James (1989):   "The Current Land Tenure System and its Impact on Long Term Performance of (the) Farming Sector: The Case of Modern China", paper presented to the AEA Annual Meetings, Atlanta, December 1989

World Bank (1991): "Poverty in China: An Issues Paper," January 1991

World Bank (1990a):   Working Paper No. 1 -- "Grain Consumption in China: Structure and Trends," (background paper, available upon request).

World Bank (1990b):   Working Paper No. 2 -- "Consumer Food Subsidies," (background paper, available upon request).

World Bank (1990c):   Working Paper No. 3 -- "Grain Production Prospects and Constraints," (background paper, available upon request).

World Bank (1990d):   Working Paper No. 4 -- "Fertilizer Sector Performance, Prospects and Policy," (background paper, available upon request).

World Bank (1990e):   Working Paper No. 5 -- "An Overview of China's Grain Sector," (background paper, available upon request).

World Bank (1990f):   Working Paper No. 6 -- "China's Domestic Grain Trade," (background paper, available upon request).

World Bank (1990g):   Working Paper No. 7 -- "Grain Marketing, Price Policy and Foreign Trade," (background paper, available upon request).

World Bank (1990h):   Working Paper No. 8 -- "Investment in Agriculture," (background paper, available upon request).

World Bank (1988a): "Rural Sector Performance Outlook", Working Paper No. 2 in the supplemental volumes to Report P-4801-CHA: The President's Report and Recommendation For a Loan & Credit to Support Rural Sector Adjustment in China, June 1988

World Bank (1988b): "Grain System Reform", Working Paper No. 3 in the supplemental volumes to Report P-4801-CHA: The President's Report and Recommendation For a Loan & Credit to Support Rural Sector Adjustment in China, June 1988

World Bank (1987): China: The Livestock Sector, Report 6589-CHA, Jan. 1987

Year 2000 Research Group (1984):   China in the Year 2000 (Beijing: Science and Technology Documents Publishers, 1984) translated by JPRS as CEA-86-023, March 6, 1986

Resource Base and Institutional Configuration

Resource Base and Institutional Configuration

Table of Contents

RESOURCE BASE AND INSTITUTIONAL CONFIGURATION

I.   GRAIN PRODUCTION SYSTEMS

-Resource Base

1.   Cultivated Area. The agroecology of grain production in China is rather complex. The continental extent of the land mass and the range of altitude leads to a broad spectrum of geophysical, soils and climatic conditions (World Bank [1990c], Appendix 1). Only about 10% of the total land area is suitable for cultivation, and 1988 statistics indicate a total cultivated area of 95.7 million ha. About 50% of this is located in the Northern Production Region and the Middle and Lower Reaches of the Yangtze River (MLYR-see Map). About 17% is located in the Northeast, 13% in the Northwest, 12% in the Southwest and the balance in the south. Available data indicate that cultivated area declined in the period 1979-1988 by 3.5 million ha (3.5%) at an average rate of 389,000 ha per year. 1/ The rate of decline in the period 1984-88 was higher at 500,000 ha per year. There was a loss of cultivated area in all regions except the Northwest. Prime causes include losses to rural and urban housing and industrialization; service infrastructure; transfer to forest and grassland and other soil conservation programs and abandonment of uneconomic land due to saline-alkaline problems, erosion and low soil fertility. With increasing population and industrialization, losses can be expected to continue at a rate of 4-500,000 ha per year.

2.   Water Resource Development. China is quite well endowed with water resources with an estimated net volume of 2800 billion cubic meters available annually. However, 82% of run-off finds its way to the Yangtze and Pearl River systems to the south in the higher rainfall zones where water requirements are lowest. Much of the good agricultural land is to the North, in drought prone areas away from the major water resources. Extensive ground water basins occur in association with the river systems. In the North these are being over exploited in some areas and groundwater levels are dropping.

3.   The location and changes in the effective irrigated area for the period 1980-1988 are presented in World Bank (1990c), Appendix 1, Table 2. The total effective irrigated area was 44.4 million ha in 1988 which represents about 46% of the total cultivated area. About 64% of the irrigated area is in the Northern and MLYR production zones. The South, Southwest and Northwest each command 9-11% of the total area and the Northeast has 5%. There was a net decline in irrigated area of about 100,000 ha in the period 1980-88. About 45% of the country's total land area is located in regions with less than 400 mm annual rainfall, mostly in the north, west and northwest. Thus, China's expansion of irrigated farmland up to the mid-1970s must be considered one of the major achievements of the country since 1949. The significance of irrigation for overall agricultural production is highlighted by the fact that

---

1/   The Agricultural Natural Resources and Planning Institute of the Chinese Academy of Agricultural Sciences reports a gross cultivated area of about 133 million ha based on satellite imagery. Although this area may include land which has been abandoned due to uneconomic production, it is large enough to have major implications regarding actual and projected crop yields and grain production projections to the Year 2000.

irrigated areas account for 2/3 of overall farm output and 3/4 of cash and industrial crop production.

4.   Most of the reported irrigation aggregates turned flat from the late 1970s. Shifting priorities in central (state) investment tell part of the story. Irrigation and agriculture had dropped to about 6% of total state investment by 1981 and fell further each year in relative terms to 3% in 1987: in real terms this was about half the level of the mid-1970s. The rapid abolition of the communes and devolution of expenditure authority substantially weakened local ability (and incentive) to promote investment in rural public works. Long-term targets have, however, been developed for further irrigation development. These envisage expanding total irrigated area by some 5.3 million ha. by the Year 2000 and an eventual stabilization of irrigated farmland at about 60 million ha. However, irrigation efficiencies are low, ranging from 30-55% for surface water irrigation systems. Inadequate investment in operation and maintenance has acted as a further constraint to productivity over much of the irrigated area.

5.   Drought, flooding, water logging and saline/alkaline soils are important constraints on existing cultivated land and on undeveloped land with production potential. The Ministry of Water Resources (MWR) estimates that there are 24 million ha of land affected by flooding and waterlogging, and 13.3 million ha that are affected by saline-alkaline soil problems, with about 6-7 million ha of the area being agricultural land. According to published statistics (World Bank [1990c], Appendix 1), 23.8 million ha had been improved by 1988. The implementation rate for irrigation and drainage improvements in recent years has been about 260,000 ha per year.

-Production Regions and Cropping Systems

6.   Regions For National Planning. A regionalization system used by the Institute of Agricultural Economics (IAE) of the Chinese Academy of Agricultural Sciences (CAAS) 2/ for its grain supply and demand analysis has been adopted by the present study, and production data have been aggregated on the basis of the six IAE production regions: Northeast, North, Northwest, MLYR, Southwest, and South. The regions are shown on the Map. 3/

7.   Rice Production Regions. The total planted area of rice is 32 million ha and most of the area is irrigated. The production area is divided into six regions. The South China Rice Region covers Guangdong, Guangxi, Fujian and South Yunnan. It is a warm high rainfall area producing indica rice. In the lowlands the main cropping systems are double rice followed by green manure or fallow or wheat followed by rice. Average paddy yields are reported to be in excess of 4 tons per ha. The Central Region represents about 60% of the total planted rice area. It embraces the single and double crop rice areas of the MLYR and the single crop rice areas of the Sichuan-Shanxi basin. Indica rice is the main rice type since the introduction of the hybrid varieties, but

---

2/   The IAE participates in the analysis and planning of grain production at national level.

3/   Locations of major grain production centers are displayed in World Bank (1990c), Map 2.

Japonica is popular in the eastern sections of the region. Common cropping systems are rice-rice-wheat and rice-wheat. Rice yields are reported to be within the range 4.5-7.5 ton per ha. The **Southwestern Region** includes Yunnan, Guizhou and Sichuan and constitutes 15% of the total planted area of rice. This is a higher altitude area with single crop *Japonica* rice at higher elevations and double crop *indica* rice at lower elevations. Reported yields are within the range of 4.2-6.4 ton per ha. The **North China Region** includes Hebei, Tianjin, Beijing, Shandong, N. Shaanxi and N. Henan, and represents about 3% of the planted area. It is a single crop *Japonica* rice area, but a fair percentage of the crop is now grown in a 2 crop system with winter wheat. Reported yields are within the range of 5.0-6.7 tons per ha. The **Northeast Region** includes Heilongjiang, Jilin and Liaoning and represents about 5% of total planted area. It is a single crop *Japonica* rice production region. Rice is either direct seeded in May or transplanted in June and is harvested in September. The **Northwest Region** includes Xinjiang and parts of the Gansu-Ningxia-Mongolian plateau. It represents less than 1% of the total planted rice area.

8.   Wheat Production Regions. The total planted area of wheat is about 29 million ha., divided into three major regions: the spring wheat, winter wheat and spring/winter wheat regions. The **Spring Wheat Region** covers the Northeast, North and Northwestern provinces and accounts for about 17% of the wheat production area. It is a low temperature single crop region. Average yields are low and in the range of 1.5-2.3 ton/ha. The **Winter Wheat Region** accounts for 60-70% of the sown wheat area. This extends from the North winter zone covering Beijing, Tianjin, Hebei and Shanxi, through the Huang-Huai-Hai zone (North China Plain), embracing the middle and lower reaches of the Yellow River, through the Yangtze River zone to the Southwest zone (Guizhou, Sichuan, Yunnan) and the South China wheat zone located in Fujian, Jiangxi, Guangdong and Guangxi. Temperature and rainfall increase and the planted area of wheat and its importance in the farming system decrease from north to south.   Depending on the length of growing season and the availability of water, wheat is grown as a single crop, or in a 2 crop system with corn, millet, beans or rice. The average yield is about 3.5 ton/ha., though yields in the south are considerably lower: 1-2 tons/ha. The **Spring & Winter Wheat Region** is located in Xinjiang and the Qing-Zang plateau in Qinghai and Tibet. This is a high altitude low rainfall zone with rather poor soils and limited growing season, and one crop per year is the norm. Fertilizer supply is limited and yields are low.

9.   Corn Production Regions. The total planted area of corn is about 20 million ha. The production area runs in a broad band from Northeast China to the Southwest. Almost 80% of the corn is grown under rainfed conditions and 80% is planted to hybrids or high yield varieties. The production area is divided into six regions. The Northern and Huang-Huai-Hai Plain Regions constitute about 70% of the planted area and contribute about 80% of national corn production. The **Northern Spring Corn Region** includes Heilongjiang, Jilin, Ningxia, Inner Mongolia, and the northern parts of Shanxi, Shaanxi, Hebei and Gansu. Due to the short growing season corn is planted as a single crop in April-May and is harvested in late August-September. Average yield in the region is 5.3 tons per ha. The **Huang-Huai-Hai Region** is the main corn production region constituting 43% of total planted area and contributing 50%

of national production. A large percentage of the corn is planted after winter wheat in late June. Average yields are about 3.8 ton per ha which is below potential due to low soil fertility, substandard management, limited fertilizer supply and vulnerability to drought. **The Southwestern Region** centered on Sichuan, Yunnan and Guizhou has a favorable rainfall and temperature regime. Corn is planted in spring, summer and autumn in a range of cropping systems with wheat, rice, tubers and beans. Average yields are low at 3.0 ton per ha. The **South China Region** is centered on Guangdong, Fujian, Jiangxi and East Guangxi. This is a warm humid area where spring, summer, autumn and winter corn are planted, usually in rice-based cropping systems. Average yield is about 3.4 ton per ha. The **Northwest Region** includes Xinjiang and parts of Gansu in the Hexi Corridor. Average yield is 3.3 ton per ha and is reported to be constrained by low rainfall and limited input supply.

10.   Soybean Production Regions. About 8.1 million ha of soybean are planted per year. About 85% of planted area and production is located in the Northeast, North and Yangtze River area. Three main production regions are recognized: the Northern Region, the Huang-Huai-Hai Plain and the South China Production Region. The **Northern Soybean Region** includes the Northeast, and the northern parts of Hebei, Shanxi, Shaanxi and Gansu. This is a low temperature single crop zone. Soybean is planted in early May and harvested in September. Average yields are about 1.7 ton/ha. The **Huang-Huai-Hai Plain Region** plants 90-100 day varieties in mid-late June following winter crops e.g. wheat, and harvest the crop in September. Average yield is about 1.2 ton per ha. The **South China Region** covers a number of scattered production areas, mostly south of the Yangtze river. Soybean is planted in spring, summer and autumn in a range of mixed cropping systems with wheat, rice and a range of upland crops. Winter soybean can be grown, south of Latitude 21°N. Yields vary with location, but range from 0.6 ton per ha in Guangxi up to 2.0 tons per ha in Jiangsu.

-Available Technology and Application

11.   China has a good **varietal base** for the major cereal crops and has pioneered the development of high yielding dwarf and hybrid rice varieties. About 42% of the rice area is reported to be planted to high yielding hybrid rice. High yielding corn varieties and hybrids are available for most production zones and 80% of the corn production area is reported to be planted with these high yielding lines. There is a wide range of high yield wheat varieties available and an on-going program to develop superior hybrids. A range of high yielding soybean varieties is also available. However, available data suggests the need to improve the disease and lodging resistance of wheat, the insect and disease resistance of rice and the disease resistance of soybean. There is also scope to develop early maturing varieties with improved cold resistance and drought resistance for some of the marginal production areas and to produce short duration high yield varieties suitable for intensive cropping systems.

12.   The agronomy of all crops is well known and documented in more detail than in most countries in the Asia Region. In areas with small farm size and high labor availability, labor intensive techniques to increase cropping

intensity and yield have been developed and are quite widely applied. Consistent reports of low soil fertility or declining soil fertility especially in the lower rainfall areas indicates a need for more research on **farming systems** in those areas. Also reports of low irrigation water use efficiency and saline-alkaline problems indicates a need to increase research on water management and irrigation technique at farm level in problem areas.

13. A great deal of work has been carried out at regional and provincial level on sources of nutrients, method and timing of application, and crop response on soils with different production capabilities. Although there appear to be deficiencies in the plant nutrition information available to farmers, lack of reasonable **fertilizer recommendations** is not likely to be an important constraint. The main constraint appears to be the availability of the fertilizer required at the time that it is needed.

14. All crops in China are subject to attack from the range of **pests and diseases** common to the Asian Region. The Crop Protection Institute, Beijing, reports that field production losses in rice due to pests and disease are high and in excess of 10%. It is possible to breed resistance into the crop varieties for most of the major pests and diseases encountered by Chinese farmers, and this approach has been adopted as the first line of defence. However, it would appear that in the case of wheat, rice and soybean, that there is still considerable room for improvement since the earlier--and quite successful--breeding programs emphasized yield response to nitrogen. Breeding for pest and disease resistance has lagged behind since 1980. The Crop Protection Institute has sound technical recommendations for most of the common pests and diseases and since the late seventies has focussed research on integrated pest management. However the Institute lacks adequate budget for research. At field level the main constraints appear to be a lack of adequately trained extension personnel and budget to launch an effective pest management campaign, and a lack of adequate supply of appropriate agrochemicals for strategic chemical control.

15. Excepting the high **rate of adoption** of high yielding varieties, anecdotal evidence suggests that only 20-50% of known technology is being applied effectively in the field. Rates of application vary with component and locality. In most areas, the lack of effective extension services to reach a majority of small farmers is clearly a common factor, and applies particularly to items largely independent of input supply, e.g. time and method of planting, optimum plant population, method of fertilizer application, use of organic manure. In the case of activities tied to input supply, e.g. use of good seed and fertilizers, the timely and adequate supply of the required inputs appears to be the primary constraint.

II. THE INSTITUTIONAL CONFIGURATION FOR PRODUCTION SUPPORT

16. Production Planning. The Agricultural Regional Planning Commission (ARPC) established in 1979 under the purview of the State Planning Commission (SPC) is a central unit for agriculture planning in China. This commission has representatives from key ministries and is in a position to coordinate data

collection, studies and planning exercises between key agencies. The Ministry of Agriculture (MOA) as the principal agency for agriculture administers the central ARPC unit, supported by subordinate units in each province. The MOA relies on the ARPC, the Chinese Academy of Agricultural Sciences (CAAS), its own bureaux and provincial agencies to collect and analyze data and prepare plans to meet government requirements.

17.   Within CAAS, the two key agencies involved in planning are the Agricultural Natural Resources and Planning Institute (ANRPI) and the IAE. A key role of the ANRPI is the collection and storage of basic data from the provinces, maintenance of a central data bank, and research and studies relevant to national planning requirements. The Institute collects basic resource, production, and economic data from all provinces and has 300 monitoring stations at the county-level collecting very detailed information under a State-financed program. The IAE took the lead in studies on grain production to the Year 2000. The work programs of both institutes are governed by study and planning contracts with MOA, and both draw upon the resources of other institutes within CAAS for specialized technical input.

18.   Agricultural Services. MOA is the lead agency for agricultural production. The Ministry has been undergoing some reorganization, but it is believed that the Chart attached to World Bank (1990c) represents MOA's current structure. The Bureaux and General Stations are responsible for monitoring their areas of activity and supplying information and technical advice at national level. They prepare recommendations on policy, regulations, and national programs and administer and supervise centrally financed programs. They also participate in national planning.

19.   There are several levels of **agricultural research** in China with differing responsibilities and sources of funding. At the top, the Chinese Academy of Sciences (CAS) supervises 122 national research institutes, some of which carry out research in the agricultural sciences. At the ministerial level, much of the research is carried out in 31 agricultural research institutes which operate under the supervision and general professional guidance of the CAAS, within MOA. About 11% of the research conducted by institutes under the guidance of CAAS is classified as basic research, while the balance generally relates to specific problems encountered in agricultural production and processing. There also are smaller, specialized institutes under MOA which carry out highly specialized research on aquatic products and tropical crops. The MWR oversees 33 affiliated research organizations which carry out research related to water use in agriculture. The CAAS system has some 4,000 research scientists, while the MWR system has 5,000. Funds for the CAS, CAAS and other ministerial level institutes are allocated from the national budget.

20.   Providing the base of support at the next level are the Provincial Academies of Agricultural Science (PAAS) and associated research institutes. Nationwide, there are about 1,340 research institutes operating under PAAS guidance at the prefectural level and above, staffed by some 15,300 scientists. These institutes focus mainly on solving production problems, but also participate in national and regional research projects. Provincially managed projects are financed by the province and national and regional

projects by the central government. Finally, the university-affiliated institutions undertake basic and applied research according to teaching and local research needs. The 60 agricultural colleges and universities receive research funds from the State Education Commission.

21.   Although much progress has been made to improve China's agricultural research capabilities since 1980, work at many research institutes continues to be hampered by inadequately qualified staff, especially at the middle and senior levels and in the areas of experimental design and statistical analysis, and poor research facilities. Experimental fields need to be established or upgraded and there is a general need for better equipped laboratories, libraries and workshops. Linkages between research institutes and the agricultural colleges and universities tend to be weak. Expenditures on agricultural research in China are comparatively low. In 1987, support for agricultural research was equivalent to only 0.5% of agricultural GDP, compared with nearly twice that amount in Korea and other nearby Asian countries. Budget shortfalls and cutbacks have forced many institutes to solicit an increasing share of their funds from production units. An unfortunate side effect has been a diversion of staff efforts from priority research programs to the search for funds and sometimes less-than-priority contract research, often little more than agricultural extension.

22.   Within the technology transfer nexus, an effective organization for **agricultural extension** and its financing have yet to be fully implemented. Organizational reforms in rural areas, and the abolition of services formerly provided by the production brigades have necessitated a new organization (and new approaches) for extension. The main problem lays with the vastly expanded number of end-users with whom both the research staff and extension agents must deal, a consequence of decollectivization and introduction of the PRS. In 1982, a decision was taken to convert the existing county research institutes into agrotechnical extension centers, to combine the formerly separate county level stations for research, extension, plant protection and animal husbandry services, seeds multiplication, crop/soil/fertilizer analysis and machinery services. Presently, extension operates as an independent system under MOA's general guidance, or completely separate from MOA in some counties. MOA's National Technical Extension Center is responsible for overall planning, allocation of central level funds, and evaluation of extension programs. Likewise, a series of provincial and prefectural extension centers are under their respective agricultural bureaux and are solely responsible for administering provincial and prefectural extension programs. Below the prefectures are county-level agrotechnical extension centers (CATEC), which are supposed to coordinate all extension activities at the county level and below. Within this impressive hierarchy, points of contact with farmers consist of a network of agrotechnical stations and demonstration farms at the township, village and farm levels. All levels of the system receive budget allocations from the central government. As in research, contracts are entered between units of the CATEC and local production units.

23.   The CATECs' major functions include training, demonstration and oversight of input distribution programs at the farm level. Their plans for extension training are typical ones: demonstrations, field days and short courses for farmers, and longer courses for lead farmers and extension

technicians. Mass media are also utilized to disseminate extension advice, which is reported to be fairly common and effective. Higher level technical support to the CATECs is provided by agricultural colleges and the PAAS.

24.   The new arrangements to provide extension services vary widely among locations and continue to evolve. To reach China's 190 million farm households, the Government plans eventually to establish a CATEC in each of China's 2,300 counties. So far, less than one third have been established, and only 80% have some form of extension program. Most extension personnel require further training to update their knowledge, and most of the CATECs lack facilities, transportation and simple equipment. There is also a need to establish--and adequately service--more demonstration centers and participating lead farmers in key locations. Also, effective means for transmitting research findings to farmers through the extension centers have yet to be devised. In consequence, effective feedback from their farmer clientele has been inhibited. Meanwhile, extension, like many other of China's agricultural support services, appears to remain underbudgeted in respect of the state's ambitious production objectives.

25.   Other Services. The MWR is the lead agency for water conservation. The Ministry and its service units play a similar role to the MOA at national level in the fields of water resources, irrigation, drainage and reclamation of saline-alkaline land. The supply of inputs and marketing and distribution of agricultural produce is dominated by government bureaux and parastatals which operate under the administrative umbrella of the Ministry of Commerce (MOC). The MOC network consists of three subsystems: (a) The National Agricultural Means of Production Corporation, also referred to as the "Agricultural Inputs Corporation" (AIC), which is responsible for the supply of inputs, (b) The General Grain Bureau (GGB) and provincial and local affiliates, which control the purchase and processing of grain; and (c) the Commercial Bureaux and Supply & Marketing Cooperatives, which manage the bulk procurement of grains and sales at administered prices. The MOA's National Seed Corporation is responsible for the import and export of seed and, together with the Bureau of State Farms, for national seed production and distribution. In recent years, state and collective joint ventures, rural cooperatives and procurement and sales agents have developed and participate in marketing. Nevertheless, the MOC largely controls input supply, grain procurement, processing and marketing. The Agricultural Bank of China provides credit for procurement of inputs and produce by government agencies, and supplies credit to farmers largely via the Rural Credit Cooperatives. 4/

26.   The provinces are responsible for implementing national programs but have a degree of autonomy, and are able to plan and implement their own programs within the policy guidelines set by the central government. As a result there are variations between provinces in their organizational structure and implementation of national programs. However most provinces have a similar organizational structure. The Provincial Planning Commission is the central economic body. A governor assisted by a number of vice-governors (with one vice-governor responsible for agriculture) have overall

---

4/   cf. Appendix to World Bank (1990h) for a synoptic view of China's rural financial markets.

responsibility for implementing State Council approved programs through provincial bureaux and corporations representing the ministries and key agencies at national level e.g. Bureaux of Agriculture and Water Resources, GGB affiliates, Materials Supply Companies for supply of inputs, Seed Corporations etc. The provincial agricultural bureaux usually have an agricultural technical institute for research and training and coordinate with the Provincial Academies of Agricultural Sciences for additional services through agricultural training colleges run by the PAAS. The CAAS is represented in most provinces, either directly, or through the network of PAAS. Most provinces also support an agricultural university or an agricultural faculty within the provincial university system.

27. Large provinces are divided into regions or prefectures. Most agricultural service units maintain an office at this level, but the function is largely supervision of county programs within their jurisdiction. The structure at province level is repeated at county level. Again, counties have some autonomy in program planning and implementation within the guidelines provided by the central and provincial governments. Cooperatives play an important role at township and village level in the supply of inputs, services and credits to farmers and the procurement of produce.

III. GRAIN PROCUREMENT AND DISTRIBUTION

-Institutions and Operation

28. Pricing. Two government agencies directly subordinate to the State Council, the State General Commodity Price Bureau (SPB) and the State Administration of Industry and Commerce (SAIC), are responsible for administering agricultural prices. The SPB's principal task is the determination, in consultation with the Ministries of Finance (MOF), Agriculture, and Commerce, and enforcement of administered agricultural prices. The setting of administered prices for major commodities is subject to review and approval by the State Council. Through its system of provincial Price Bureaux and local government Price Departments, the SPB monitors official procurement and sales at the local level to ensure compliance with national price policies. SPB also monitors free market prices. The SAIC has principal responsibility for the regulation and administration of free market trade and prices. The SAIC owns and regulates most of China's urban and rural free markets, the number of which has increased from about 40,000 in 1980 to more than 72,000 in 1989. Its more than 400,000 central and local level staff also collect a 1% management fee and a 2% ad valorem tax on free market sales and monitor free market prices on a country-wide basis for about 150 agricultural inputs and outputs. These fees and taxes are used to offset the SAIC's local operating costs and, in combination with local government and private funds and loans, as investment funds for the expansion of free markets and associated infrastructure.

29. Domestic Trade. At its peak, the state-run trading system procured and distributed more than 230 agricultural commodities and controlled as much as 85% of China's total marketed agricultural production. During the 1980s, however, the state system sharply reduced its share of the trade in most

commodities other than grain, vegetable oil, sugar, cotton and some other industrial crops. Within the state system, the MOC now has principal responsibility for the planned domestic procurement and distribution of China's grain, vegetable oil and industrial crop output. More than four million MOC staff, mostly employees of branch provincial and county level grain bureaux and their network of more than 40,000 rural grain stations, are directly involved in the procurement and distribution of grain and vegetable oil. Other specialized bureaux of the MOC operate commercial agencies and trading companies which control much or most of the domestic trade in cotton, fruit, vegetables, sugar, tobacco, tea, animal feed and other products. The MOC's commercial system is also associated with provincial and local level Supply and Marketing Cooperatives (SMC). 5/ The SMCs supply farmers with most of their agricultural inputs and some consumer goods (including processed grain) and are the nation's most important purchasing agents for vegetables, fruit and handicraft items.

30.   International Trade. The administration of China's foreign trade was streamlined in 1982 with the amalgamation of the Ministry of Foreign Trade, the Ministry of Foreign Economic Relations, the Foreign Investment Commission, and the State Import-Export Commission into the newly established Ministry of Foreign Economic Relations and Trade (MOFERT). MOFERT supervises the local Foreign Trade Bureaux of each province and municipality and 15 product-specific national foreign trade corporations (FTCs), including the China National Cereals, Oils and Foodstuffs Import and Export Corporation (CEROILS), which controls most of China's international trade in grain and vegetable oil.

31.   The FTCs engage directly in international trade and, operating on a commission basis, are reportedly now responsible for their own profits and losses. Decentralization of foreign trade began in 1979 with the partial authorization of provincial and municipal governments and some individual enterprises to directly engage in foreign trade. However, foreign trade policy has alternated during the 1980s between decentralization and recentralization, and it was recently reported that CEROILS has regained full control of China's foreign trade in grain and vegetable oils.

32.   Foreign trade is an integral part of China's national economic planning. The State Planning Commission (SPC) first sets preliminary annual and long term targets for broad categories of imports and exports. MOFERT subsequently prepares more detailed plans for import and exports on the basis of the SPC targets and in consideration of trends in the world market, and then transmits these plans as guidelines to the FTCs.

-Procurement and Distribution

33.   Official **grain procurement** figures shown in World Bank (1990g), Appendix

---

5/   The SMCs, established in the early 1950s as autonomous farmers' collectives, were brought under direct state control in the late 1950s. Ownership and control of the SMCs switched repeatedly between the state and farmers over the following three decades. The SMCs are now officially considered to be nongovernmental, but the MOC continues to exert considerable control over SMC operations.

1, Table 1, indicate that total procurement ranged between 20-26% of total grain production during 1952-1982, and then increased to between 30-35% of production in 1983-1988. In absolute terms, annual total procurement increased from 39 million tons (trade grain) in 1952 to an annual average of 114 million tons during 1983-88. Annual procurement by the MOC's grain bureau system, other state-owned commercial agencies, and the SMCs, herein referred to as "state procurement," increased from 80% of total procurement in 1952 to 100% during the 1960s and 1970s, and then declined to about 85% at present. State procurement of grain at negotiated prices increased rapidly in the 1980s, from less than 15% of total procurement in 1980 to 35% in 1987, and now accounts for more than 40% of total state procurement. Urban and rural free market trade accounted for about 6% of total grain procurement in the 1980s, with rural markets accounting for the majority (85%) of total free market trade. "Other" procurement, *viz.* the difference between total procurement and known procurement through state channels and the free market, was negligible until 1985 when it increased to about 10% of total procurement. During the period 1983-88, state procurement averaged 99 million tons, free market trade accounted for another 7 million tons, and "other" the remaining 8 million tons.

34. Official **grain distribution** figures in World Bank (1990g), Appendix 1, Table 1 reportedly include all urban and rural sales through both state-owned and free market channels except farm-to-farm sales and barter trade. State sales at negotiated prices grew rapidly during the 1980s, increasing from about 5 million tons in 1980 to about 27 million tons in 1987, or from less than 10% of total sales by state-owned agencies to almost 30%. Despite this rapid increase, however, negotiated sales have not kept pace with negotiated procurement. On average about one-third of total state grain distribution is "resold" to rural households through grain stations and the SMCs, though rural resales' share of state distribution was as low as 20% in the early-1950s and temporarily surged to 50% in 1985. Lastly, the figures in the above referenced table indicate that free market trade has accounted for between 6 to 9% of total grain distribution during the 1980s.

-A Sketch of the Grain Distribution System

35. China's grain distribution system is grounded in a near monopoly of off-farm stores and interprovincial movements, managed by the system of grain bureaux enterprises. Though detailed information about China's grain storage and handling capabilities is not readily available, it is reported that the grain bureau system currently operates about 127 million tons of off-farm storages, of which only 87 million tons are considered fully serviceable. Exacerbated by transportation constraints, stocking ratios are high. Because of siting problems and a failure of local investment to keep abreast of developments in regional supply and demand, a severely unbalanced regional distribution of storage capacity exists. As a result, about 25 million tons are being held in open stores.

36. Physical losses are high, perhaps equivalent in value to US$ 1.5 billion in imports. Financial losses also are high. In 1988, the GGB system's accumulated losses amounted to ¥ 9.2 Billion. These financial losses increased in 1989 and are expected to have further escalated in 1990. The causes are

manifold, but collectively, the operating losses of public agencies in the grain distribution system accounted for nearly one-third of the total grain subsidy in 1988, and were nearly equivalent to subsidies provided for financing the difference between farm-gate procurement prices and urban sales.

37.   China's official grain procurement and distribution system is made up of the following components:

> **Rural collection points**, which are the primary point of entry into the commercial, public grain system and which possess by far the largest amount of grain storage;
>
> **Urban distribution depots**, serving as the principal entry point for grain arriving at major cities and which provide processing as well as storage and distribution facilities;
>
> **Urban/Transfer depots**, a combination of urban distribution center and assembly point for grain being trans-shipped for export or inter-provincial trade;
>
> **Urban retail shops**, which provide the primary outlet for grain sold to consumers, and
>
> **Rural storage points**: a special group of facilities that have been set up to hold longer-term grain reserves.

In addition to these components there are the parts of the "double track" or market system which are operated by (or on behalf of) independent traders. The wholesale grain markets licensed and/or run by the SAIC are one part of this system while private retail markets in cities and small farmers markets in rural areas are the other two principal parts.

38.   Essentially all of the **rural collection points** only have flat warehouse storage--much of it in need of major maintenance--with little or no power equipment for grain handling and conditioning. Grain is brought by farmers to these points in sacks. After visual inspection for quality, foreign material and moisture the grain is either accepted for storage or it is rejected. However, the average country point is not equipped to cope well with grain receipt, particularly when a significant amount requires conditioning. The extent of double handling also is very high. A very few **urban collection depots** may be equipped with bulk grain storage and handling facilities - almost all will have a rice or flour mill which will operate a limited amount of bulk handling capacity, the use of which is restricted to operations of the mill. In most instances the bulk of storage will be flat storage and the extent of mechanical handling between transport modes and storage may be limited to bag elevators and simple cranes for emptying or loading boats.

39.   Urban or other **transfer depots** generally ship grain by rail but receive by a mixture of road, rail and water. Storage and handling will be very similar to urban distribution depots except for a small number of recently improved stores. Milling is of less importance, on average, in a transfer

depot than in an urban distribution depot. The facilities in **urban retail shops** vary greatly, but the amount stored is equivalent to only a few days' sales. The **rural storage points** have been selectively sited to hold longer term reserves. Their storage is typically flat warehouse space--reportedly in good condition--in which grain is stored either in bags or in bulk. Handling facilities are minimal and only grain in good condition is accepted by such facilities.

40.   Within the distribution system, all of the storage, handling and processing/ distribution facilities are linked by rail, road or water transport or a combination of **transportation modes** and it is commonly argued that transport network capacity is a binding constraint on the movement of grain and other major commodities. The total volume of grain moved through the several transportation modes is not known with accuracy **6/** but a large share of inter-provincial shipments (80% or more) move by rail with most of the remainder by water. Road shipments make up a very large percentage of the shorter, intra-provincial hauls.

41.   The role of China's nascent **free markets** in grain seems to be concentrated on market exchange. They do not offer much storage capacity and mainly serve farmers and consumers within specific locales, although there is some evidence of grain assembly and movement over long distances. This latter function has never really been encouraged in China and is now actively being discouraged as a matter of government policy. Without ready access to rail transport, good market information, and the ability to hedge purchases against expected sales, the fact that free market operatives have been able to function at all, interprovincially, is prima facie evidence that the public system had allowed significant price distortion to occur between provinces. **7/**

IV.   THE URBAN GRAIN RATION SYSTEM

42.   Fears that rising wages among the growing industrial and government work force would push demand for grain and other basic foodstuffs above available supply and perhaps drive up prices to unacceptable levels prompted adoption of the ration system in 1955. Access to the ration system is restricted to

---

6/ According to MOC, the total volume of grain moved by rail in 1986 was 47 million tons of which 30 million were shipped inter-provincially. World Bank (1990f), pp 7-16 contains a discussion of available data and analyses.

7/ One of the most important actions which could be taken to encourage non-official investment in grain storage and handling would be to establish regional grain futures market in China, and indeed, considerable official interest has already been shown. In 1989, the State Council authorized the commissioning of a feasibility study for setting one up in Zhengzhou, Henan with the assistance of experts from the Chicago Board of Trade, to operate alongside a recently established national wholesale market for wheat in Zhengzhou. Though a decision was made to postpone implementation for the time being, it is widely recognized in China that a successful grain futures market could substantially reduce the need for holding excessive stocks within the official system.

China's registered "nonagricultural" population. 8/ The nonagricultural population includes current and retired employees (and their dependents) of state industrial enterprises and government agencies, students, and other permanently registered residents of cities and towns. Preliminary estimates, discussed in World Bank (1990b), Appendix 2, suggest that the total urban population numbered about 304 million in 1987, and that about 116 million of these urban inhabitants were not entitled to rationed foodstuffs.

43.   The MOC's urban grain bureaux distribute milled rice, wheat flour and flour products, corn and other grains, beans, vegetable oil, salt, soy sauce and other staple foods to the nonagricultural population through their networks of urban grain ration shops. 9/ The grain ration shops sell premium, standard and low grades of these products, but premium grades are generally in limited supply and, on most days, not available for purchase. The MOC also distributes a portion of the urban supply of nonstaple foodstuffs, including soybean curd, sugar, pork, other animal products, and vegetables, through "nonstaple" food stores and markets operated by other MOC commercial agencies and trading companies. Each urban household entitled to ration grain receives a grain purchase booklet which is used to secure the ration coupons required when purchasing grain and vegetable oil at the ration shops. The majority of ration coupons are valid only in the locality in which they were issued. Entitled urban households also receive ration booklets and coupons for nonstaple foods.

44.   "Base" grain ration allotments, which average about 180 kg per person per year, are determined by the age, sex, and occupational structure of the household. Heavy laborers receive substantially greater base allotments than do office workers and students. Some workers and other employees also receive a "variable" allotment in addition to their base grain ration. These variable grain rations can be quite substantial in some industries -- coal miners, for instance, receive a variable allotment of up to 300 kg per year. The base grain ration allotment significantly exceeds actual levels of urban per capita consumption. Income and expenditure survey data for a large number of urban households indicate that the average urban resident now purchases about 135 kg of grain annually. Since about 8 kg of this quantity is purchased on the free market, actual per capita purchase of ration grain averages only about 127 kg, or about 70% of the base allotment. 10/ Ration coupons not used to purchase grain can be deposited in banks and exchanged for new coupons at the end of the year. The overhang of unused grain ration coupons nationwide was equivalent to about 12 million tons in 1980, and is now estimated to be equivalent to 20 million tons (World Bank [1990b]). Unused ration coupons are also now commonly bartered in the free market for pork, eggs and other

---

8/   Since alternative sources of grain and other basic foodstuffs were sharply curtailed in urban areas (private trade in grain was legally enjoined) and only registered urban households were allowed access to rationed foodstuffs, the ration system also functioned as an effective means of controlling rural to urban migration from the mid-1950s until private free market trade in grain was legalized in the early-1980s.

9/   In southern China ration grain is sold through grain ration shops and vegetable oil, salt, soy sauce and other staple foods through separate "vegetable oil" ration shops.

10/ See World Bank (1990a).

nonstaple foods and, though the practice is illegal, sold for cash. Ration coupons have in effect been monetized and are currently worth about ¥ 0.8 per kg of grain.

V. FERTILIZER DISTRIBUTION

45.   Price Determination. China's fertilizer distribution system is highly regulated and operates completely within a framework of administered pricing. Fertilizer price setting in China attempts to take into account the cost of fertilizer production and/or imports, returns to farming and the prices of other fertilizers. SPB, the central price-setting organization in China, acts in consultation with SPC, MOF, MOA, MOC and MOFERT, as price decisions must be approved by the highest levels in government. Pricing is based on several principles, including (a) maintenance of price uniformity -- pan-national for national fertilizers, at the provincial level for provincial fertilizers and at the county level for county fertilizers; (b) maintenance of price stability (e.g. maintaining a fixed price for several years); (c) maintenance of low prices in order to provide incentives to farmers and support agriculture; (d) maintenance of low but positive profit margins for commercial agencies; and (e) reduction of adverse movement in the terms of trade for industrial and agricultural products. Historically, however, the price policy has been applied to transfer resources from the rural-agricultural to urban-industrial sectors.

46.   Distribution System. Located under the MOC, and centered in the AIC, the system distributes fertilizers in accord with annual distribution plans. The central AIC purchases fertilizer from factories, receives imports from MOFERT's China National Chemical Industries Import-Export Corporation (SINOCHEM) and distributes fertilizer to AICs at the lower level wholesale stations. The AIC operate at three different administrative levels, including national, provincial and county levels. Approximately, 90% of the total fertilizer is controlled and distributed by the AIC and the remaining 10% by non-AIC agencies (World Bank [1990d]). 11/ After the AIC monopoly was reimposed in January 1989, fertilizer distribution is now managed by central and provincial government agencies only. A schematic of the fertilizer distribution system in China is provided in the Chart attached to World Bank (1990d).

47.   The central AIC has its headquarters in Beijing and, in addition, operates five first-level wholesale stations at the regional level. The national level AIC (a) works out the annual plan for fertilizer allocation at the national level; (b) controls and supervises the implementation of policies established by government; (c) establishes rules and regulations regarding the management of enterprises within the AIC system; (d) manages and distributes fertilizer, produced in large scale plants and imported by SINOCHEM, based on

---

11/ The non-AIC agencies involved in fertilizer marketing included: (a) direct sale by factories to farmers; (b) fertilizer sale by factories to farmers through township and village level SMCs (supply and marketing cooperatives), and (c) fertilizer purchase and sale by other government organizations.

unified planning, distribution and price; and (e) purchases, receives, allocates and transports fertilizer according to production and distribution plans established by government. About 20% of total AIC fertilizer is handled by the national-level AIC.

48.   The **provincial level AIC** have 200-300 second level wholesale stations -- generally sited at prefecture levels. 12/ These AIC (a) work out the plan for circulation of fertilizer within the province; (b) implement policies established by government and rules and regulations established by the central AIC; (c) control and supervise county level AIC; (d) manage and distribute fertilizers purchased from small and medium scale plants, fertilizer received from the national AIC, and fertilizer imported by local governments with their own foreign exchange with central government approval; and (e) receive, on behalf of the central government, imported fertilizer in secondary ports. Approximately, 30% of total AIC fertilizer is handled by provincial AIC.

49.   The **county level AIC** have about 2,200-2,300 third level wholesale stations -- at least one for each county. The county AIC is responsible for several activities, including the management of fertilizer purchased from small scale plants and fertilizer received from provincial AICs, the wholesale distribution of fertilizer to SMC at the basic level, and some retailing of fertilizer through county level AIC warehouse retail shops. Approximately, 50% of total fertilizer distributed through the AIC system is handled by the county-level AIC.

50.   At the **retail level**, AIC fertilizer is handled by the county AIC, and SMC at the basic level. The county AIC sells fertilizer directly to farmers through county warehouse retail shops. There are about 10,000 such shops, handling approximately 15% of the total AIC fertilizer that is sold at the retail level. The remaining 85% is mostly retailed through the SMCs' means of production shops--64,000 at the township level, and the SMCs' retail kiosks--110,000 at the village level. Small amounts are also sold by commission agents. AIC officials believe there is adequate number of sales points in the country. Farmers are issued "supply (ration) cards" by the SMC which enables them to purchase fixed quantities of subsidized fertilizer at SMCs' retail outlets.

51.   Government authorities believe that physical losses in China were 1-2% in 1982 and 3-4% in 1984. 13/ The actual physical and chemical losses may be much higher than these estimates because (a) a large share of fertilizer in China is of low grade and relatively poor quality, (b) packaging is not very good, and (c) fertilizer is handled several times before it reaches the farmer. Volatilization of the widely used ammonium bicarbonate (AmBC) is a major source of loss. One study carried out by CAAS reports that fertilizer losses could be over 20% nationally and 30-40% in some areas. These losses

---

12/ By the end of 1988, China had 29 provinces/municipalities/autonomous regions (excluding Taiwan); 156 prefectures; 378 cities (out of which 170 equivalent to prefecture and 208 equivalent to county); 1986 counties; and 632 districts under cities' administration.

13/ The experience from other developing countries indicates that physical losses of fertilizer in the marketing chain amount to about 5% of total fertilizer sale.

include losses incurred during packaging, storage and transport.

52.   Accurate information on annual fertilizer **stocks** is not available. According to AIC, fertilizer stocks account for about 20-25% of total annual sales volume measured in product weights. Approximately 90% of these stocks is designated to meet peak season fertilizer demand and the remaining 10% is designated as emergency stock. Fertilizer stocks were relatively high in 1984 due to a decline in the demand for low grade fertilizers, primarily AmBC. Then government imposed an import moratorium in 1985 and 1986. Consequently, fertilizer stocks dropped to about 18% of annual sales in 1987.

53.   The total fertilizer **storage capacity** in China is about 14 million square meters. Over 80% of the existing fertilizer storage capacity is at the village, township and county levels, some of it being shared with the local grain bureaux. The AIC and SMCs each account for about 50% of total storage. Over time, there has been a gradual shift away from paper bags to stronger polyethylene bags. Consequently, China can now store about 20 million tons, almost equalling the level of fertilizer stocks in recent years. However, as fertilizer production and consumption expands there will be a need to expand fertilizer storage capacity.

54.   Owing to rapid growth in fertilizer use during the 1980s, total consumption reached the level of 89.3 million product tons in 1988. **Fertilizer transportation** is now becoming a serious constraint and is expected to be even more serious in the future. The principal modes of fertilizer transportation are rail and road, although river (water) transport also plays an important role, especially in southern China. Fertilizer is given priority within the national transportation network to ensure timely delivery to the farm level. Although fertilizer transport costs in China are highly subsidized, transportation accounts for the largest share of fertilizer marketing costs in China. The estimated fertilizer transport tariffs (both economic and financial) in China are reported in World Bank (1990d), Table 27. As expected, fertilizer transport by road is the most expensive but it is the most convenient at the county level. The importance of fertilizer transport costs varies by nutrient content of a given fertilizer (World Bank [1990d], Table 28).

Performance in the Real Sector: 1979-1990

Performance in the Real Sector: 1979-1990

Table of Contents

PERFORMANCE IN THE REAL SECTOR: 1979-1990

1.   From the inception of the reforms in December 1978 until 1988, the main
sources of growth in crop agriculture fell in two patterns. Institutional
change, principally the spread of the PRS, dominated the initial years, while
price policies, liberalization in the markets for higher valued commodities,
and a continued expansion of fertilizer consumption (albeit at a slower pace)
were largely responsible for growth that ensued after 1984. Benefitting from
extraordinarily favorable weather conditions, production in 1989 regained the
level realized in 1984 (407 million tons), then increased further to 425
million tons in 1990, which is a new record. Following the return of normal
weather in 1991, however, it is anticipated that production will decline. Thus
the technological basis for growth in crop production in the coming years will
largely depend on the continuing diffusion of yield enhancing improvements
associated with fertilizer responsive plant varieties, improved water control
and efficient fertilizer use. This generalization applies both to grains and
to non-grains. In view of the importance of chemical nutrients in this schema,
developments in the fertilizer sector are reviewed below corollary to
performance in the grain sector.

I.   TRENDS IN THE GRAIN SECTOR

-Production and Supply

2.   Grain Production and Supply. Excluding changes in stocks, China's grain
supply (cf. Table 2.1 of the main report) steadily increased until 1984, then
declined. With the exception of 1984 and 1985, however, China has been a net
importer of grain. Though quantities have been large relative to total world
trade, the contribution of net grain imports to total supply has never
exceeded 3.9% (in 1981), which had fallen to 2.0% by 1988. Per capita
production (with rice expressed in unmilled form) gradually increased from
293 kg in 1970 to a peak of 394 kg in 1984, and then declined to 360 kg in
1988. However, per capita availability has consistently been higher.

3.   With reference to the structure of production at the farm level, there
remains a marked lack of diversification in Chinese agriculture. Though it has
declined since the onset of the reforms, from 121 million ha. in 1978 to 110
million ha. in 1988, the total area under grain crops continues to occupy 76%
of the total sown area. In view of the already high yields enjoyed in China,
these data reinforce an impression that the best options to pursue while
stimulating agricultural growth may not reside in China's grain sector.

4.   Trends in Production. The major grain commodities in China are rice,
wheat, corn and soybeans. 1/ Grain production performance (Table 2.1 of the
Main Report and World Bank [1990c, 1990e]) has been remarkable by any
standard, both during the decade preceding initiation of China's rural
reforms, and even more so during the first half-decade of the reform era.
Average annual incremental grain production between 1979-84 was 17.1 million

---

1/ Chinese definition of grains (footnote to para 1.12 of main report)

tons, twice the amount of the pre-reform period. It was during this period
that China reattained basic self-sufficiency in grain and, briefly, became a
net exporter. The subsequent euphoria led to changes in national grain policy
(reviewed below), stagnation in grain production and, in the late-1980s, a
perceived "grain crisis" among China's leaders. Grain production in 1989
registered 407.6 million tons, a new record after five years, and increased
further to 425 million tons in 1990. However, because of population growth,
per capita grain production was still lower in 1989 than in 1984.

5.   **Regionally,** about 60% of China's total grain production originates in
the Middle and Lower Reaches of the Yangtze River (MLYR) and Northern
Production Regions (map). There have been no major changes in the regional
distribution of grain production in the period 1979-1988. Small increases
occurred in the Northeast and Northwest and there was a reduction in the
contribution from the South.

Total Grain Production
(million tons)

	Grain Production			Annual % Change		Distn (%)	
	1979	1984	1988	79-84	84-88	1979	1988
Northeast	35.6	48.2	46.4	7.0	-1.0	10.7	11.8
North	84.1	100.5	99.0	4.0	-0.3	25.3	25.1
Northwest	15.5	18.9	22.0	4.2	4.3	4.7	5.6
MLYR	113.6	140.5	136.0	4.8	-0.8	34.2	34.5
Southwest	46.6	58.9	54.2	5.2	-2.0	14.0	13.8
South	36.7	40.4	36.4	2.0	-2.5	11.1	9.2
China	332.1	407.4	394.0	4.6	-0.8	100.0	100.0

6.   There have been significant changes in **total grain production** in the
period 1979-1984. Total grain production rose from 332.1 million tons in 1979
to 407.4 million tons in 1984, the record harvest year. In this period
planted area fell by 5% and production increases were due to a 30% average
yield increase with significant yield increases occurring in all regions. By
Chinese standards, production fell back dramatically in 1985 (by about 9%) due
to a reduction in the area planted in grains of 4 million ha and a slight
reduction in yield. By 1987, grain production had largely recovered to about
404 million tons due to a partial recovery of planted area and a slight
increase in average yield. However, average yields appear to have plateaued
since 1984 and planted area has thereafter been the main determinant of
production trends.

7.   The contribution to total production of the individual grain crops is
shown in the table over page. Rice is the major component with wheat and corn
the other major contributors. All the major crops exhibited substantial
growth in production in the period 1979-1984 and contributed to the large
increase in total grain production. The production of rice, wheat, tubers and
other grains declined by from 0.8 to 1.5% per year between 1984-88, while
soybeans and corn registered increases.

8.   An analysis of production data for the major grain crops (World Bank [1990c], Appendices 2-5) indicates that the **rice** planted area declined by about 0.6 million ha in the period 1979-1984 and by a further 1.2 million ha in the period 1984-1988. Most of the reduction in planted area occurred in the MLYR and the South, and the only region showing a significant increase was

Total Grain Production
(million tons)

	Production			Annual % Change		Distribution (%)	
	1979	1984	1988	79-84	84-88	1979	1988
Rice	143.8	172.3	169.1	4.8	-1.3	43.3	42.9
Wheat	62.7	87.8	85.4	8.0	-0.8	18.9	21.7
Corn	60.0	73.4	77.4	4.4	1.0	18.1	19.6
Soybean	7.5	9.7	11.6	6.0	5.0	2.3	2.9
Tubers	28.5	28.5	27.0	0.0	-1.3	8.6	6.9
Others	29.6	29.6	23.6	0.0	-1.5	8.8	6.0
Total	332.1	407.3	394.1	4.6	-0.8	100.0	100.0

the Northeast. An average annual increase in yield of 5.7% was the sole source of production growth for the period 1979-1984. Yield has tended to plateau since 1984 and the reduced production in 1985-88 could be largely attributed to continued decrease in planted area.

9.   The planted area of **wheat** has been fairly stable at 28.8 million ha although it reached a high of 29.6 million ha in 1984. Reduction in planted area in the Northeast, Southwest and South has been offset by increases in the North, Northwest, and MLYR. Most of the production growth in the period 1979-1984 came from yield which increased at an average rate of 7.9% per year. Average yield levelled off at about 3.0 ton per ha since 1984. The record wheat harvest of 89.4 million tons in 1986 represents a combination of large planted area and good average yield.

10.   In the period 1979-1984 the area planted to **corn** decreased by 1.6 million ha due largely to reductions in the North and Northwest and an expansion of cotton area. Production increases are entirely due to yield which grew at an annual rate of 6.5%. Since 1984, production slumped in 1985 due to a significant reduction in planted area and yield, which appears to be partly due to excessive rainfall in the Northeast. It partly recovered in 1986 and a record corn harvest was achieved in 1987 due to a combination of large planted area and good average yield. Seasonal conditions mask yield trends for the period 1984-1988. There are indications that yield continues to increase but at a slower rate.

11.   The production of **soybean** has grown steadily in the period 1979-1988. Planted area grew at an average annual rate of 1.4% and yield showed an average annual growth rate of 4.3% and shows indications of further increase. Planted area shows marked fluctuations due primarily to variable planted area in the North and MLYR regions. This is probably due to the fact that the short

duration varieties grown in these areas fill short-term gaps in the standard crop rotations when they get out of phase due to late harvest, and need to be put back on schedule. No detailed information is available on **tubers and other grains**. Statistical data available for tubers indicates a decline in planted area of about 1 million ha in the study period and a yield increase of 0.4 ton per ha resulting in little change in total production.

12. A long-term performance summary for production, area and yield for individual grain crops is provided in World Bank (1990e), Tables 5-7. In general, between 1960-84, there was a steady increase in grain production, a decrease in grain area and an increase in grain yield, though a marked increase in all three performance indicators (negative in the case of area) occurred after the reforms began. The increase in grain yield was more than enough to compensate production losses owing to declining area. Since 1984, production and yields have fluctuated, though area continued to decline, albeit at a slower pace.

13. Trends in **cultivated area** and **effective irrigated area** are reviewed in World Bank (1990c), Appendix 1. Key parameters (all crops) are summarized below.

	Changes in Area (Million ha)		
	1980	**1983**	**1988**
Cultivated area	99.6	98.3	95.7
Sown area	145.2	144.2	144.1
Irrigated Area	44.5	44.6	44.4
Cropping Index (MCI)	146	147	151

Total cultivated area has declined and at an annual rate of about 0.5 million ha in the period 1983-1988. Total area planted to all field crops has been fairly stable at 144 million ha since 1983. Effective irrigated area has not changed significantly, but the MCI increased from 147 to 151, indicating more intensive cropping on the reduced cultivated area. These data indicate that reduction in cultivated area due to demand for land for housing and industrial development is the prime reason for the reduction in planted area of rice. Most of the reduction in rice area has occurred in the densely populated areas of the MLYR and South production regions.

14. The key technical inputs influencing **yield** are variety, fertilizer input, water control, pest and disease control and standards of crop management. Currently most of the wheat, rice, and corn is reported to be planted to improved varieties. About 80% of the corn area is reported to be planted to hybrids or high yielding lines and about 46% of the rice area is planted to high yielding hybrids. The technical basis for the dramatic increases in yield in the period 1979-1984 largely result from the development and dissemination of improved high yield varieties and a substantial increase in the use of nitrogen fertilizers during the period. Farmers also improved standards of crop management, once they were able to reap the full benefits of

their expertise and labor under the PRS. The slow down in yields post-1984 is difficult to explain with reference to strictly technical factors, since overall, China has developed a good technical base and pool of technology to increase and maintain yields and production. For most grains, on the other hand, yields are already high by international standards and additional increments on farmers fields may be difficult to achieve except at high cost.

15.   The increases in nutrient use in the period 1980-1988 are summarized in para 59. Unfortunately, there are no data available to indicate actual usage by crop. The MOA reports that about 66% of total nutrients used in China are applied to grain crops. Numbers from MOA's 1987 Farm Survey indicate that most of the fertilizer is applied to rice, wheat and corn. Only scanty information is available on the use of organic manure, an important source of phosphate and potash (paras 66-68). The reported run down in the effectiveness of irrigation, drainage and water control facilities could be expected to have a significant effect on planted area, response to fertilizer and yields. With investment in maintenance declining during the 1980s, it is reasonable to assume that the full effects would not be felt until the late eighties, the period in which there were large reductions in the planted area of rice, and the yields of rice and wheat levelled off. The main physical constraints are variable rainfall and the quite frequent occurrence of drought in the drier northwestern part of the country, the high intensity rainfall accompanying typhoons which lead to flooding and waterlogging in lower lying and poorly drained areas, and the cold temperature regimes in the north and high altitude areas that restrict the growing season and sometimes cause crop damage. Apart from reduced investment, irrigation infrastructure may have deteriorated due to lack of adequate revenue and, in some areas, insufficient expertise at county and township level to maintain systems in good order. However, a field survey is required in representative production areas to determine the relative importance of the above factors in constraining yield and production.

16.   Farm Level Economics of Grain Production. Future government policy on the farm gate price of product and inputs can be expected to play an even larger role in determining the structure and level of agricultural production than it has thus far. With the exception of grain production under "contract", small farmers in China generally are free to choose the crops they will grow. Choice will depend on many factors, but important determinants will be profitability, net profit in relation to cash input requirements (net revenue/cost ratio) and risk, and return per labor day.

17.   The **profitability** of main crops, such as wheat, rice, corn, soybean, cotton, rapeseed and peanut were compared in the Northern Production Region at 1984 prices (the bumper harvest year), at 1987 prices (latest farm survey data) and at 1989 border price equivalents when evaluated at the prevailing official exchange rate (World Bank [1990c], paras 5.02-5.04).

18.   The comparison among main grain crops at current average yields for the Northern Region are shown below. The outstanding feature of this data is the dramatic increase that occurs in net revenues and net revenue/cost ratios for wheat and rice when 1989 border prices are applied to the four main grain crops. MOA's 1987 farm survey for the Northern Region gave a range of ¥ 1.74-3.22 per day as the average wage rate, the higher rates occurring near

industrial centers. On this basis, the daily "cash" return to labor for crop
production generally is competitive with off-farm work in the Northern Region,
though hours may be longer and the returns in farming more variable. The high
return to labor for soybean reflects the low input approach adopted for
soybean production in the Northern Region. Although official farm gate
procurement prices have been increased in nominal terms by about 18% since
1987, the average farm gate price for wheat and rice still remains
significantly below international price parities (World Bank [1990g], Table
4). Thus farmers in actuality continue to face very tight net revenue/cost
ratios for wheat and rice at current low farmgate price levels, while corn and
soybean appear more attractive as current prices are closer to international
prices.

Crop	Net Revenue (¥/ha)		Net Rev/Cost Ratio		Return/Labor Day (¥)	
	financial prices /a	border prices /b	financial prices /a	border prices /b	financial prices /a	border prices /b
Wheat	973	2142	1.31	2.64	5.41	11.90
Rice	897	3489	0.84	3.01	2.99	11.63
Corn	912	906	1.73	1.71	4.56	4.53
Soybean	881	814	4.79	4.55	9.79	9.05

/a evaluated at 1987 mixed average farm gate procurement prices and actual prices paid
    for chemical fertilizers.
/b evaluated at 1989 border price parities for crops and fertilizers.

19.   Regional comparisons of the **cost of production** of wheat, corn, rice and
soybean shed some light on regional comparative advantages for production
planning purposes (World Bank [1990c], Appendix 8, Tables 8-11). The results
indicate that in general terms, rice and corn have the lowest unit production
costs. The Northern and MLYR have a regional advantage for wheat production.
Production costs of wheat are high and net revenue is low in the Northeast
raising doubts about the promotion of wheat in that region. Rice give a
satisfactory net revenue in all regions. The MLYR is the lowest cost producer
which is mainly due to lower irrigation costs. The North and Northeast, the
two major corn production regions, have a regional comparative advantage for
corn production. While some of the base data available for soybean is suspect,
it is reasonable to conclude that currently, the Northern region and the MLYR
are the lowest cost producers.

-Consumption and Utilization

20.   Grain Consumption and Utilization. The evolution of grain consumption
(Table 2.1 of the main report and World Bank [1990e], Table 4) shows a
pronounced shift since 1960 from direct consumption of table grains to feed
grains. Within the table grains category (where direct human consumption has
generally declined relative to indirect since 1960, and in absolute terms
since 1984), a marked consumer preference for wheat has evolved, at the
expense of all other grains except rice--whose relative share has remained
about constant. The shift in relative demand from table to feed grains has not
been matched in recent years by shifts in production and net import patterns.
Thus an imbalance exists between the supply and demand for various grains.

21.   During the 1980s, roughly ¼ of the grain consumed annually in China was distributed to urban consumers, the army, civil institutions and agroprocessing industries through China's grain bureau system and free markets of various sorts. The remaining 3/4 has been consumed in rural areas. Of the so-called "commercial grains", about half, or upwards of 50 million tons per year have been distributed well below cost to urban households and enterprise work forces through China's grain ration system. Ration prices have been kept constant at their early-1960s levels and, with the sharp increases in official grain procurement prices and volumes procured beginning in 1979, subsidies to urban consumers have increased dramatically.

22.   Within the grain sector, and in contrast to the wealth of official data for grain production, official estimates of grain utilization are incomplete and inconsistent. The evolution of China's estimated grain demand and its components from 1970 to 1988 are summarized in Table 2.1 of the main report. 2/ Direct consumption of food grains increased from 158.1 million tons in 1970 (unprocessed weight) to 271.9 million tons in 1988; accounting for 81% of total grain demand in 1970 (excluding stocks and miscellaneous forms of utilization) but only 70% in 1988. The major increase in grain use has been in the form of feed grain. Feed grain consumption between 1970-88 increased from 23.5 million tons to 104.3 million tons, and showed marked acceleration after the reforms were introduced. During this period, the implied relative share of feed grain in total grain demand increased from about 12% to 27%. The use of grain as seed is about 14 million tons.   In absolute terms, seed grain use remained stable over time whereas its relative share in total grain demand declined from 7% in 1970 to 4% in 1988.   The relative share of food, feed and seed grain in total grain consumption (excluding changes in stocks) has changed as follows:

	Relative Share:			
Year	Food Grain	Feed Grain	Seed Grain	Total
		---(%)---		
1970	81	12	7	100
1980	80	15	5	100
1984	77	19	4	100
1985	74	22	4	100
1988	70	27	4	100

Derived from Table 2.1 of the main report

23.   Consumption of Table Grains. In response to various factors such as shift in domestic production patterns, changes in total availability, changes in per capita income and income distribution patterns, an increase in free market grain prices, shifting food preferences and the government's grain rationing policies, the relative shares of different grains in total food

2/ For a longer term perspective from a different data base, see World Bank (1990e), Table 9.

grain consumption has been changing. The relative share of potatoes, coarse grains, other grains and soybeans in food grain consumption declined over time; the relative share of corn increased from 10% in 1960 to 20% in 1978 and then declined again to 10% in 1988. In the case of rice, however, the relative share declined from 36% in 1960 to 34% in 1978 and then increased to 38% in 1988. Finally, the relative share of wheat in food grain consumption increased from 16.5% in 1960 to 22% in 1978 and 38% in 1988. Clearly, during 1988, wheat became as important as rice for direct food consumption. The increase in wheat consumption over time, especially during the post-reform period has been spectacular. Total wheat consumption more than doubled during the post-reform period from 46 million tons in 1978 to 98 million tons in 1988.

24.   According to results reported in Annex 2 Table 1 (last column), **per capita consumption** of table grains increased between 1970 to 1984, and then declined.   Since 1984, the impact of negative price elasticities of demand for food grain appear to have reinforced the impact of China's negative income elasticity of demand. 3/

Annex 2 Table 1 Estimated Direct Per Capita Consumption of Grain
(kg unprocessed grain per year)

	National Average	Urban			Rural		Population Share (%)		Estimated Weighted Average National Consumption
Year	Trade Grain /a	Trade Grain /b	Fine/b Grain	Expressed In Unprocessed Equivalent	Total	Fine /c Grain	Urban	Rural	
1970	187					na			193
1975	191					na			197
1980	214				257	163			243
1981	219	145		217	256	178	17	83	249
1982	225	145		°216	260	192	17	83	252
1983	232	144	135	216	260	197	18	82	252
1984	251	142	135	212	267	209	19	81	257
1985	254	135	129	201	257	209	20	80	246
1986	256	138	130	206	259	212	20	80	248
1987	251	134	127	200	259	211	20	80	247
1988	249	137		205	260	211	20	80	249
1989	242	134		201	262	213	21	79	249

Source: World Bank (1990a), Table 2 and SSB (1990)

/a Rice expressed in unprocessed form.
/b Rice expressed in milled form.
/c Primarily rice and wheat.

25.   Implications of changes in total consumption patterns are highlighted by some interesting shifts in direct per capita consumption which occurred during the 1980s. The estimates of direct consumption of **table grain** have been calculated from SSB's figures for urban and rural average per capita

---

3/ Additionally, some grain is allocated administratively for institutional consumption. Consumption in this segment of the "market" is unlikely to be very responsive to changes in per capita incomes and prices.

consumption of grain and midyear population. A weighted average of SSB's urban and rural estimates indicate that average national per capita consumption of table grain increased (by 26%) from 193 kg in 1970 to 257 kg in 1984 and then declined (by 3%) to 249 kg in 1989. However, **urban** direct consumption of table grain (expressed in trade grain equivalent) declined by 8% from 145 kg per capita in 1981 to 134 kg/cap in 1989. The SSB urban household survey data also indicate (not shown in Annex 2 Table 1) that direct grain consumption was 167 kg per capita in 1957, or 125% of the 1989 figure. Direct consumption of fine grain (*viz.*, rice and wheat) remained roughly constant at 95% of total direct urban grain consumption during 1983-87.

26. The **rural** data indicate that direct per capita consumption of table grain (expressed in unprocessed equivalent) remained roughly constant at about 260 kg during 1980-88. The share of fine grains in rural per capita direct consumption increased from 63% in 1981 to 81% in 1989. Available data indicate that urban direct per capita consumption of wheat declined by 3 kg (-9%) from 35 kg in 1984 to 32 kg in 1987, while urban direct per capita consumption of rice declined over the same period by only 1 kg (-2%) from 66 kg to 65 kg. (Urban consumption of fine grain by province in 1984 and 1987 is reported in World Bank [1990a], Appendix 1, Table 1.) In conjunction with trends in total wheat consumption noted above, stagnant per capita consumption of both wheat and rice in urban areas during the 1980s suggests that most of the incremental supply of wheat has been consumed by the rural population. If true, the latter hypothesis suggests that wheat has played a key role in the increase in rural consumption of fine grain during the 1980s.

27. <u>Utilization as Animal Feed</u>. Production of all animal products and of pork, beef and mutton increased by 370% and 290% respectively between 1970-89. The number of draft animals increased by 50% during 1970-89. Backstopping the rapid increase in feed grain consumption that was associated with increased production of animal products has been a shift in the composition of feed grains. In China, rice is fed to livestock in large quantities. During 1988, 18 million tons of rice was used as livestock feed, accounting for 19% of total feed grain consumption. **4/** There may be other reasons, such as lack of available corn at reasonable prices as an input to pig production, but the low ration price of rice (rice has been generally cheaper than animal feed) is responsible for much of this misuse. About 3% of wheat was also used as feed grain during 1988. The relative share of corn in feed grain has increased from 33% in 1960 to 47% in 1988. Soybeans and other grains are also used as feed grain but in relatively small quantities. The relative share of coarse grains (minus corn) in feed grain has dropped from over 20% in 1960s to less than 10% in 1980s. Potatoes are also fed to animals in large quantities. However, corn has been and continues to be the most important feed grain.

28. Estimates of animal feed requirements have been calculated as (a) the product of assumed feed conversion ratios (FCR) and official production data for animal products, plus (b) maintenance feed requirements for draft animals (Appendix 1 of World Bank [1990a]). The production and animal number data,

---

4/ cf. World Bank (1990e), Table 11. This is appalling especially when China believes it faces a serious grain problem.

FCRs and maintenance requirements used in the calculations are shown in Annex 2 Table 2. These calculations indicate that total animal feed requirements increased by 270% from 39 million tons in 1970 to 144 million tons in 1989. Utilization of bran and meal as animal feed is estimated to have increased by only 100% over this same period and, consequently, the volume of grain utilized as animal feed is estimated to have increased by the greater margin of 350% -- from 23 million tons in 1970 to 112 million tons in 1989.

Annex 2 Table 2 Estimated Utilization of Grain as Animal Feed

(million tons unprocessed grain)

	Unit	1970	1975	1980	1981	1982	1983	1984	1985	1986	1987	1988	1989	Feed Conversion Ratio
Animal Products:														
Pork	mil.t	5.4	7.2	11.3	11.9	12.7	13.2	14.4	16.5	18.0	18.3	20.2	21.2	4.35
Beef	mil.t	0.3	0.4	0.3	0.2	0.3	0.3	0.4	0.5	0.6	0.8	1.0	1.1	9.03
Mutton	mil.t	0.3	0.4	0.4	0.5	0.5	0.5	0.6	0.6	0.6	0.7	0.8	1.0	1.20
Poultry	mil.t	0.5	0.7	1.1	1.1	1.2	1.3	1.4	1.6	1.9	2.0	2.2	2.8	2.60
Eggs	mil.t	1.2	1.6	2.5	2.6	2.8	3.3	4.3	5.3	5.6	5.9	7.0	7.2	2.34
Milk	mil.t	0.6	0.9	1.4	1.5	2.0	2.2	2.6	2.9	3.3	3.8	4.2	4.4	0.39
Fish	mil.t	0.6	0.8	0.9	1.0	1.2	1.4	1.8	2.4	2.9	3.5	3.9	4.2	0.87
Draft Animals	m head	49.4	51.2	50.9	54.7	58.3	61.3	64.0	66.5	69.1	71.1	72.2	74.3	150 kg
Feed Requirements:														
total	mil.t	38.7	49.4	69.9	73.3	78.6	83.1	92.8	106.8	116.3	122.1	135.2	144.0	
of which:														
grain	mil.t	23.1	31.6	46.2	48.1	52.2	55.8	64.1	78.3	87.1	92.1	104.3	112.0	
bran	mil.t	14.2	16.2	21.5	22.3	22.9	23.2	23.9	23.1	23.7	23.9	24.5	25.0	
meal	mil.t	1.3	1.6	2.3	2.9	3.6	4.1	4.9	5.4	5.5	6.1	6.5	7.0	

Source: World Bank (1990a), Table 3.

29.   **Other Forms of Utilization and Disappearance.** During 1970, approximately 14 million tons of grain was used as seed and this amount has remained more or less stable over time. Such stability in the face of measurably enlarged production is another reflection of the widespread diffusion of genetically improved seed that has occurred in China, and increased use of modern farm inputs, which results in higher grain yield and grain production for a given amount of seed. Estimates of storage losses and waste of grain range from as little as 0.5% ("China Leads in Storage of Grains," in China Daily 8/5/88) to more than 11% (CAAS estimate) of total production. Accurate figures are not available, but it is likely that storage losses and waste amount to more than 10% of production or at least 40 million tons. Use of grain in food and non-food manufacturing is reported to have amounted to only 4 million tons in 1980 (Year 2000 Research Group, 1984), but increased to more than 15 million tons by 1988. About 14 million tons of grain were reportedly used in the production of alcoholic beverages alone in 1988 ("Alcoholic Beverage, Tobacco Production Soars Out of Control," in China Daily 5/29/89).

30.   **Ending Grain Stocks.** The evolution of grain stocks is reviewed in World Bank (1990e) and (1990f), Appendix 2. The level of end-year stocks has fluctuated from one year to another but, overall, there has been a general increase from 10 million tons in 1960 (in the wake of China's disruptive "Great Leap Forward") to 111 million tons in 1984, a record grain harvest year. However, it is worth reiterating that the level of grain stocks in China is extremely high, equivalent to about 70% of all grains marketed in

1988. **5/** These levels do provide food security for bad production years but primarily to urban consumers at very high economic and financial costs.

-The Structure of Domestic Grain Prices

31.   Procurement. Presently, China's marketed grain surplus, roughly 100 million tons or 25% of annual production, is sold through a three-tiered structure of grain procurement prices: the mandatory (or "planned") prices and the negotiated prices offered by GGB, and free market prices for a much smaller share of sales. Mandatory procurement, at quota and above-quota prices prior to 1985, and at contract prices thereafter, declined from more than 90% of total procurement in 1978 to just under 50% in 1987 (World Bank [1990b], Appendix 1, Table 1). Procurement of grain at the above-quota price is estimated to have increased from about 20% of total mandatory procurement in 1978 to perhaps 70%. With the increase in quota and above-quota prices in 1979, this increase in above-quota procurement's share of total mandatory procurement during 1984 pushed the average mandatory procurement price for grain to more than 150% of its level in 1978.   The switch to contract prices reduced the inequities of the previous system (the accrual of above-quota premiums differed widely by locality), but also reduced the average return to farmers from mandatory procurement. The contract price was increased in each year 1986-1989, and now surpasses the old above-quota price.   While the temporary reduction in the marginal mandatory procurement price may have contributed to the decline in grain production in 1985, it may be argued that, with the more than four-fold surge in negotiated procurement from less than 10 million tons in 1984 to more than 40 million tons in 1987, **negotiated prices supplanted planned prices as the operative marginal price to producers** in the second half of the 1980s.   Negotiated and free market purchases together amounted to 50 million tons in 1987 (see World Bank [1990g], Table 1), or nearly 50% of total procurement in that year. Since mandatory procurement at the contract price will be held to no more than 50 million tons through 1992, furthermore, it also appears that negotiated and free market sales are becoming the dominant source of grain revenues to China's producers.

32.   Distribution. On the sales side in China's grain markets, grain (in its whole, milled, and processed forms) and vegetable oil also are sold at administered ("planned"), negotiated, and free market prices to urban and rural consumers, industry, and other end users. Sales at planned prices increased from 55 million tons in 1979 to 65 million tons in 1987 (World Bank [1990g], Appendix 1), but declined as a share of total commercial trade from over 90% in 1980 to about 65% in 1987. **6/** The ration sales volume is known to have amounted to at least 36.9 million tons in 1987, accounting for at least 57% of total planned price sales in that year.   This volume of grain was distributed by the GGB's network of urban grain ration shops to China's nonagricultural population, which is mostly comprised of registered urban households.   The GGB provided another 10.6 million tons of grain at planned

---

5/   Normal grain stocking rates in a well-run food security system range between 2-4 months of annual sales.

6/   Planned price sales include sales at highly subsidized ration prices and sales at the mandatory procurement price plus a small margin to cover handling.

prices to urban consumers, urban industry, and other urban end users in 1987, and most or all of that grain may have been supplied at the ration price. Another 17.7 million tons of grain were supplied by state agencies at planned prices to the rural population in 1987. Most of this grain was sold at the contract price plus a small marketing margin to farm households specializing in the production of vegetables, industrial and other nongrain crops, and animal husbandry. A lesser portion was distributed at little or no charge to rural households suffering extreme poverty or having lost much of their harvest to natural disasters.

33. Negotiated and free market sales together increased from 12 million tons in 1981 to 34 million tons in 1987, more than doubling as a share of total commercial trade in grain from 16 to 34%. The role of negotiated and free market retail sales may extend beyond their share of commercial trade, furthermore, since available evidence suggests that the near complete monetization of the subsidy value of ration coupons has made the **urban free market price the effective marginal price** to the urban consumer.

34. <u>Input Prices</u>. Farmers purchase fertilizer, pesticides, diesel fuel, seeds and other current inputs at planned prices from the SMCs, at negotiated prices from the SMCs and local private and collective enterprises, and on the free market. Sales of farm inputs at planned prices is the most important form of distribution, and has been linked to delivery of farm products to the state since the early-1960s through a variety of crop specific sales encouragement programs. During the mid-1980s, the sale of farm inputs at negotiated prices made significant inroads in the share of total trade--in Xinxiang (Henan) Municipality, for instance, distribution of fertilizer at planned prices declined from more than 45% of total fertilizer sales in 1981 to 15% in 1986. **7/** Negotiated sales were sharply curtailed in 1989, however, when the government recentralized input supplies. Aside from widespread leakage in official channels, authorized free market sales of farm inputs more than doubled during the 1980s, from ¥ 0.7 billion in 1980 to ¥ 1.8 billion in 1988, but still account for less than 2% of total sales of farm inputs.

-<u>Domestic Price Trends</u>

35. <u>Price Estimates</u>. Quota, contract and negotiated procurement, rural and urban free market sales, and urban ration price data for standard grades of (indica paddy) rice, wheat, corn, soybeans and rapeseed oil are summarized in Annex 2 Table 3 for selected years 1978-89. Based on the quota prices shown in this table, the average **mandatory procurement prices** of rice, wheat, corn, soybeans and rapeseed oil in 1978 were 208, 288, 187, 425 and 1760 ¥/ton respectively. On this basis, the 1988 average mandatory procurement prices (i.e. 1988 contract prices) of rice, wheat, corn, soybeans and rapeseed oil ranged from 50-80 percentage points above the nominal 1978 average mandatory procurement prices. Increases to contract prices in 1989 added another 37% to the mandatory procurement price of rice, and 7% and 6% respectively to wheat and corn. Though substantial, these increases are significantly less than the 110% increases in the mixed average procurement prices of grain and vegetable

---

7/ See World Bank (1988b), Annex 1, Tables 26 and 27.

oil reported in World Bank (1990g), Table 3 for the period 1978-88. The sharp increase in procurement at (substantially greater) negotiated prices during 1984-87 (para 31) presumably accounts for most of the difference.

Annex 2 Table 3 Structure and Pattern of Domestic Grain Prices for Standard Grades

(Yuan/ton)

| | Mandatory Procurement | | | Free Market | | | | Urban Ration |
| | | | | Rural (Producer) | | Urban (Consumer) | | |
Year	Quota	Contract	Negotiated	Surplus	Deficit	Surplus	Deficit	
Indica Paddy Rice								
1978	196			574				196
1980	231		525	546				196
1985		312	462	322	462	378	448	196
1987		312	651	518	658	560		196
1988		312		602	980	770	896	196
1989		427						196
Whole Wheat								
1978	272			680				276
1980	314		620	580				276
1985		424	440	420	480			276
1987		424	590		700			276
1988		454		660	920			273
1989		486						273
Maize								
1978	176			500				194
1980	214		310	400				194
1985		289	320	280	380	400	400	194
1987		336	520	400		500		194
1988		336		400	675	540	900	194
1989		356						194
Soybeans								
1978	401							
1980	461		760					
1985		600	670	620	720	720	900	
1987			910	940	940	1000	1180	
1988					1160	1080	1500	
Rapeseed Oil								
1978	1660							1600
1980	2120							1600
1985		2760						1600
1987		2760						1600
1988		2968						1540
1989		2968						1540

Source: World Bank (1990b), Table 2.

36. Available data indicate that **negotiated procurement prices** for grain have actively responded to market conditions during the 1980s. Negotiated procurement prices declined by 20-30% in the early-1980s in response to the record grain harvest of 1984, and then increased by a greater margin of between 35% to 110% by 1987 in response to stagnating production. Negotiated procurement prices for grain have generally exceeded average mandatory procurement prices, and in 1987 were 110, 40, 55 and 50 percentage points greater than the respective contract prices for rice, wheat, corn and soybeans. (Similarly, the negotiated sales price of fertilizer in 1988 was as much as 90% greater than the planned distribution price. See World Bank [1990d], p. 41.) The negotiated procurement prices reported in Annex 2 Table 3 also closely track rural (producer) free market prices.

37. The government does not release detailed information on **free market prices** but indices of nominal free market retail grain prices have been reconstructed for 1978-88 from official data in Annex 2 Table 4. The national average price index indicates that, with the surge in production beginning in the late 1970s, free market prices declined by about 25% during 1978-84. With the subsequent stagnation of production and mounting general inflation in recent years, free market prices then surged by more than 75% during 1984-88.

Overall, the official data indicate that the free market retail price of grain increased by just over 30% during 1978-88. As shown on the right hand side of Annex 2 Table 4, there appears to have been little difference between price trends in urban and rural free markets, though as expected, urban free market prices are moderately (about 25% to 35%) greater than rural free market prices (see World Bank [1990g], Appendix 2). The absolute price data also document substantial differences between free market prices in grain surplus and deficit areas, and suggest that the differences in rural markets increased during the second half of the 1980s.

Annex 2 Table 4 Index of Free Market Retail Price of Grain, 1978-88

(1978=100)

Year	National Average	Urban	Rural
1978	100.0	100.0	100.0
1981	85.1	87.7	84.4
1982	85.4	88.8	84.4
1983	83.3	86.8	81.6
1984	74.5	76.8	73.9
1985	75.9	78.2	75.1
1986	91.5	91.7	92.2
1987	106.4	107.3	107.1
1988	132.2	138.5	131.3
1988/84	177.3	180.4	177.8

Source: World Bank (1990g), Table 5.

38.   In contrast to the sharp fluctuations and general increase in mandatory procurement, negotiated procurement, and free market prices since 1978, **urban ration prices** have been kept fixed and, hence, declined sharply in real terms. The margin between official urban sales and farm procurement prices gradually eroded during the 1960s and 1970s, then turned sharply negative after the reforms were introduced. Further adjustments in procurement prices during the 1980s, to offset rising input costs and--more recently--price erosion induced by inflation, coupled with a refusal to announce off-setting price hikes for urban ration sales has caused the discrepancy in nominal price levels to widen. Overall, available price data document substantial and, since 1985, markedly increasing distortions in average producer and consumer prices. The price data reported in World Bank (1990g), Table 6 indicate that the average mandatory procurement price of rice increased from 36% of the rural free market price in 1978 to 68% in 1985, but then declined to only 32% of the market price in 1988. Similarly, the ratios between the average mandatory procurement and rural free market price of wheat and corn more than doubled during 1978-85, but then declined sharply in subsequent years. The distortion in consumer prices is even more extreme. The ratio between the urban free market and urban ration prices of rice and corn doubled from 2.3 and 2.1

respectively in 1985 to about 4.6 each in 1988. These trends in price relatives were broadly confirmed by a cross-section developed from MOA's 1987 farm survey (World Bank [1990g], Table 7).

-Comparison With World Market Prices

39.   During the 1980s, China's agricultural foreign trade system continued to be highly administered, showing large real distortions between domestic and border prices for the more important traded commodities. As shown in World Bank (1990g), Table 19 the rural free market prices for milled rice, wheat, maize and soybean in 1987 were roughly equivalent to the import and export unit values which China realized from foreign trade in these commodities, with the exception of corn exports (which were over-valued domestically) at the prevailing **official exchange rate**. However, procurement for export at administered quota and contract prices and sales of imports at ration sales prices, being considerably lower than free market prices, accounted for the bulk of the commodities traded. Thus the effective price relatives were considerably more distorted than a comparison of free market and border prices would indicate. In 1988, corn prices were brought back into line with border prices, but the prices of wheat imports and rice exports remained considerably distorted. The official exchange rate was overvalued in 1988, **8/** thus a different picture in 1988 is shown when domestic and border prices are compared at a **shadow exchange rate**. At the official exchange rate, rural surplus free market prices of rice, corn and soybeans about equalled or moderately exceeded border prices in 1987 and 1988. The rural free market price of wheat in 1988, on the other hand, surpassed the unit import price of wheat by 50%. At a shadow exchange rate of ¥ 6.5/US$, the 1988 rural free market prices were only between 51% (rice) to 85% (wheat) of the corresponding border prices. **9/** This comparison implies that substantial economic rents are accruing to the state in the exporting of rice and corn. Similarly, large economic subsidies are being absorbed in the importation and marketing of imported wheat and corn.

40.   This picture is corroborated by international comparison. The Trade Analysis Division of USDA's Economic Research Service has computed producer subsidy equivalents (PSEs) and consumer subsidy equivalents (CSEs) for 22 agricultural commodities in 13 regions and countries including China. Determined by sign, PSEs and CSEs are estimates of the degree of subsidization or taxation (direct and indirect) placed on a commodity as a result of government incentives, the country's foreign trade framework, domestic marketing and incomes policies, tax policies and the regulatory framework. Estimates for China between 1982-1987 are reported in Webb (1989) and, on the basis of observed differences between domestic and border price equivalents, are compared with other countries for the trade year 1986/87 in Dixit and Webb

---

8/   Subsequently, the combined effects of a nominal devaluation in December 1989, and curtailment of inflationary pressures have helped to realign the value of the Chinese currency unit with international parities.

9/   It has been pointed out that use of a shadow exchange rate of ¥ 6.5 likely exaggerates the extent of overvaluation in 1988, since this rate doesn't reflect the influence of non-tradeables and is influenced by demand from marginal buyers.

(1989). As shown below, the pattern of PSEs and CSEs in China is very different than that in most industrial market economies (IMEs) and the USSR. While producers in industrial economies tended to be supported (positive PSEs), producers in China are severely taxed. Conversely, while consumers in the industrial market economies bear high taxes (negative CSEs), though not in the Soviet Union, consumers in China enjoy substantial subsidization. The Chinese pattern is similar to many low income developing countries that subsidize consumers and tax producers, though the magnitudes of taxation and subsidies appear to be much higher in China.

The Direction of Agricultural Support and Taxation in Selected Economies

	USA	EEC	Japan	USSR	Other Developing Importers	China
CSEs	–	–	– –	++	+	++
PSEs	++	++	++	++	–	– –

Legend: (i)   + < 20%,
        (ii) ++ ≥ 20%,
       (iii) – < 20%,
        (iv) – – ≥ 20%

Source: World Bank (1990g), Table 8

-China's Position in the International Grain Trade

41.   These trends in the internal structure of the Chinese economy and the changing composition of foreign trade also were reflected in the evolution of China's position in the international grain economy. Aided by decollectivization, pricing and inputs policies and by rising consumer incomes since 1978, China's domestic grain production by 1988 had increased by nearly one third. As discussed in Section B above, there also occurred a profound shift in the utilization of grains from consumption as table food to its use as livestock feed, mirroring growth in live animal and meat exports and a rapid expansion since 1978 in the availability and consumption of animal products by the Chinese population. During the 1980s, China joined the USA, EEC and USSR as a dominant force in the international grain economy, whose importance to the production and utilization of various grains is shown in World Bank (1990g), Table 14. China is now the world's largest producer of grains, accounting for nearly 20% of the world's output in recent years. With 22% of the world's population, China is also the largest consumer of agricultural products. By the end of the 1980s, China had become responsible for more than one-third of the world's rice production and utilization, about

20% of its wheat, about 15% of its corn, and as a producer--more than 10% of the world's soybeans and one-third of the world's total feed grains.

42. Though the rapid growth in China's grain production is of immense international significance, China's net imports of grains have none-the-less increased substantially since inception of the reforms, no doubt reflecting agriculture's declining importance to the Chinese economy at large, and--within agriculture--even faster growth in the production of non-grains. During the 1980s, China's position as a major net exporter of rice steadily eroded until, in 1989, China became a net importer (World Bank [1990g], Table 15). With the exception of a puzzling spike in 1984 (a peak production year), China's net wheat imports rose steadily, and in 1988, China surpassed the Soviet Union as the world's largest net importer of wheat. On the other hand, China increased its exports from the rapidly growing production of corn and soybeans during the 1980s. These figures mask an anomaly that is occurring, however, caused by lack of transportation capacity between the main production centers in the Northeast and the main feeds consumption centers which are located inland and to the south. Coupled with China's irrational producer price policies for the main grains, the constrained availability of locally produced feeds has seen the considerable diversion of fine grains during the 1980s to the feeding of pigs and poultry, which is an inefficient feeding regime at best, but has no doubt contributed substantially over the decade to the build up of net imports of rice and (to a lesser extent) wheat.

43. Net Imports. The trends of the 1980s derive from and show forcefully in China's changing position in world trade figures for grains (World Bank [1990g], Tables 16-17). Since 1975, China's share of world total rice exports declined from over one fifth to only 2.6% in 1989. In parallel its share of world imports rose from 1.0 to nearly 10%. China's wheat exports have been negligible, though its total imports increased from only 5.4% of world exports in 1975 to over 15% by the end of last year. Performance in the foreign trade of other grains has been mixed. China captured more than 10% of the corn export market in the mid-1980s which has since tapered off to about 5%, while accounting for only a minimal share of world corn imports. A small but growing share of world soybean exports (5.6% in 1988), negligible soybean imports, and minimal but growing barley imports completes the picture. As a result, China has moved from being a price setter in the international rice markets (which are thin in any event--cf. World Bank [1990g], Appendix 4, Table 1) to a passive influence, but through its import programs in wheat and its large but fluctuating export volumes in corn, has begun to exert fairly significant pressure on the levels and trends in international pricing of these commodities.

44. Self-sufficiency. The longer run decline in China's earnings from agricultural exports has not altered the fact that the country remains essentially self-sufficient in staple foods, but it has meant that the self-sufficiency ratios have shown a moderate decline since the 1970s (World Bank [1990g], Table 18). Grain self-sufficiency fell from 102% in 1970-74 to 94% in 1985-1986 and has since remained at about that level. Part of the decline has been because of the rapid increase in effective demand for wheat and livestock products. While these comparatively small declines in agricultural self-sufficiency might seem minor, the direction of change is towards more import

dependence, a trend exacerbated by rising incomes, China's growing population, and limited land endowment. Because China's shares in world production and consumption have become so large, changes in China's self-sufficiency ratios have had profound effects on international markets, which could become even more profound during the 1990s, a point taken up in World Bank (1990g).

II. PERFORMANCE IN THE FERTILIZER SECTOR

-Production and Supply

45.   Fertilizer Production. Though China is a major fertilizer importer, its fertilizer industry development strategy is based on the principle of self-reliance. [10/] This is due to China's desires to reduce its dependence on others in order to meet domestic fertilizer needs to become self-sufficient in food production, minimize foreign exchange needs to import fertilizer, and minimize exposure to relatively unstable international fertilizer markets. However, despite serious efforts to increase domestic production, fertilizer consumption has generally been greater than domestic production (World Bank [1990d], Table 2 and Figure 2). The deficit was met through imports.

46.   Fertilizer production is dominated by indigenous technology and broadly dispersed small scale fertilizer plants which generally produce low quality, low grade nitrogen and phosphate fertilizers. Until the mid-1970s, almost all of the domestic fertilizer was produced in the locally designed and fabricated plants. In the early 1970s, when energy prices skyrocketed, China decided to import 13 large ammonia/urea fertilizer plants which came on-stream in the late 1970s. Since then China has imported several new plants to produce nitrogen, phosphate and compound fertilizers. Despite a major push to establish large-scale fertilizer plants, the small-scale fertilizer sector still accounts for about 55% of nitrogen and 80% of phosphate fertilizer production.

47.   All of China's fertilizer production is in the public sector. However, ownership, financing and management is highly fragmented among the central, provincial and county governments which, as a general rule, respectively control the large, medium and small scale fertilizer plants. The national fertilizer production and investment strategy is prepared by the Ministry of Chemical Industry (MCI), in consultation with other government agencies. Provincial and county governments are expected to adhere to national strategy, plans and guidelines. A small number of small-scale plants, organized as Township and Village Enterprises (TVEs), are coordinated by the MOA. These plants have been blamed for substandard fertilizer quality and are now required to obtain licenses for operation from MCI.

[10/] From an international perspective, China in 1987/88, accounted for 11% of the world's fertilizer production (third after USSR and USA), 12% of fertilizer imports (second after USA), and 16% of fertilizer consumption (second after USSR). Because of the volume of China's imports, but also because of her established reputation as a reliable business partner, China plays an important role in influencing the international fertilizer market in terms of supply, demand and prices. Most other developing countries (including India and Indonesia) pay higher prices for their fertilizer import requirements.

48.   The development of fertilizer production in China from 1949 to 1988 is shown in World Bank (1990d), Table 3. During 1988, total fertilizer production in China was about 17.4 million nutrient tons, of which 78.5% was N, 21.2% P_2O_5 and 0.3% K_2O.   The fertilizer industry is dominated by nitrogen fertilizer. With the exception of 1987 and 1988, incremental fertilizer production has not been as impressive since the reforms were introduced (World Bank [1990d], Table 4). Part of the decline in incremental production was due to the euphoria of record grain production in 1984, excess supply of low grade fertilizers in 1985 and fall in investment in the fertilizer industry. At present, priority is being given to expanding the production of P_2O_5 and NPK compound fertilizers in order to improve the balance of available nutrients.

49.   Nitrogen fertilizer needs in China are met by several different fertilizers produced domestically. However, the relative importance of these fertilizers in total production has changed over time (World Bank [1990d], Table 5).   From 1970 to 1988, the relative production share of ammonium bicarbonate (AmBC) increased from 40% to 60%; ammonium nitrate declined from 25% to 4%; aqua-ammonia declined from 22% to 1%; and urea increased from 4% to 32%. Nitrogen fertilizers other than AmBC and urea are highly specialized for certain crops and soils.

50.   The composition of domestically produced phosphate fertilizers consists mainly of single superphosphate (SSP) and fused calcium magnesium phosphate (CMPh).   The relative share of SSP increased from 63% in 1970 to 69% in 1988; whereas, the relative share of CMPh declined from 37% to 27% during the same period.   The relative share of other phosphate fertilizers is still very small but increased from 0.1% in 1970 to 5.0% in 1988.   These others consist of high grade triple superphosphate, nitrophosphate and diammonium phosphate.

51.   <u>Provincial Production and Supply Gaps</u>.   The principle of self-reliance has also been applied at the provincial and county levels. The main economic advantages of such a strategy were to reduce dependence on an over-burdened railway system for long distance fertilizer transport and also to reduce fertilizer distribution costs. On the other hand, lacking economies of scale, many small fertilizer plants were established irrespective of their inherent inefficiency. Since grain and other crop procurements are tied to fertilizer supply, many counties preferred to have their own plants in order to use fertilizer as leverage for compliance by farmers with official programs.

52.   The seven major fertilizer producing provinces are Hebei, Henan, Shandong, Jiangsu, Hubei, Hunan and Sichuan.   During 1988, these seven accounted for 54% of nitrogen production, 56% of phosphate production, and 54% of total fertilizer production.   However, with the exception of Tibet, all of China's provinces have some production facilities (World Bank [1990d], Table 6).

53.   Estimated supply gaps are reported in World Bank (1990d), Tables 7-9 for nitrogen, phosphates and aggregate fertilizer. The degree of dependence at the provincial level on other provinces for purchase or sale are reported in World Bank (1990d), Appendix Tables 6-8. The results indicate that even some of the major fertilizer producing provinces are net importers.   Supply gaps have also

changed over time due to several factors, including growth in fertilizer consumption and production. However, actual gaps may be larger (for deficit provinces) or smaller (for surplus provinces), owing to carry-over stocks, losses, substandard production and diversion of fertilizer to industrial/ nonagricultural uses. Supply gaps in the deficit provinces are met through allocations of centrally managed fertilizers, imports from surplus provinces and international trade.

54.   Small Scale Fertilizer Sector.   Small scale fertilizer production remains a vital component of the fertilizer industry in China. An innovation by the Nanjing Chemical Fertilizer Company in 1962 set the stage for rapid development of small scale AmBC plants. These spread rapidly, but with the introduction of large imported plants, the Chinese government has discouraged additional investment in small scale plants until only recently. At present, small scale fertilizer plants account for about 55% of nitrogen production (World Bank [1990d], Table 10) and 80% of phosphate production. The maximum number of small scale fertilizer plants was 2,333 during 1979. 11/

55.   As a result of recent improvements, MCI believes that the quality of AmBC, SSP and CMPh has been improved. The high moisture content and easy volatilization of AmBC has been reduced, and measures to improve the quality of phosphate fertilizers have been implemented since 1987. Still, the MCI reports that product quality does not always meet design standards. As a result, farmers prefer high-grade fertilizers when given a choice, and when pricing is not distorted. Clearly, there are trade-offs between the advantages and disadvantages of small fertilizer plants.

56.   Until 1986, government discouraged the further development of small plants and even encouraged the closure of many inefficient plants. The present number of small plants is less than 2000. Since the gap between fertilizer demand and domestic supply has widened, government now is promoting rehabilitation to improve their efficiency or their conversion to produce high-grade fertilizers such as urea and diammonium phosphate (DAP). By December 1988, about 400 small plants had closed after running at a loss due to low ex-factory prices fixed by the government, high prices for most raw materials, and lack of timely availability of raw materials. In early 1989, however, central government intervened to provide priority allocation of raw materials to small plants at plan prices. For better or for worse, many have now reopened.

-Use of Fertilizers

57.   Evolution and Performance. The evolution of fertilizer consumption (in terms of nutrients) in China is reported in World Bank (1990d), Table 16. Fertilizer consumption increased from a mere 78,000 tons in 1952 to 21.4 million tons in 1988, implying a 275-fold increase over a period of 36 years.

11/ Nitrogen plants generally produce AmBC, a poor quality and low grade fertilizer that will literally evaporate if not handled properly. As a result, AmBC suffers from large storage and distribution losses. The P_2O_5 content in production by small scale phosphate plants is highly variable and sometimes very low (range 10-20%). This variability is due to the variability in the P_2O_5 content of phosphate rock used as raw material.

By developing-country standards, this performance has been quite remarkable and has resulted in relatively high levels of fertilizer use. 12/ Incremental fertilizer consumption for different time-periods is reported in World Bank (1990d), Table 17. The average annual increment in fertilizer use during 1978-84 was 1.42 million tons, which then fell back to about 1 million tons between 1984-88.

58.   This spectacular increase was made possible by at least two key factors: (a) the introduction of the PRS and other agricultural reforms, which led to an increase in fertilizer demand; and (b) an increase in fertilizer supply through imports and domestic fertilizer production after the 13 imported large ammonia/urea plants came into production in late 1970s. However, the decline in incremental consumption during 1984-88 followed a drop in fertilizer supply due to imposition of an import moratorium in 1985 and 1986 and the closing of several small-scale fertilizer plants. At present, policies to again accelerate fertilizer consumption and improve its use efficiency, especially in grain production, are being given high priority.

59.   As with production, fertilizer **nutrient use** in China has been dominated by nitrogen (World Bank [1990d], Tables 18 and 19):

Year	Total Nutrient Consumption					Average Nutrient Consumption				
	N	P_2O_5	K_2O	Compound	Total	N	P_2O_5	K_2O	Compound	Total
	'000 tons					kg/ha of sown area				
1980	9,342	3,733	346	272	12,694	64.4	18.8	2.4	1.9	87.4
1984	12,153	3,286	694	1,265	17,398	84.6	22.9	4.8	8.8	121.1
1988	14,171	3,821	1,012	2,412	21,416	98.3	26.5	7.0	16.7	148.6

Although nitrogen deficiency remains widespread, the production and availability of nitrogen have been growing very rapidly. However, the relative share of nitrogen in total consumption has been declining in response to government programs to achieve an improved balance of applied nutrients:

Year	Share in Nutrient Consumption:			
	N	P_2O_5	K_2O	Total
	(%)			
1980	80.3	18.7	1.0	100
1984	74.9	20.6	4.5	100
1988	69.3	24.3	6.3	100

12/ The level and growth in nutrient use in China from 1971 to 1987 is compared with other Asian countries in World Bank (1990d), Table 22. Fertilizer use in Japan and Republic of Korea is very high but China is catching up fast. For example, as compared to Japan, the level of nutrient use in China was only 13% in 1971 but has increased to 55% in 1987. Even by Chinese standards, fertilizer use in other Asian countries is rather low. As an example, nutrient use in India was only 32% of nutrient use in China during 1971, which had declined to 23% by 1987.

60.   The most important **fertilizer products** consumed in China are AmBC, urea, SSP and potassium chloride (KCL). Over 80% of nitrogen consumption is from AmBC (still dominant) and urea. SSP alone accounts for over 50% of all P_2O_5 consumption.   About 70% of all K_2O is supplied by KCL. The supply of large quantities of low analysis fertilizers, including AmBC (16% N) and SSP (12-18% P_2O_5), puts a tremendous strain on the fertilizer distribution system. However, there is a trade-off between relatively high production cost (and high nutrient-unit transportation cost) but low total distribution costs, since the small plants which produce these fertilizers are dispersed throughout China and located close to market areas.   Another emerging trend is the expanding use of compound fertilizers, whose share in total nutrient consumption has increased from 2.1% in 1980 to 11.3% in 1988. Since a proper nutrient balance becomes increasingly important to yield development at high levels of nutrient use, China's gradual shift in favor of compound fertilizers is in the right direction.

61.   On average, the **nutrient content** in applied fertilizers also has increased over time in China, owing to the fact that most of the new fertilizer plants are designed to produce high analysis fertilizers, while the bulk of fertilizer imports consist of high analysis fertilizers. **Crop use:** Aside from grains, the other heavy fertilizer user is cotton. As the derived demand for feed grains and other high value crops (vegetables, fruits, oil seed crops and sugar crops) increases over time, farmers--if given free choice--could be expected to divert more and more fertilizer to these crops. Even today, a substantial leakage appears to be occurring, and government may not be able to control the actual use of fertilizer as well as it would like to.

62.   The **regional pattern** of fertilizer consumption has been highly variable among provinces, within provinces and over time. The level of use of different nutrients varies across provinces depending on the level of agricultural development, cropping pattern, and prevailing nutrient deficiency in soils. The nutrient use is also higher in regions with relatively high grain yields and multiple cropping index since more nutrients are being taken up from the soil by crops. Provincial and regional fertilizer consumption levels from 1980 to 1988 are reported in World Bank (1990d), Table 20. Since the major share of fertilizer is used on grain crops (rice, wheat and corn) and cotton, the provinces which grew these crops account for most of the fertilizer use. Much of this area is south of the Yangtze and between the Yangtze and Yellow Rivers.

63.   At the regional level, there exist large variations in the level of fertilizer use. During 1988, the two main agricultural regions (Northern and MLYR) accounted for 63% of total fertilizer consumption, though their combined share of total cultivated area (51%) and cropped area (58%) were considerably lower. On the other hand, two relatively poor agricultural regions (the Northwest and Southwest) accounted for 25% of the cultivated area and 22% of the cropped area, but only 15% of the fertilizer use. Regional differences also exist in the uses of different nutrients which do not appear to be entirely commensurate with regional soil deficiencies, but may again reflect transportation constraints.

64.   Intensity of Fertilizer Use.   Overall nutrient use has increased from 0.6 kg/ha (cropped area) in 1952 to about 59 kg/ha in 1978 and to about 149 kg/ha in 1988.   This spectacular increase in fertilizer use intensity is partly a reflection of the decline in cropped area since 1978, but mainly was stimulated by the agricultural intensification spawned by the reforms, increased fertilizer availability, the provision of economic incentives (especially since 1978) to stimulate fertilizer use, and a gradual slowdown in the growth of nutrient supply from organic manures. At the provincial level, average nutrient use per ha from 1980 to 1988 is reported in World Bank (1990d), Table 21. Average use is the highest in coastal provinces and lowest in the northeastern, northwestern and southwestern provinces.   Ranging in 1988 from 57.0 kg/ha (cropped area) in Inner Mongolia to 277 kg/ha in Guangdong, the national average in 1988 was 149 kg/ha. Large variations in nutrient use have also been reported in different counties within a province (Stone-1986a). Low application areas generally have been allocated only the low quality, low grade fertilizers, whereas high application areas have access to high quality and high grade fertilizers.

65.   Nutrient Balance.   The provincial average nutrient balance for China during 1980, 1984 and 1988 is shown in World Bank (1990d), Table 23. The data indicates that the nutrient balance has been improving over time, but that there still is a long way to go to achieve the full balance.   Although fertilizer use in China continues to be dominated by nitrogen, government is making special efforts to make more P_2O_5 and K_2O available to farmers.   In this context, there is a need to determine nutrient deficiencies and nutrient requirements through nationwide soil surveys and soil testing laboratories, to persuade the fertilizer industry and importers to supply appropriate fertilizers, preferably compounds, and to provide needed incentives and knowledge to farmers.

66.   Use of Organic Matter.   China has a long history of using organic matter to support intensive agriculture.   Chinese scientists and farmers have been able to develop very sophisticated and scientific methods to collect, mix, store, transport and apply organic manures, both excreta and green manures. Organic manure is a good source of organic matter, plant nutrients, and energy when organic waste is processed through biogas plants, and it improves the texture and structure of soil.   However, its use is very labor intensive, even by the standards of rural China, given the need to apply 15-25 tons per ha to make an appreciable impact.

67.   Alternative estimates of nutrient supply from organic manures are set forth in World Bank (1990d), Table 24. Since 1949, the relative share (not the absolute amount) of organic manure in total nutrient supply has declined.

Share of Organic Manure in Total Nutrient Supply:

Year	N	P_2O_5	K_2O	Total
		------ (%) ------		
1957	99.6	100.0	100.0	99.0
1975	53.0	54.6	97.3	66.4
1983	26.2	35.5	88.5	42.0

Farmers (understandably) prefer to use chemical fertilizers. On the other hand, government is making serious efforts to promote the use of organic manure for crop cultivation, since organic manure and fertilizers are complements (not substitutes) in production.

68.   The other important source of organic matter and nutrients is green manure (World Bank [1990d], Appendix Table 24), rapeseed and cottonseed meal. The main green manure crops are milk vetch, especially around the Yangtze River. About 15 years ago, azzola was also a good source of nitrogen. However, its use as fertilizer has now declined since its use as animal and fish feed has become relatively more profitable.

69.   <u>Economics of Fertilizer Response</u>. Despite the rapid increase in fertilizer use during the past few years, **nutrient deficiencies** in China appear to have increased over time and are becoming more widespread. About 80% of agricultural land was deficient in nitrogen in the 1950s. At present, nitrogen deficiency exists throughout China with different degrees of severity. Lands deficient in phosphate have increased from about 50% in the 1950s to almost 70% in the 1980s, though the degree of phosphate deficiency has become a more serious problem north of the Yellow River. 18/ The proportion of soils deficient in potash also has increased, from 15% in the 1950s to over 30% in 1980s, with a large proportion of the deficient soils being located in China's southern rice belt. In addition, deficiencies of sulfur and micronutrients (especially zinc) are emerging in high intensity crop areas. As shown in World Bank (1990d), Appendix Table 33, nutrient uptake increases with an increase in cropping intensity as well as changes in the cropping pattern.

70.   The Institute of Soil Science in Nanjing and the national network of the Soil and Fertilizer Institute of CAAS in Beijing are responsible for basic and applied research on soil fertility in China. Their main conclusions on soil fertility and **fertilizer response** in the various regions of China can be summarized as follows:

<u>Physical Crop Response To:</u>

N	P_2O_5	K_2O
High response throughout China	High response in north	High response in south
Response declining in northeast and south China	Response declining in south and increasing in north	Response increasing in south and other parts of China

In general, though, the CAAS has concluded that (a) the average incremental crop response to unit nutrient application is comparatively low (World Bank [1990d], para 8.06), less than 10 kg per kg of nutrients, the minimum level generally assumed to exist for other developing countries (Mudahar-1978); (b) the average response to nitrogen is higher than potash, which, in turn, is

---

18/ This is partly due to transportation constraints. Most of the phosphate reserves in China are in the south and southwest, as are many of the phosphatic fertilizer factories.

higher than phosphate; (c) the average response for corn is higher than for paddy rice, which, in turn, is higher than wheat (this may not be true for rainfed conditions in the north with no assured supply of water); and (d) crop response to balanced nutrient application is much higher as compared to the use of individual nutrients.

71.   A common indicator of the **profitability of fertilizer use** is the value cost ratio (VCR), which is computed by dividing the estimated average fertilizer response ratio by the prevailing nutrient/crop price ratio. The estimates presented in World Bank (1990d), para 8.08 suggest that among crops, fertilizer use is relatively less profitable on corn than on wheat and rice; among nutrients, the use of K_2O is relatively more profitable than N and P_2O_5; and at plan prices, fertilizer use is more profitable on grain crops than at market prices. Based on a large amount of field level response and price data from developing countries, FAO has concluded that a VCR > 2 provides adequate incentives to farmers in order to adopt and expand fertilizer use. Since China's VCRs for various crops and nutrients are above two, it would appear that the use of additional fertilizers in China would be profitable, even at market prices.

-Price Levels and Trends

72.   Since the 1950s, China's fertilizer price policy has featured low prices to farmers, low profit to factories and low profit to commercial agencies. The fertilizer pricing system in China is very complex. The following list typifies the broad range of (largely administered) prices being used in China:

by Administrative Level:	-First wholesale level (AIC - national) -Second wholesale level (AIC - provincial) -Third wholesale level (AIC - county) -Retail (SMC)
by Level of Market Activity:	-Ex-factory transfer (fertilizer plants) -CIF transfer (SINOCHEM) -Wholesale (prices paid by different agencies) -Retail (price paid by farmers)
by Level of Government Intervention:	-Plan (subsidized) -Negotiated (subject to maximum price ceiling) -Market (reflects supply and demand situation)

With the exception of a brief period in 1985-86, when small quantities of fertilizer were traded at market prices, the distribution of fertilizer in China has been based on administrative prices.

73.   Price relationships between 1982-88 in Xinxiang, Henan, are illustrative of how prices have moved during the 1980s (World Bank [1990d], Tables 29-31). Xinxiang is an important prefecture which is located in China's wheat belt. The key points which emerge from this and other price data include: (a) the real value of planned purchase and sales prices have declined during the 1980s; (b) negotiated prices (prices close to market prices but still subject to government price guidelines) increased much faster and fluctuated within a wide band; (c) the subsidized sale prices, on a nutrient

basis, were fixed in 1988 to encourage a more balanced nutrient application, the use of nutrients that were not popular with farmers, and the use of low grade fertilizers produced by small local fertilizer plants to enable these plants to remain in operation; (d) fertilizer prices and marketing margins are established arbitrarily with little consideration of production costs, the cost of imports, or of the marketing and demand/supply situation for a particular fertilizer; (e) the national fertilizer (urea and imported fertilizers) prices are fixed by the central government and are kept uniform throughout China. Provincial and county-level prices are set by local authorities, held within the maximum price guidelines established by the central government, and kept uniform within the jurisdiction (province or county).

74.   Historically, relatively low retail fertilizer prices have been maintained in China to partly compensate for artificially low procurement prices for grain and other agricultural commodities, and to popularize and encourage the use of fertilizers. For example, subsidized prices at the retail level for national fertilizers apply to about 20% of the fertilizer handled by the national AIC and have not changed since 1986. At relatively high levels of fertilizer use, price policy generally loses its value as a stimulant to consumption. However, the situation in China is rather unique. Fertilizer use is high in high yield grain areas since historically these areas were given priority in fertilizer allocation. But many areas remain where fertilizer use is still very low. Furthermore, nutrient use is not properly balanced (para 65). In this context, fertilizer price policy can still be used to encourage more effective and efficient use of fertilizer. However, there is a need to remove existing distortions in administered prices, implement non-price policies which would shift the fertilizer response function upward, improve fertilizer availability at the farm level, and, ultimately, encourage a shift towards market-based allocation and pricing.

75.   Price Administration. Under the dual pricing policy for fertilizers that was introduced in 1985, fertilizer "within plan" is sold at subsidized plan prices and fertilizer "outside of the plan" is sold at negotiated prices. Fertilizer sold at negotiated prices consists of small and medium fertilizer plant output, out-of-plan imports, and above plan fertilizer production. The negotiated prices are fixed by the government but are assumed to reflect market conditions. In principle, there are no limits on fertilizer sales at negotiated prices, but in practice, this is not the case. The difference between plan and negotiated prices is often large, indicating large financial subsidies. The available evidence indicates that about 60% of the total and 90% of the high analysis (local production and imports) fertilizer is sold at AIC fixed plan prices which are more or less the same throughout China. The remaining 40% is sold at negotiated prices, which have very little uniformity. Generally, grain farmers purchase fertilizer at plan prices as part of the 3-linkage policy. On the other hand, cash crop farmers purchase fertilizer at negotiated prices. As reported below, in the last few years, negotiated prices have been as much as 100% higher than plan prices for similar products. Thus in January 1989, the government fixed maximum prices for different fertilizers and for different locations.

76.   Ex-factory and retail prices and fertilizer marketing margins are
regulated by government at the central, provincial and county levels. However,
the actual prices paid by farmers are not always equal to those fixed by the
government, especially in the case of 'plan' prices. Ex-factory and retail
prices fall into two categories. Prices of centrally managed fertilizers
(urea, ammonium sulfate, ammonium nitrate and imported fertilizers) are fixed
by the central government and are kept uniform throughout the country. Prices
of AmBC and SSP, which are produced by a large number of small plants, are
fixed by provincial or county governments and vary across plants within a
small price range. The State does not interfere in price determination at the
provincial and county levels but these prices must follow established
guidelines. The marketing margins, on the other hand, vary considerably
depending on the type of fertilizer, marketing costs and size of fertilizer
plant and its location.

77.   Uniformity in the pan-national retail prices is obtained through
subsidization of transport costs. China is divided into 9 fertilizer marketing
regions. Fertilizer transport costs are different for each of these regions
but are assumed the same within each region. The subsidization of transport is
accomplished by adjusting the state's "within plan" fertilizer allocation
price. The underlying justification for pan-national pricing is to reduce
discrimination against farmers located in remote areas far from fertilizer
supply sources. At the provincial and county levels, however, it is very
difficult to implement a uniform price policy since there is always a
possibility of illegal fertilizer trade across provincial or county borders
depending on the price differences.

78.   There are several other factors which influence fertilizer price levels
(World Bank [1990d], para 7.08). Fertilizer prices vary by type of fertilizer
product and its nutrient content. On nutrient basis, the unit price of potash
(K_2O) is generally lower than the price of N or P_2O_5. Fertilizer prices
increase with an increase in nutrient content. Price also depends on the
quality of a particular type of fertilizer. Higher prices are charged for
fertilizer sold in braided bags, which are more durable than paper bags. The
ex-factory price also is influenced by the cost of production of a particular
fertilizer which in turn is influenced by the prices paid by factories for
procuring fertilizer raw materials and intermediates. 14/ Lastly, retail
prices for provincial-level fertilizers vary across provinces, due to
differences in either the average production and marketing costs or in the
rate of fertilizer subsidy given by different provinces. 15/

-Fertilizer Imports

79.   Trends and Administration. The value of fertilizer imports since 1982
is reported in World Bank (1990d), Table 13. With the exception of 1986,

---

14/ The plan prices for raw materials and intermediates at the national level have not changed
since 1979, but factories which are unable to obtain adequate amounts of raw material at plan prices
pay higher prices which result in higher production costs and hence higher ex-factory prices.

15/ Thus, prices for provincially regulated fertilizers are generally higher than national price
equivalents in poor provinces since they are unable to afford high fertilizer subsidies.

China's total outlay on fertilizer imports has been increasing gradually. In 1988, China imported fertilizer valued at US$2.34 billion, and urea alone accounted for 52% of the import bill. In international trade circles, SINOCHEM--the FTC responsible for importing all of China's fertilizers--is known to import fertilizers on reasonably good terms and is considered to be an extremely reliable and responsible customer. During the 1980s, China's fertilizer consumption has increased faster than production. In turn, the volume of fertilizer imports has increased (World Bank [1990d], Table 12). As a result, the share of fertilizer imports in total fertilizer consumption increased from 16% in 1980 to 21% in 1984. Following a ban on imports in 1985, these dropped precipitously to only 15% of total supply, and further to only 10% in 1986. But after the government reversed its import policy, the share of fertilizer imports in consumption increased to 21% in 1987 and 27% in 1988.

80.   Fertilizer import decisions are made jointly by SPC, MOA, MCI, MOF and MOFERT. MOA determines fertilizer requirements and the type of fertilizers needed to meet those requirements. MCI determines the amount and type of fertilizers which will be produced domestically. Based on the projected gap between consumption, production and stocking requirements, SPC and MOF allocate the foreign exchange required to complete the annual importation plan. Within MOFERT, SINOCHEM transfers all the imported fertilizer to MOC's national AIC at fixed prices which may be higher or lower than the corresponding CIF prices. 16/

81.   Import Patterns. China's fertilizer imports consist mainly of three nutrients: nitrogen, phosphate and potash. Other relatively more specialized fertilizers are imported to meet specific needs. In the 1980s, the share of nitrogen in total fertilizer imports declined whereas the shares of P_2O_5 and K_2O have increased, a trend that is expected to continue. With reference to product composition, urea in 1988 made up 35% of total imports, followed by DAP (25%), KCL (8%) and triple super-phosphate ([TSP]-7%). Imports of NPK compounds accounted for the remaining 25%. Supply sources are diverse. As reported in World Bank (1990d), Table 10, urea was imported from 27 different countries in 1987; from some in uneconomically small quantities.

82.   Fertilizer Production vs Imports. The following characteristics of China's "fertilizers economy" would be significant elements in any assessment of potential trade-offs between decisions to produce and decisions to import, including the one which follows. For example, raw materials for the fertilizer industry are allocated under annual plans at fixed plan prices. Labor costs are generally low. (Fertilizer production costs would be much higher if all the inputs were priced at market prices or at their opportunity costs.) Further, ex-factory prices are set at low levels to enable the supply of fertilizers to farmers at low prices. China currently is vigorously promoting the development of the phosphate industry to produce straight phosphates and compounds containing P2O5. According to Kreuser and Sheldrick (1988), annual P_2O_5 demand in China by the Year 2000 could exceed 9 million tons. They also

---

16/ In the early 1980s, provincial trading companies were also allowed to import fertilizer provided they used their own foreign exchange and followed MOFERT guidelines. However, such imports were banned in 1985.

have evaluated the economics of domestic production vs imports to meet the projected demand for phosphate fertilizer, and conclude that there is a strong case (base case) for meeting increased phosphate fertilizer demand by domestic production rather than imports. If China chose domestic production rather than imports by the Year 2000, it could reduce its potential fertilizer import bill by more than ¥ 9.0 billion/year and net savings to the country would be ¥ 2.0 billion/year.

83.   The immediate effect of the devaluations of December 1989 and November 1990 was to make domestic production more attractive. At the new exchange rate, and with a constrained transport system, it will be economic to meet only small quantities of phosphate needs through imports. In the case of potash, there is limited raw material and most of the K_2O requirements will have to be met through imports.

84.   <u>Fertilizer vs Cereal Imports</u>. China imports both cereals (especially wheat) and fertilizers. Nearly 70% of fertilizer is used for grain production. Barring additional (and unlikely) major breakthroughs in cereals production technology, China will have to continue its grain importations to meet domestic grain supply requirements. However, China can reduce its import bill on the margin by importing larger quantities of fertilizer to increase domestic grain production and by reducing grain imports. The comparative economics of cereal and fertilizer imports depend on several factors but three are critical: the price of cereals on international markets, international fertilizer prices and the incremental productivity of fertilizers on grain crops, as indicated by the average physical fertilizer response ratios.

85.   International prices during 1988 and 1989 are reported in World Bank (1990d), Appendix Tables 12 and 13 for selected fertilizers and cereals. As shown earlier, China primarily imports wheat. The cif price of wheat in 1989 was $245/ton, which is higher than all the five fertilizers generally imported by China. Thus, for the value of 1 ton of wheat in the international marketplace, China in 1989 could have imported an additional 1.63 tons of urea, 1.26 tons of TSP, 1.69 tons of KCL, 1.09 tons of DAP or 1.20 tons of 15-15-15, the application of which would have resulted in increments to crop output amounting to several times the value of additional nutrients applied. As shown in World Bank (1990d), Table 15, the average incremental response ratio in wheat production in China is 6-9 kg per kg of applied nutrient. Comparing the incremental output value in 1989 from additional fertilizer imports with the corresponding import bill for 1 ton of wheat suggests that it would have been more economic to import fertilizers than wheat since additional fertilizers could have led to an increase in wheat production of 3.5-6.0 times the incremental fertilizer input. <u>17</u>/

86.   <u>Implications for the Longer-Term</u>. During 1987/88, the share of China in world fertilizer imports was as follows:

_____

<u>17</u>/ This simple analysis does not include instability in international prices, internal distribution costs and the cost of any other complementary inputs needed to produce wheat. However, it does demonstrate that any import moratoria on fertilizers--no matter what the current justification may be--can result in substantial loss in potential agricultural output to China.

Nutrient	Share in World Imports (%)
N	18
P_2O_5	13
K_2O	7
NPK /a	12

/a Quantity weighted average.

Should China pursue a strategy of importing more fertilizers, however, the relative share of imports by China in the world fertilizer trade could also be expected to increase from its already high level. Though fertilizer supply is not expected to be a problem in the near and medium-term since the world's existing fertilizer capacity is not being fully utilized, an expansion of imports could have a major impact on the international fertilizer market over the longer term. Prices may go up when China increases fertilizer imports, partly due to the oligopolistic nature of the international fertilizer market. This is particularly the case for phosphate and potash. However, China has always done well in negotiating very good terms for fertilizer imports and is expected to continue to do so in the future. But since several years are required to install new production capacity, China may be well advised to begin negotiating longer-term contracts with major fertilizer exporters, which would reduce import prices and also guarantee a still important segment of total supply that otherwise could fall hostage to a sometimes capricious international marketing situation.

Developments in Grain Distribution, Trade in Fertilizers
and Agricultural Public Expenditures

CHINA

OPTIONS FOR REFORM IN THE GRAIN SECTOR

Developments in Grain Distribution, Trade in Fertilizers
and Agricultural Public Expenditures

Table of Contents

DEVELOPMENTS IN GRAIN DISTRIBUTION, TRADE IN FERTILIZERS AND AGRICULTURAL PUBLIC EXPENDITURES

I. DISTRIBUTION AND MARKETING: GRAINS

-China's Domestic Grain Trade

1.   Compelled by the socialist tradition of egalitarian distribution, though still influenced by the Maoist principle of regional self-sufficiency, China's provincial per capita grain balances and the derivative classification of China's provinces into "grain surplus" and "grain deficit" areas are key planning criteria for determining the annual program of inter-regional grain transfers. An increasingly significant criterion during the 1980s, however, has been the rapidly changing levels of per capita production at the provincial level. 1/

2.   The setting of annual targets in China, be they financial, fiscal or real sector targets, is rife with bargaining among all levels of administration. Perhaps the most contentious negotiations in agriculture occur when setting annual targets for interprovincial grain movements within the state commercial system, the pricing of official transfers, and the terms and conditions for settling attendant financial obligations. Involved are negotiations between the officially designated exporting (i.e. "grain surplus") provinces and importing ones, and negotiations with the state concerning the assignation of foreign trade targets and the allocation of subsidized grain transfers to poor areas. Thus, China's inter-provincial grain "trade" is a highly administered system. The volume and location of grain stocks is considered to be very sensitive information, while a detailed accounting of the domestic grain trade--both time series and cross-sectional estimates alike--are incomplete and difficult to interpret. Lacking access to complete information, the report's conclusions on this topic should be interpreted with care. 2/

-Grain Production and Trade

3.   Available evidence documents a several-fold increase in domestic grain trade during the 1980s, first recovering to and then greatly surpassing the

---

1/ See World Bank (1990f), Tables 1 and 2 for estimates of per capita production at the provincial and regional level.

2/ Transport data published in the Chinese Statistical Yearbook (SSB-1989) yield a partial understanding of the total volume of domestic grain trade movements during the 1980s, but do not identify interprovincial grain flows. A second source of data, provincial matrices of grain inflows and shipments by rail in 1982 and 1986 (World Bank [1990f], Tables 5 and 6), provides useful indicators of interprovincial grain trade in those years. Since rail shipments account for the bulk of interprovincial grain trade, these matrices likely identify the most important trade flows. The provincial grain trade matrices are supplemented by a third source of data, provincial net trade of grain through MOC's General Grain Bureau, available for each year 1984-87 (World Bank [1990f], Appendix 4). Since the GGB dominates domestic grain trade, the MOC data should reasonably approximate provincial net trade in grain. In addition to these official data, Walker (1984) has used data gleaned from Chinese journals, newspapers and other sources to assemble a relatively complete provincial breakdown of net grain trade in 1953/57 and a somewhat less complete breakdown for 1979/81. Lardy (1989) recently completed a similar exercise which includes an incomplete provincial breakdown of domestic grain trade in the mid-1980s.

interprovincial flows of the 1950s (Annex 3 Table 1). Further, the provincial grain trade balances have been positively correlated with provincial per capita grain production. Thus, most of the major exporting provinces in the 1950s, (Heilongjiang, Inner Mongolia, Jiangxi and Jilin) and in 1986 (Jilin, Hubei, Anhui and Jiangsu) were also the leading producers of grain on a per capita basis. Most of the major importers in the 1950s (Hebei and the three municipalities) and 1986 (Liaoning, Inner Mongolia, Guangdong, Guangxi, Guizhou, Fujian, Yunnan and the three municipalities) had levels of production well below the national average. Major exceptions to this generally positive relationship between provincial grain production and trade balances are: Sichuan, the nation's leading exporter in the 1950s but only a slightly (103%) greater than national average grain producer at that time; Liaoning, the leading importer in the 1950s but only a slightly (98%) below national average grain producer in 1953/57; and Henan, the number two exporter in 1986 with below (94%) national average grain production.

4.   Norms in Distribution Planning. For political and other reasons, the criteria used to program China's domestic grain transfers have never been transparent. On the basis of simple regression analysis, however, it is apparent that unprocessed per capita grain production has been (and remains) a more powerful predictor of net provincial grain trade than the more appropriate indices of adjusted grain production 3/ (World Bank [1990f], Appendix 3). Provincial per capita unprocessed grain production in 1985/87 explained 65% of the variation in 1986 provincial per capita net grain trade; adjusted grain production, by comparison, explained 49% of the variation. Provincial grain procurement per nonagricultural resident is, as expected, negatively correlated with net grain imports at the provincial level. Other less powerful explanatory variables of provincial per capita net trade in grain are gross social product (positively correlated), total production of fine grains (negatively correlated) and the extent of urbanization (negatively correlated). Surprisingly, the extensiveness of extreme poverty explains none of the variation in provincial net grain trade. Unprocessed grain production, gross social product and urbanization together explain 74% of the variation in 1986 provincial per capita net grain trade (though regional transportation constraints may be a factor). Adjusted grain production and urbanization together explain 65% of the variation in 1986 provincial per capita net grain trade.

5.   Total Domestic Transfers. Total, regional and provincial net grain trade for selected years are summarized in Annex 3 Table 1. The data indicate that total net provincial exports declined by more than half between the 1950s and 1979/81, when the drive for regional self-sufficiency determined policy, but then recovered sharply in the mid-1980s. Total net provincial grain exports are estimated to have amounted to 8.6 million tons annually during the 1950s, or about 5% of total grain production. About three quarters of these exports, or about 6.3 million tons, were directed to other provinces with most of the remainder being sold on the international market. In contrast with the 84% increase in total grain production achieved over the two and a half

---

3/ Adjusted grain production includes rice at milled weight and accounts for animal feed requirements.

decades that followed, net provincial grain exports by 1979/81 had dropped to about 4 million tons annually, or less than 1.5% of total grain production. Lardy (1989) reports that, as part of the central government policy of provincial and local self-reliance, net provincial grain exports were maintained at very low levels throughout the Cultural Revolution period (1966-76). Total net provincial grain imports, on the other hand, increased to 10 million tons annually by 1979/81. Grain purchased on the international market supplied more than half of provincial imports during 1979/81.

6. Although total domestic grain trade during the 1980s is not known, the provincial rail transport matrices indicate that interprovincial grain trade recovered sharply beginning in the mid-1980s. As shown in Annex 3 Table 1, total net provincial grain exports by rail jumped to 18 million tons in 1986, or about 5% of total grain production. The GGB's grain trade data for 1986, viz., net provincial imports of 16.9 million tons and net exports of 12.2 million tons, roughly corroborate the rail trade figures for that year. The MOC data also indicate that net provincial exports of grain through the GGB trade network increased from 6.5 million tons in 1984 to more than 12 million tons in each year 1985 and 1986. The figure for 1987 suggests a sharp decline in exports to less than 2 million tons in that year, but the decline has almost certainly been exaggerated by an incomplete reporting of negotiated exports. Net provincial imports through the GGB network, on the other hand, have been relatively steady, ranging between 14 million tons to 17 million tons annually during 1984-87. 4/

7. The published national transport data summarized in World Bank (1990f), Table 4 provides further evidence of the resurgence of interprovincial grain trade in the 1980s. Although official total grain traffic data are not available, traffic in grain by rail and by water are known for each year 1984-88 and grain tonnage by rail for all years. These data indicate that a 50% increase in tonnage and 30% increase in average distance boosted railway traffic in grain by just over 100% in only three years from 28 btkm in 1984 to 57 btkm 1987. Grain tonnage and average distance both dipped slightly in 1988, and rail traffic in grain declined by 3% in that year. Water traffic in grain is substantial and increasing, having reached 220 btkm in 1988. However, long distance international shipments comprise most of the water traffic in grain, and actual internal tonnage may be less than one-fourth that moved by rail. Grain's share of road traffic is not known, but given that road traffic accounts for only 14% of total traffic and that inter-provincial shipment of grain by truck would in most cases be prohibitively expensive, it is likely that interprovincial grain shipments by road are not substantial. In sum, the data suggest that rail transport accounts for at least 80% to 90% of total interprovincial grain tonnage. 5/

4/ Net provincial imports through the GGB network should, by identity, equal net exports. However, GGB net provincial imports exceed net exports in all years 1984-87. This anomaly may reflect the influence of China's international grain trade.

5/ In this connection, the recent CAAS study (para 12) notes considerable inefficiency in grain transport including circuitous routing, back flows of the same grains, and excessively long hauls.

Annex 3 Table 1   Net Provincial Grain Imports by Mode of Transport and Marketing Channel (million tons)

	All Modes & Channels		Mode of Transport (all channels)			Marketing Channel MOC's General Grain Bureau (all modes)				
	1953/57 Average	1979/81 Average /a	1981 ocean /b	1982 rail	1986 rail	1984	1985	1986	1987	1985-87 Average
Northeast										
Heilongjiang	-1.43	-0.53	--	1.14	-0.97	-0.30	-1.60	-0.42	0.46	-0.52
Liaoning	1.66	1.30	3.00	-1.31	4.14	1.68	-0.36	1.48	1.48	0.87
Jilin	-0.64	(X)	--	-0.24	-3.53	-1.09	-0.04	-0.50	-0.10	-0.21
subtotal	-0.41	na	3.00	-0.41	-0.36	0.29	-2.00	0.56	1.84	0.13
North										
Beijing	1.20	(M)	--	1.76	2.32	1.87	2.27	2.20	2.08	2.18
Tianjin	1.20	(M)	2.50	-1.07	0.87	1.43	1.63	2.00	1.53	1.72
Hebei	1.11	0.43	1.70	-1.27	0.69	1.04	0.62	0.11	0.09	0.27
Shanxi	-0.04	0.34	--	0.85	0.67	0.99	0.54	0.48	0.89	0.64
Henan	-0.25	(~)	--	-0.40	-3.09	-1.60	-2.95	-2.09	-0.35	-1.80
Shaanxi	-0.14	0.60	--	0.76	0.26	0.25	-0.07	0.09	0.37	0.13
Shandong	0.00	(~)	1.60 /c	-0.10	0.03	0.63	0.10	-0.12	0.11	0.03
subtotal	3.08	na(X)	>5.80 /c	0.53	1.75	4.60	2.16	2.69	4.70	3.18
Northwest										
Inner Mongolia	-0.78	1.40	--	0.99	1.33	1.14	0.87	0.75	0.89	0.84
Gansu	-0.11	0.60	--	0.74	0.11	0.19	0.06	0.21	0.50	0.26
Qinghai	0.00	0.20	--	0.28	0.33	0.20	0.28	0.30	0.23	0.27
Ningxia	NA	0.07	--	-0.06	-0.08	-0.03	-0.16	-0.05	0.00	-0.07
Xinjiang	0.00	0.23	--	0.14	-0.15	0.10	0.03	-0.13	-0.15	-0.09
subtotal	-0.89	2.50	0.00	2.09	1.54	1.60	1.08	1.07	1.47	1.20
MLYR										
Shanghai	1.20	(M)	2.50	0.26	0.26	1.29	2.16	1.99	1.71	1.95
Jiangsu	-0.35	-1.00	na /c	-1.46	-2.20	-0.79	-1.89	-2.53	-0.56	-1.66
Zhejiang	-0.42	(X)	--	0.21	0.03	0.25	0.13	0.44	0.35	0.31
Anhui	-0.32	-0.80	--	-0.94	-2.35	-0.73	-1.64	-1.87	-0.20	-1.23
Jiangxi	-0.73	-0.63	--	-0.53	-1.63	-0.53	-1.14	-1.18	0.07	-0.75
Hubei	-0.05	-0.36	--	-0.47	-2.82	-0.73	-2.04	-2.47	0.01	-1.50
Hunan	-0.55	-0.67	--	-0.78	-1.17	-0.69	-0.82	-0.81	-0.13	-0.58
subtotal	-1.21	na(X)	>2.50 /c	-3.71	-9.88	-1.94	-5.24	-6.44	1.26	-3.47
South & Southwest										
Guangdong	-0.29	0.35	1.60	-0.19	2.00	1.15	2.25	2.70	0.88	1.94
Guangxi	-0.14	(M)	--	0.42	1.58	0.34	0.78	1.14	0.65	0.86
Fujian	-0.03	0.10	na /c	0.20	1.10	0.59	0.96	1.07	0.79	0.94
Sichuan	-1.84	-0.04	--	0.23	0.20	0.03	0.01	0.05	0.02	0.03
Guizhou	-0.29	0.60	--	0.58	1.15	0.50	1.15	0.99	0.70	0.95
Yunnan	-0.16	0.33	--	0.26	0.92	0.12	0.52	0.87	0.52	0.64
Xizang (Tibet)						0.13	0.04	0.00	0.07	0.04
subtotal	-2.75	>1.34	>1.60 /c	1.50	6.95	2.86	5.70	6.82	3.63	5.39
Total Net Trade:										
provincial imports	6.3	10.0	na	8.8	18.0	13.9	14.4	16.9	14.4	14.9
provincial exports	8.6	>4.0	na	8.8	18.0	6.5	12.7	12.2	1.5	8.4
international imports	-2.1	12.0	13.5	15.3	-1.7	7.2	-3.3	-1.7	8.9	1.3
Gross Trade:										
provincial imports				16.5	29.9	20.0	23.7	25.1	18.5	22.4
provincial exports				16.5	29.9	12.6	22.0	20.4	5.6	16.0

Source: World Bank (1990f), Table 3.

Note: In the above table, positive numbers indicate net imports and negative values represent net exports.

/a   "M" indicates province known to be a net importer, "X" a net exporter, and "~" provincial imports and exports about equal. China's three municipalities together had net grain imports of 3.4 million tons annually in the late-1970s.

/b   International imports by ocean going vessels.

/c   A total of 2.2 million tons of grain were discharged in 1981 at the ports of Yantai (Shandong), Lianyungang (Jiangsu) and Xiamen (Fujian). Figure for Shandong (1.60) is discharge at port of Qingdao only.

8.   Interregional Trade. The data in the above table show the following
shifts in the magnitude and direction of domestic grain trade:

   1953/57: The two dominant features of domestic grain trade in the
   mid-1950s were that most (19) provinces were net grain exporters
   and all importing provinces and municipalities, except Shanghai,
   were located in North and Northeast China. The four importers in
   Northeast and North China, viz., Beijing, Tianjin, Hebei and
   Liaoning, together accounted for 81% of total net provincial
   imports (Shanghai accounted for the remaining 19%);

   1979/81: Domestic grain trade at the end of the 1970s differed
   from that of the 1950s in three important ways: (a) the number of
   provincial net grain exporters declined from 19 to 9 while the
   number of net importers increased from 5 to 16, (b) except for
   Sichuan, all provinces in Northwest and South-and- Southwest China
   became net importers of grain and the two regions together
   switched from net grain exports of 3.6 million tons in 1953/57 to
   net imports of 3.8 million tons in 1979/81, and (c) Northeast
   China became a net importer of grain following a sharp decline in
   net exports from Heilongjiang and Jilin. Grain trade in China's
   two other regions was largely unchanged -- North China remained a
   large net importer and MLYR a net exporter;

   1984-87 The GGB's provincial trade data indicate that, although
   trade levels fluctuated sharply on an annual basis, North,
   Northwest and South-and-Southwest China were consistent importers
   of grain throughout during 1984-87. The MLYR was a major net
   exporter during 1984-86. The figure for 1987 suggests that the
   MLYR had net imports of 1.3 million tons in that year, but this
   switch is most likely the result of the incomplete reporting of
   negotiated exports in the GGB trade figures and not a true
   reversal in trade posture. The GGB data also indicate that the
   Northeast was a moderate net importer of grain in each year except
   1985. However, the GGB figures appear to exclude international
   exports of grain, and may not accurately portray the Northeast's
   grain trade posture.

9.   Estimates at the Provincial Level. China's four leading grain exporting
provinces in the 1950s were Sichuan (1.84 million tons), Heilongjiang (1.43
million tons), Inner Mongolia (0.78 million tons), and Jiangxi (0.73 million
tons). By the 1980s, however, Sichuan and Inner Mongolia had become net
importers of grain and Heilongjiang's net exports were greatly reduced.
Jilin, Henan, Hubei, Anhui and Jiangsu, on the other hand, all substantially
increased grain exports to become China's five leading exporters in the
mid-1980s, with Jilin primarily exporting to foreign markets (maize) while the
other four were leading exporters to the domestic market during 1985-87.

10.   The leading grain importers in the 1950s were the three municipalities,
with combined net imports of about 3.6 million tons, and Liaoning and Hebei,
with net imports of 1.66 million tons and 1.11 million tons respectively. The
rail trade data suggest that in 1986 (a) the three municipalities had net

imports of 3.5 million tons, (b) Liaoning had net imports of 4.1 million tons, **6/** and (c) the other leading importing provinces were Guangdong, Guangxi, Inner Mongolia, Guizhou, Fujian and Yunnan. The latter 6 provinces, all of which were net grain exporters in the 1950s, together imported 8.1 million tons of grain (more than 10 million tons when accounting for net international trade) in 1986. The GGB data indicate a moderately different pattern of interprovincial trade. On an average annual basis, domestic grain trade through the GGB system in 1985-87 included (a) net imports of 5.9 million tons to the three municipalities, (b) net imports of 0.9 million tons to Liaoning, and (c) net imports of 1.9 million, 1.0 million, 0.9 million, 0.9 million, and 0.8 million tons respectively to the other leading importing provinces of Guangdong, Guizhou, Fujian, Guangxi and Inner Mongolia. **7/**

11.   Major flows of grain from leading exporting to importing provinces and municipalities can be roughly discerned through an examination of the interprovincial grain trade matrices presented in World Bank (1990f), Tables 5 and 6. About 90% (3.2 million tons) of Jilin's 1986 net grain exports of 3.5 million tons were shipped to Beijing, Tianjin, Inner Mongolia and Liaoning. Liaoning alone received 2.2 million tons or more than 50% of Jilin's total net exports, though much of this was presumably transshipped to Japan and other foreign markets. More than 50% (1.5 million tons) of Hubei's 1986 net exports of 2.8 million tons were shipped to Guangdong, Guangxi, Guizhou and Yunnan. More than 40% (1.3 million tons) of Henan's 1986 net exports of 3.1 million tons were shipped to Beijing, Tianjin and Inner Mongolia. More than 35% (0.8 million tons) of Jiangsu's 1986 net exports of 2.2 million tons were shipped to Liaoning. Anhui's grain exports (2.4 million tons), and the remaining portions of Hubei, Henan and Jiangsu's exports, were shipped quite widely throughout the country.

-Interprovincial Transfers: By Type of Grain

12.   The interprovincial grain trade flows identified in the preceding section are corroborated in a detailed study, "Regional Balance of the Supply and Demand of Grain" in Research on China's Grain, recently completed by the CAAS. Major importing and exporting provinces during the early-1980s are listed over-page. The study also notes that Northwest Xinjiang produces a surplus of wheat, but that there is at present no economic way to export it out of the area. Lastly, the wheat import requirements of Tianjin, Liaoning, Jilin, Fujian, Guangxi, and Guangdong were mostly met through international imports.

6/   The net trade figures for Heilongjiang and Liaoning do not fully reflect international trade across the border with the USSR and through the port of Dalian.

7/   Since they include domestic inter-coastal and riverine imports and exports, the GGB trade figures almost certainly provide a more accurate portrayal of the three municipalities and Liaoning's net grain trade posture than do the rail trade data.

Grain	Importers	Exporters
Rice	Three Municipalities, South-and-Southwestern, Gansu, Inner Mongolia and Shanxi	Jiangxi, Hubei, Hunan, Anhui, Jiangsu, & Zhejiang
Fine Rice	World Market	Liaoning, Jiangsu, Anhui, Jiangxi, Hubei & Hunan
Wheat	Beijing, Shanxi, Inner Mongolia, Guizhou, Yunnan, Hebei, Shandong & Gansu	Henan, Jiangsu, Hubei, Anhui & Sichuan
Corn	South-and-Southwestern & most other nonexporters	Jilin, Hebei & Liaoning
Soy	South-and-Southwestern & most other nonexporters	Heilongjiang, Jilin & Inner Mongolia

-Marketing Channels and Prices

13.   **Planned Trade.** The central government maintained nearly complete control of China's domestic and international grain trade until the early-1980s, and continues to closely regulate the larger share of such trade today.   In accordance with annual and long-run plans drafted by the SPC and approved by the State Council, planned domestic grain trade is managed by the GGB and its network of local grain bureaux, and planned international grain trade is carried out by CEROILS. The GGB and CEROILS directly manage the procurement, processing, storage and sales of grain, and arrange for the domestic and international transport of grain through agencies and corporations of the Ministry of Railways and the Ministry of Communications (mostly domestic and international shipping) as well as local government transport departments (trucking). 8/

Annex 3 Table 2. Domestic Planned and Free Market Grain Prices, 1988

(yuan per ton)

	Contract Procurement	Inter-provincial Transfer /a	Free Market	Difference: Free Market Price Minus Transfer Price
paddy rice	312	372	980	608
wheat	454	514	920	406
corn	336	396	675	339
soybeans	692	752	1160	408

Source: World Bank (1990f), Table 7.

/a   Wholesale price paid by importing province.

8/ Grain procurement, distribution, handling and storage are discussed in World Bank (1990b, 1990g).

14.   Planned interprovincial grain trade is transacted at below market planned prices which involve large losses of revenue for farmers in grain exporting provinces and a substantial financial windfall to importing provinces. Farmers' loss of revenue on grain sales for planned interprovincial trade can be roughly approximated as the difference between the contract procurement price, which is the price received by farmers for mandatory planned procurement, and the free market price, which is an indicator of the price the farmer would receive were domestic grain trade fully liberalized. As shown in Annex 3 Table 2 for 1988, the differences between the interprovincial transfer and free market prices are substantial. The greatest difference -- more than 600 yuan per ton -- is for paddy rice, the contract procurement price of which was only about one-third the free market price. Contract procurement prices for the other major grains, viz., wheat, corn and soybeans, were each only about 50% to 60% of the prevailing free market price. For planned interprovincial transfers, importing provinces pay only the contract price for the grain plus a small marketing margin. 9/ At these planned interprovincial transfer prices, the loss of potential revenue suffered by farmers of exporting provinces and the subsidy to importing provinces ranged between about 340 yuan per ton of corn, to 400 yuan per ton of wheat and soy, to more than 600 yuan per ton of paddy rice traded. Planned provincial exports, which amounted to 4.25 million tons annually during 1976-80, increased to perhaps 15 million tons by 1986 before declining sharply in 1987. Assuming planned interprovincial grain exports recovered to at least 10 million tons in 1988, farmers in grain exporting provinces suffered a loss of potential revenue of about ¥6 billion, or on average at least ¥ 120 per farmer.

15.   Negotiated Trade. In 1982 the government initiated a process of liberalizing China's domestic and international grain trade. An important first step was the relaxation of restrictions on domestic trade in excess of the state plan ("above-plan") for both state (including the GGB system and commercial units of other state agencies) and nonstate agencies and companies (including rural collective enterprises and farm households). Secondly, provincial trade companies were granted limited authority to negotiate grain purchase and sales on the world market. However, the volume of above-plan international grain trade is thought to have remained quite limited. Since above-plan trade is transacted at negotiated prices closely approximating free market prices, surplus grain producing regions have a strong incentive to maximize the share of above-plan shipments in total interprovincial grain exports. Above-plan shipments have increased as a share of total interprovincial grain trade since the initiation of these reforms, though the full extent of this increase is not known. The sharp reduction in net provincial exports (of more than 10 million tons) between 1986 and 1987 indicated by the GGB's trade data (Annex 3 Table 1), suggests a near total collapse in net planned provincial exports in 1987. This trend is

---

9/ The price differential, which averages about 60 yuan per ton, covers only the transaction and handling costs of the Grain Bureau supplying the grain. Transport costs are reportedly borne by the central government (Lardy [1989], p. 24).

corroborated by scattered evidence at the local level. 10/

16.   Though the impact on intra- and interprovincial grain trade is unclear, the State Council took action in late-1988 and 1989 to reverse the liberalization of domestic and international grain trade. Full control of the domestic grain trade was returned to the GGB and transfers in all channels other than the GGB system was disallowed (China Daily, "State Acts to Ensure Calm Grain Market," November 17, 1988). It is suspected that net planned interprovincial grain exports recovered to at least 10 million tons in 1989. It was also recently reported (Business China, "MOFERT Tightens Control," July 31, 1989) that CEROILS has regained full control of China's international grain trade. The situation appears to be quite fluid, however, since the State Council also appears to be considering a MOC plan to open a wholesale grain market in Zhengzhou with the eventual aim of trading up to 50 million tons of grain in such markets (China Daily, "Pioneer Market for Grain Marks a Major Reform," June 27, 1989).

-Transportation Capacity

17.   In "The Transport Bottleneck Problem in China," Watanatada (1988) argues that the inadequacy of the transport system is one of the most binding constraints to China's economic development. He contrasts the 125% increase in total freight traffic during the period 1978-87 with the much smaller increase in total route lengths of the railway and highway systems of only 8% and 10% respectively over the same period. Available evidence suggests that the binding constraint is the low network capacity of the railway and highway systems, not the shortage of locomotives, rolling stock and trucks. The paper's prospective analysis indicates that inadequacies in the transport system will get worse in the 1990s before getting better.

18.   Given the large investment costs and long construction period required for expansion of railway network capacity and assuming that coal continues to comprise 30% of China's rail traffic, further growth of the interprovincial grain trade over the next decade may in some cases become severely constrained by transport limitations. One possible means of partially overcoming the transport constraint would be to utilize the often empty back hauls from coal shipments to move grain. An examination of matrices of interprovincial coal trade and total trade (World Bank [1990f], Appendix 2, Tables 1 and 3) indicates good potential for moving grain out of Northeast China (net coal imports of about 28 million tons in 1986) and the MLYR provinces of Jiangsu, Anhui, Jiangxi, Hubei and Hunan (net coal imports of about 53 million tons in 1986). The transport constraint may not be so easy to resolve in South-and-Southwest China since the region is a net importer of both coal and grain.

19.   In this connection, a view held by many transportation experts in China and in the Bank in worth noting: that China's inter-coastal and riverine

---

10/ In Henan province, for instance, the Xinxiang Municipal GB's above-plan grain exports increased from 22,000 tons in 1985 to 124,000 tons in 1987 -- or from 10% to 75% of total shipments -- while planned exports declined from a peak of 206,000 tons in 1985 to only 39,000 tons in 1987.

shipping potential has barely been exploited. In order to do so, China would have to expand its fleet of coastal vessels, both general cargo and bulk carriers, and possibly investment in port improvements and handling capabilities. But in addition to removing pressure from the over-burdened rail system on North-South hauls, inter-coastal shipping would measurably facilitate grain movements between provinces in the North and South (and vice-versa), and by river between East and West, particularly the movement of animal feeds (corn and soybeans) from northern production areas to the main feed deficit areas located in the South and rice in the other direction.

-GGB Financial Balances

20.   It has been noted elsewhere that the GGB system incurs exceedingly large financial losses in its grain distribution operations. To name a few, the underlying reasons appear to be inefficiencies in organization and management, over-staffing, outmoded facilities and equipment, high physical losses in handling and distribution, inefficient transport routing, and reliance on bagged handling for the most part rather than on bulk handling which is more economical. These losses are quite apart from losses owing to the price differential between official procurements and urban ration sales, and are met either by the state and the state banking system, provincial and municipal governments, or covered by profits from the GGB's more remunerative non-grain marketing activities.

21.   An incomplete financial balance statement for GGB grain operations is presented for each year 1978-87 in World Bank (1990b), Table 5. Profits from negotiated sales, feed processing, and other activities grew steadily from ¥ 0.6 billion in 1978 to ¥ 4.5 billion in 1987. The increase in profits was more than offset by the increase in **gross losses**, which surged from ¥ 3.8 billion in 1978 to ¥ 23.4 billion in 1984, lessened slightly to about ¥ 21 billion in 1985 and 1986, and then increased again to ¥ 24.4 billion in 1987. About 20% lower than gross losses, the GGB's **net losses** showed similar trends.

22.   In World Bank (1990b), Appendix 1, Table 2 the GGB's gross losses are disaggregated as either operating losses, which comprise transport, storage, interest, maintenance, and labor costs, or price subsidies, which by convention correspond to the difference between procurement costs and sales revenue. Operating losses have increased each year, from ¥ 2.5 billion in 1978 to ¥ 9.6 billion in 1987, but declined as a share of total GGB gross losses from more than 65% in 1978 to less than 40% in 1987. Transport costs comprise about one-third, interest about one-quarter, labor about one-fifth, and storage and maintenance each about one- tenth of the GGB's 1987 operating losses.

II. DISTRIBUTION AND MARKETING: FERTILIZERS

-Evolution of China's Fertilizer Distribution System

23.   Timely procurement, adequate storage and transportation, careful handling and effective sales promotion, and efficient distribution are several attributes of a well-functioning fertilizer distribution system. China's

fertilizer distribution system performs all the above activities, some reasonably well and others not so efficiently. Since the reforms were introduced, the system has evolved through several phases:

Prior to 1982	-Complete centralization
Early 1982	-Partial decentralization
Mid 1985	-Partial liberalization
October 1987	-Partial recentralization
January 1989	-Complete centralization

During the last several years, the fertilizer distribution system has shown both rapid growth and reasonably efficient performance, then, towards the end of the 1980s, experienced considerable chaos and became relatively less efficient.

24.   Fertilizer Procurement. The procurement of domestic production and imports in China is the responsibility of two separate agencies. The AIC at different levels are responsible for procurement from factories at the national, provincial and county levels. SINOCHEM is responsible for all fertilizer imports. When it arrives in China, imported fertilizers are transferred by SINOCHEM to the AIC at the various ports of entry. Fertilizer is unloaded from ship and put in transfer warehouses controlled by AIC. Most of the fertilizer in China is imported, not in bulk, but in bags. The fertilizer transfer prices, from factories (under the MCI) or from SINOCHEM to AIC, are determined by the State Price Bureau (SPB) in consultation with other relevant ministries.

25.   Fertilizer Allocation. Owing to continuous shortage, the allocation and pricing of fertilizers remains subject to central planning in China. The State Planning Commission (SPC), MOA, MOC and MCI in consultation with provincial planning and agricultural departments prepare annual fertilizer distribution plans. Once this plan is prepared and approved by the relevant agencies it becomes a blueprint for fertilizer distribution. Any divergence from the planned allocation is discouraged and must be approved by authorities at the highest level. This process applies to both "plan" (fertilizer sold at subsidized prices) and "above plan" (fertilizer sold at negotiated prices) allocations. From time to time, factories are allowed to sell small quantities of fertilizer directly to farmers. Several criteria are used to determine fertilizer allocations to the different provinces and counties. These criteria include (a) allocation by total cropped area (at a fixed rate per unit of area under certain crops in different locales), (b) assigning priority to high and stable yield areas in order to maximize agricultural production, (c) linking allocations to crop procurement priorities, especially grains, and (d) special (though comparatively limited) allocations to remote, impoverished and disaster prone areas. Through the years, the emphasis given to these priorities has been changing. From the mid-1950s to the early 1960s, most of the fertilizer was allocated to cereal crops or to cereal areas having high and stable yields. From the early 1960s to the late 1970s, priority was given to supporting the production of agricultural commodities controlled by the central government. In the 1980s, fertilizers were allocated to areas not

only with high economic returns (as defined by the Chinese authorities) but also with relatively high production potential. Further, according to Stone (1986b), county officials sometimes allocate fertilizer to reward compliance with various government programs such as birth control campaigns. With the exception of a few years in the mid-1980s, however, decentralized markets have played only a very limited role in determining fertilizer allocation and use.

26.   When first introduced, the strategy of allocating fertilizer to high and stable yield areas was an appropriate one since fertilizers were limited in supply and crop response was generally quite high. However, with the ensuing increased use of fertilizers in high yield areas, incremental crop response declined due to an already high level of application, growing nutrient imbalance, and increasing deficiencies in secondary and micronutrients. High yield areas not only receive relatively more fertilizers than the lower yielding areas but also receive higher quality fertilizers which are sold at subsidized prices.   The key differences between the high and the lower yielding areas are summarized below:

Higher Yielding Areas	Low/Medium Yield Areas
Larger fertilizer allocation	Smaller fertilizer allocations
More high analysis fertilizers	Less high analysis fertilizers
At subsidized prices:	
More fertilizer sold	Less fertilizer sold
Relatively low fertilizer response	Relatively high fertilizer response
Low potential fertilizer response	High potential fertilizer response

It is these differences which were responsible for the chaos (e.g. fluctuating prices and extensive leakage) that occurred when the fertilizer market was partially liberalized from 1985 to 1987.   The higher yielding areas continued to receive official priority under the annual allocation plan due to their large grain procurement targets, political clout, and ability to manipulate the fertilizer distribution plan.   But subsequently, following reimposition of the state's monopoly over fertilizer distribution, the government has been trying to refocus the official distribution plan on low and medium yield areas through its grain-base development program.

27.   During the 1970s and early 1980s, the importance of government's crop procurement targets as criteria for allocating fertilizers progressively increased. The available evidence (World Bank [1990d], para 6.07) indicates that the share of fertilizer allocation in direct exchange for the sale of agricultural commodities increased rapidly after the introduction of the PRS. However, fertilizer allocations that were tied to crop procurement programs declined temporarily during the mid-1980s in response to record grain production.

28.   In the later 1980s, however, corollary with the emergence of a perceived grain problem, the government again increased the allocation of fertilizers linked to grain delivery contracts. The "3-linkage policy", first introduced in 1985 (which offers subsidized fertilizer, insecticides and diesel fuel to signed agreements for grain delivery at administered prices), was expanded considerably. Further, in 1988 and 1989, special incentive allocations were offered to rice and soybean farmers. Assuming that 50 million tons of grain

are procured every year at the low "contract" price (cf. World Bank [1990d]), approximately 6-7 million tons of urea will be sold annually at subsidized prices through the 3-linkage policy alone.

29.   Estimated Marketing Costs. In theory, fertilizer marketing costs consist of all costs incurred in the fertilizer marketing chain between factory or port to retail points of sale, including profit margins for all units involved in fertilizer marketing. In China, however, fertilizer distribution cost categories are defined and unit values are fixed by the state. Profit margins for the various official agencies (AICs, SMCs) involved in distributing fertilizers are fixed at very low levels for accounting purposes. Other costs such as storage and transportation are heavily subsidized and recorded at subsidized prices. The raison d'etre for these procedures is to maintain a ceiling on distribution costs in order to curtail price creep at the retail level.

30.   Information on the build-up of distribution costs from points of manufacture and importation to the farmgate is not readily available, thus a detailed functional cost accounting could not be constructed for this report. However, crude estimates are possible on the basis of reported ex-factory and farmgate prices. According to the headquarter's AIC, the "administered" average internal distribution costs for different fertilizers during the late 1980s have ranged from ¥ 40/ton for low analysis products manufactured by small fertilizer factories, to ¥ 100-110/ton for high analysis products and imports. For accounting purposes, these "costs" became effective in May 1986. Some profit within the official distribution system is allowed as well. But these are hardly representative of either the actual financial costs associated with fertilizer distribution or the true economic costs since the accounting definitions do not encompass the totality of distribution cost components, nor do they record cross-subsidization, principally to cover losses in manufacturing.

-Attempts to Reform Market Structure

31.   Prior to 1982, the AIC exercised a virtual monopsony on the purchase of fertilizers produced by Chinese plants and imported by SINOCHEM, and had been given monopoly privileges on the direct sale of fertilizers and over sales through the SMCs. Thereafter, reforms to the fertilizer distribution system were introduced in 1982 and further broadened in 1985. These reforms made it possible for factories and private traders to sell above-plan fertilizers directly to farmers at market prices.

32.   Several reasons lay behind the fertilizer marketing reform. However the key factors were the build-up of AmBC stocks in 1984 and 1985 owing to excessive production by small-scale plants, farmer preference for higher analysis urea as a source of nitrogen, a shortage of distribution credits for the AICs and farmers, and an increase in price of AmBC due to an increase in input prices. Thus in 1985 the Chinese government legalized private trade, allowed factories to sell AmBC directly to farmers at market prices, and refused to purchase unsold output from the AmBC factories. Initially, there were problems since these factories, being small-scale operations and geographically dispersed, had no experience in fertilizer marketing. By 1987,

however, a system to market surplus production had been set up. In parallel, a moratorium on fertilizer imports was imposed in 1985 and 1986.

33.   In 1987, the fertilizers picture reverted to scarcity. The main contributing factors were an increase in demand for fertilizer, the aforementioned reduction in imports, reduced production (over 200 small plants were closed during this period), and the expanding role of private trade in locales which were not previously served well by the AICs and SMCs.   The main distribution problems encountered during this period included the diversion of fertilizers--even those produced "within plan"--and consequent price increases, lack of fertilizers to meet planned allocations, especially of high quality fertilizers, a marked decline in quality below government standards, increased physical and chemical losses in the distribution chain, and less than optimal use of China's overstretched transportation facilities to carry fertilizers to the new demand centers.

34.   Whether these claims were valid or not (the farmers were never really consulted), the weight of official protest from the local levels carried. During the period of reassessment that followed, the government concluded that these problems were the direct result of market liberalization. There are reasons for believing, however, that this conclusion is not quite accurate. Rather, the marketing reforms led to a loss of leverage by local authorities to enforce compliance with various government programs, very vocal complaints from factories which couldn't compete in the new policy environment, and an accelerated (but predictable) diversion of fertilizers from low response to high response areas which was not acceptable to the well-positioned "high yield but low response" areas. The AICs and SMCs also did not relish the idea of losing full control over an important agricultural input, and farmers did not appreciate having to pay higher prices for the lower grade fertilizers. Thus, the main problems encountered during China's brief liberalization rather reflect the general shortage of high quality fertilizers and teething difficulties associated with the nascent status of fertilizer market development, regulation and information systems. But in view of the huge financial losses being absorbed by the official distribution system (discussed below) and the inadequacies of its centralized allocation system, it would seem worthwhile for China to again introduce a measured liberalization in order to cut some of these losses.

35.   Nonetheless, in response to complaints from various pressure groups, the government reintroduced in January 1989 the monopoly in fertilizer purchase, distribution and sales, reimposed completely unified planning and distribution management, and reissued price control regulations and price guidelines. The central AIC claims that after the reimposition of central control, price increases have been brought under control and substandard fertilizers have stopped entering the market. Meanwhile, further attempts to learn from the problems encountered during China's brief experiment with liberalized fertilizer marketing policies have been placed on hold.

III. GRAIN SECTOR SUBSIDY PROGRAMS

-Urban Ration Sales

36.   A modest source of revenue during the 1950s, the food distribution
system began suffering losses in the early-1960s as procurement and marketing
costs increased above sales revenue. With the substantial increases in
planned procurement prices and volume beginning in 1979, losses on the food
distribution system increased sharply and have become a major claim on
government finances (World Bank [1990b]). Estimates derived from government
expenditure data indicate that the annual outlays to finance the price
differentials between subsidized food sales (mainly grains) and related
official procurement averaged more than ¥ 25 billion during 1986-88,
accounting for more than 10% of total government expenditure and representing
more than six times government expenditure on capital construction in
agriculture. With the 18% increased in the contract procurement prices for
grain, expenditures on food subsidies reportedly surged to ¥ 41 billion in
1989.   Furthermore, government expenditure data substantially understate state
agencies' operating losses on the transport, handling and storage of food.
The true expenditures amounted to at least ¥ 30 billion annually during
1986-88, and at least ¥ 45 billion in 1989. The estimates also understate the
full economic value of consumer food subsidies since they do not include the
net loss of farm revenue on mandatory sales of farm products at below-market
planned procurement prices, estimated to have amounted to more than ¥ 23
billion in 1988. These large financial outlays and economic losses can not be
justified on equity grounds, since the principal recipients of the food
distribution system, *viz.*, the predominantly urban nonagricultural population,
enjoy levels of income and welfare which are unambiguously superior to that of
their rural counterparts.

37.   Financing and Fiscal Impact. Official figures for state budgetary
expenditure on price subsidies are presented in World Bank (1990b), Table 3
for 1978-88. In SSB (1989), these outlays are disaggregated for consumer
goods, farm inputs, and five subsidized imports. The first category, consumer
goods, mostly comprises subsidies for food items, including grain, vegetable
oil, vegetables, and some meats. The second category, subsidies for farm
inputs, represents the government's losses on providing farmers with
fertilizer, fuel and other inputs at below-cost planned prices. The third
category of subsidies, the five imports (grain, cotton, sugar, fertilizers and
pesticides) are also sold to urban consumers and rural producers at below-cost
planned prices.

38.   In Annex 3 Table 3, estimated state budgetary expenditure on food price
subsidies is compared to official figures for total state revenue and
expenditure, state capital investment in agriculture, and GDP. The comparison
indicates that such expenditure initially increased from 9% of total state
expenditure in 1979 to more than 22% in 1981, and then declined to about 10%
in 1988. Similarly, budgetary outlays for the subsidies were equivalent to
2.9% of GDP in 1979, nearly doubled to 5.6% of GDP in 1981, and then declined
to 1.9% of GDP by 1988. Cumulative budgetary outlay on food price subsidies
during the 1980s (¥ 224.2 billion) was nearly five times the shortfall between
government revenue and expenditure over the same period (¥ 48.1 billion), and

146

during 1979-1988 was six times the cumulative state capital investment in agriculture (¥ 39.7 billion), having increased from 185% of state capital investment in agriculture in 1979 to a peak of more than 1000% in 1981 before declining to about 560% in 1988.

Annex 3 Table 8   State Revenue and Expenditure, GDP and Consumer Food Subsidies, 1978-88

(billion yuan and %)

| | | State Expenditure | | | | Consumer Food Subsidies | | |
| | | | Capital Investment in | Revenue minus | | | as a percent of: | |
Year	State Revenue	Total	Agriculture	Expenditure	GDP	Value	State Expenditure	GDP
1978	112.1	111.1	5.1	1.0	358.8	na	na	na
1979	110.3	127.4	6.2	-17.1	400.0	11.5	9.0%	2.9%
1980	108.5	121.3	4.9	-12.8	447.2	17.2	14.2%	3.8%
1981	109.0	111.5	2.4	-2.5	477.5	25.0	22.4%	5.6%
1982	112.4	115.3	2.9	-2.9	518.6	24.3	21.1%	4.7%
1983	124.9	129.3	3.4	-4.4	578.5	26.3	20.3%	4.5%
1984	150.2	154.6	3.4	-4.5	692.4	28.3	18.3%	4.1%
1985	186.6	184.5	3.8	2.2	854.1	26.1	14.1%	3.1%
1986	226.0	233.1	3.7 /a	-7.1	972.0	24.7	10.6%	2.5%
1987	236.9	244.9	4.3 /a	-8.0	1135.7	25.9	10.6%	2.3%
1988	258.8	266.8	4.7 /a	-8.1	1385.8	26.4	9.9%	1.9%

Source: State revenue and expenditure data and GDP estimates from SSB (1989). Consumer food subsidies from World Bank (1990b), Table 3.

/a Figures are total capital investment (in the case of agriculture, "total" closely approximates state capital investment).

39.   Since only that portion of state agencies' gross operating losses which is reimbursed by the government is included, however, the official figures for price subsidies understate the true fiscal cost of consumer subsidies to the extent that gross operating losses exceed reimbursed losses. The difference between gross and reimbursed losses is substantial, amounting to at least ¥ 5 billion in recent years. Together with the GGB's operating losses, the 18% hike in the average procurement price for grain in 1989 and moderate increases in procurement volume reportedly pushed the total financial expenditure by state agencies on the provision subsidized foods to ¥ 45 billion or more.

40.   There also are food subsidies administered by municipalities and provinces. In early-1988, many urban recipients were provided with new monthly allowances of at least ¥ 7.5 to offset price increases for government supplied pork, sugar and vegetables. The annual cost of the new allowances probably amounts to ¥ 16 billion. Some municipalities also provide additional subsidies for grain consumption. Though the proportion is unknown, it is likely that official figures for price subsidies include only a small share of these amounts.

41.   Economic Impact. The estimated financial costs presented above significantly understate the full economic value of subsidies on grain and vegetable oil. Most importantly, estimated financial costs do not include the

loss of potential farm revenue on mandatory sales of farm products at below-market planned procurement prices. Rough estimates of the loss of farm revenue on mandatory grain sales (no official figures are available), shown in World Bank (1990b), Table 6 for each year 1985-88, indicate that the **gross** loss of farm revenue on mandatory grain sales increased from about ¥ 7.8 billion in 1985 to ¥ 34.6 billion in 1988. Since mandatory procurement volumes declined modestly after 1985, this sharp increase in lost revenue corresponds solely to the widening of the divergence between contract procurement and free market prices. Since roughly one-third of the grain procured by the GGB at mandatory contract prices is resold to the rural population (mostly at the contract price plus a small marketing margin), the **net** loss to the rural sector on mandatory grain sales (para 42) has been estimated as two-thirds of the gross loss. **11/**

42. <u>Welfare Effects</u>. Though not initially designed or intended as a means of redistributing income or alleviating poverty, the state-run food distribution system has evolved into a powerful redistributive force with enormous consequences for urban and rural welfare. The system now has a strong and unambiguously regressive impact on income distribution, principally by reducing rural income through procurement of grain and other agricultural products at below-market prices and by augmenting urban income through provision of these foods to the nonagricultural population at below-cost ration prices. The **net** loss of farm revenue on mandatory grain sales **12/** is estimated to have been ¥ 23.0 billion in 1988 (World Bank [1990b], Table 6), equivalent to ¥ 26 per rural inhabitant and more than 4% of 1988 average rural per capita income. This also is equivalent to about ¥ 105 per urban food ration recipient, or almost 10% of 1988 average urban per capita income. The distributional impact of this implied transfer of income is to <u>increase</u> inequality since, relative to their rural counterparts, the urban population has long enjoyed superior levels of income and food intake and greater access to health, education and other social services. **13/**

43. Since consumer food subsidies are equitably distributed to all registered nonagricultural citizens, the system does achieve a modest reduction in income inequality within the nonagricultural population and significantly increases the real income of urban residents with below average income. However, roughly one-third of the urban population, numbering 116 million people at present, is not entitled to food subsidies. According to estimates shown in World Bank (1990b), para 3.14, the **financial** value of the subsidies on ration grain in 1988 was at least ¥ 125 per recipient. Average per capita income among the lowest income decile, ¥ 627 (nominal) in 1988, was

---

11/ Further, the interest on working capital paid by the GGB may understate the economic opportunity cost of this working capital by three-fold or more. At an annualized interest rate of 4%, the GGB paid ¥ 2.4 billion in interest on working capital in 1987, or roughly 25% of total operating losses in that year of more than ¥ 9 billion. At a discount rate of 12%, the economic opportunity cost of the GGB's working capital was about ¥8 billion in 1987.

12/ Computed by deducting the estimated value of the official rural resales of subsidized grain to farm households.

13/ The food distribution system also redistributes income within the rural and urban sectors (World Bank [1990b], para 3.12).

just slightly more than half the national average but only 30% of that of the highest income decile households (¥ 2093). Thus, the estimated financial value of the subsidies on ration grain was the equivalent of more than 20% of the average per capita income (nominal) of the lowest income households, 11% of the average for the nonagricultural population as a whole, but only 6% of that of the highest income households. These figures indicate that the grain subsidies do significantly increase the real income of the lowest income members of the nonagricultural population, are not inconsequential to those with average income, but are of little importance to households with high per capita income.

44.   From the standpoint of an incomes policy, however, the important comparison would be with the status of rural population. Though the food distribution system does significantly increase the real income of the registered lower-income nonagricultural residents, available evidence suggests that a reduction of food subsidies would not depress the physical well-being of this group below levels deemed acceptable for the vast majority of China's population. In 1988, even the lowest-income nonagricultural residents enjoyed 15% more income (¥ 627 versus ¥ 545 respectively) and consumed 15% more vegetable oil (5.5 kg versus 4.8 kg), 27% more red meat (13.6 kg versus 10.7 kg), and 117% more eggs (5.0 kg versus 2.3 kg) per capita than the average rural inhabitant, which constitutes an important income buffer by Chinese standards (¥ 82) and has stimulated a considerably greater consumption of preferred foods across all levels of income by urban residents.

45.   Government Sponsored Reforms. Well aware of the enormous financial and economic losses and serious price distortions engendered by the food distribution system, the government has actively experimented with and implemented a variety of reform measures. Financial losses and price distortions on state supplied nonstaple foods have been largely controlled through a combination of increases in planned retail prices (beginning in 1979), subsequent conversion of "allowances" for these price increases to regular government and enterprise wages, and a gradual reduction of sales volume at planned prices. In addition to capping government losses and reducing price distortions, these reforms directly and indirectly encouraged the rapid growth of free market trade of animal and aquatic products, vegetables and fruits, and other nonstaple foods during the 1980s. In contrast to subsidies on nonstaple foods, however, subsidies on grain and vegetable oil continued to increase during the late-1980s. Government sponsored reforms of grain and vegetable oil subsidies, first implemented at the national level in 1985 and, on an experimental basis, in a number of regional pilot areas in more recent years, include (a) reducing the volume of sales at planned retail prices and (b) increasing planned retail prices.

46.   The government eliminated sales of grain and vegetable oil at planned prices to the food processing industry and reduced such sales to the feed industry on a national basis in 1985. However, national level data suggest that the reduction in sales volume at planned prices was only moderate. 14/ In

---

14/ It is estimated that distribution at planned prices declined from 77.5 million tons in 1984 to 65.2 million tons in 1987 (World Bank [1990b], Appendix 1, Table 1).

several regional experiments where more comprehensive reductions were introduced, the savings were subsequently offset in the face of rising consumer prices by salary supplements, new forms of cross-subsidization, or a return to the *status quo ante* in response to pressure from local residents.

47.   The first major reform of the **planned sales prices** of grain and vegetable oil was in 1985 when, in conjunction with the adoption of the contract procurement system, prices for the majority of planned rural resales were increased from the old "quota" price (plus a small marketing margin) to the new contract price (plus a small marketing margin). This change effectively increased the planned sales price for most rural resales by about two-thirds, and contributed to a temporary decline in the government's losses on grain and vegetable oil subsidies in 1985. In a number of subsequent reform experiments, the value of the subsidy to the nonagricultural population was made explicit by (a) monetizing the value of the subsidy as a direct income transfer while (b) bringing the planned urban retail price of grain and vegetable oil in line with free market retail prices. However, these experimental reforms have yet to be evaluated and woven into national policy.

-Fertilizer Subsidies

48.   Most agricultural inputs in China benefit from direct or cross-subsidization in one form or other. While small in comparison with subsidies in the food distribution system, fertilizers remain heavily subsidized and account for the major share of input subsidies at the farm level. The subsidies accrue in different forms, **15/** but broadly, fall within six categories. **Production subsidies** and tax incentives are given primarily to old, inefficient and small fertilizer plants with high production costs in order to compensate for financial losses. These subsidies are financed by provincial and/or county level governments. **Import subsidies**, offered sporadically, are determined by China's annual fertilizer import bills as well as by the profits earned by SINOCHEM. **Transportation subsidies** are advanced to maintain pan-national retail price levels for centrally managed fertilizers. **Subsidies to disaster areas**, consisting *inter-alia* of free or heavily subsidized supplementary fertilizer allocations, depend upon the nature and seriousness of the natural disaster. **Price subsidies** are applied to fertilizers sold at plan prices or linked with grain procurement and other official programs. **Interest subsidies** are in the form of interest foregone on production advances to farmers (equivalent to 20% of estimated crop procurement value) to facilitate fertilizer purchases.

49.   While some kinds of fertilizers, organizations and kinds of farmers, particular crops and even specific locales are subsidized, others are taxed. This tax revenue is used to finance many of the subsidies, by requiring (and ensuring) that most of the commercial agencies involved in fertilizer production, imports and marketing do not suffer heavy financial losses in the process of implementing government policy.

15/ Some are direct, others are indirect. Some are transparent and others are not. Some aim to benefit farmers, others are for the fertilizer manufacturing industry.

50.   Cost of Fertilizer Subsidies. The cost of fertilizer subsidy is born by
different levels of government (national, provincial, county) for different
fertilizers. Although input and output prices are now being controlled again,
it is extremely difficult to estimate the true financial and economic costs of
China's fertilizer subsidies since the various levels of government are
permitted to accrue tax revenues or pay subsidies in response to movements in
CIF prices and the exchange rates quoted in China's 60 or so regional exchange
rate adjustment centers. Both have been fluctuating a great deal recently.
Nonetheless, according to the central AIC, total subsidization in the
fertilizer sector during 1988 amounted to ¥ 7.1 billion (next table). Included
in the estimate is the 3-linkage subsidy for fertilizer, about ¥ 1.0 billion
in 1988, but coverage through cross-subsidization of the sizable share of
gross operating losses within the fertilizer importing and distribution
agencies (e.g. SINOCHEM, the AICs and SMCs) is excluded. When the final
figures become available, the volume of subsidization during 1989 and 1990 is
expected to be even higher due to an increased volume of fertilizer imports
and consumption, and no corresponding increase in plan prices.

Type of Fertilizer Subsidy	1988 Cost of Fertilizer Subsidy /a
Import Subsidies	¥ 2.1 billion or $0.565 billion
Other Direct/Indirect Subsidies	¥ 5.0 billion or $1.344 billion
Total Subsidy	¥ 7.1 billion or $1.91 billion

/a Estimated at official exchange rate of US$ 1 = ¥ 3.72.

IV.   GRAIN SECTOR EXPENDITURES AND FINANCING

51.   Public Sector Financing Channels. Public investment in agriculture, as
in other sectors, is financed by three main methods: from on-budget
allocations directed by the central government (which includes allocations to
be administered by provincial governments), off-budget allocations derived
from provincial and municipal government revenues, and self-raised funds from
state farms and agricultural collectives and cooperatives. Though allocated to
the agriculture sector as a whole, most are being directed to support the
government's grain production programs. Budgetary expenditures, strictly
defined, are supplemented by funds provided by the State-owned banks, which
sometimes administer budgetary allocations for a fee, and also intermediate
deposits and other loanable funds in accord with official lending priorities.
Though the finance bureaux at various levels continue to play an important
role in channeling appropriations to project entities, much of the on-budget
funds for capital investment is increasingly channelled through the People's
Construction Bank of China at subsidized interest rates. (This represents a
significant shift in public sector financing policy: in 1981, only 13% of
total State fixed investment was loan financed and 28% came from the central
budget, in 1987, the corresponding figures were 23% and 13% respectively).
Funds for crop purchase, working capital and medium term investments are also
channelled through the Agricultural Bank of China (ABC) and the Industrial and
Commercial Bank of China (ICBC), which sometimes serve as commissioned agents

for public sector appropriations.

52.   In recent years a number of special funds have been established which have been earmarked mainly for grain production programs. These include, for example, the Working Capital Fund, the Grain Production Development Fund, the Irrigation Fund, the Fund for Assistance to Underdeveloped Regions, the Fund for Land Reclamation, Clearing and Transformation, and the Agricultural Development Fund (ADF - established in 1987 and intended to support the production of grain, cotton and oil seed). Some of these funds were established with budgetary appropriations, some with earmarked taxation (e.g., land conversion fees), and some with retained and/or deducted income from enterprises operating in these areas of activity.

53.   In 1989 the Central Committee and the SPC decided to allocate yet more funds for grain sector programs using the mechanism of state budget adjustment. The objective is to raise at least ¥ 12 billion, of which 10% (i.e., ¥ 1.2 billion) would be earmarked for agriculture and administered through the ADF. It is MOF's desire to move many of the existing funds "on-budget" and consolidate these under the ADF umbrella. Presently, the ADF is financed through six channels: from budgetary adjustment which is a 10% surcharge on off-budgetary expenditures by local governments; 16/ by taxes on TVEs (production tax, value added tax, business tax and sales tax); from agricultural land conversion fees; from ad valorem taxes on specialized agriculture and forestry products; from incremental income taxes on self-employed individuals in rural areas as well as from private businesses; and from taxes on grain distribution (the "agricultural technology up-grading fee") raised on grain procured at negotiated prices. 17/ For the Eighth Five Year Plan the ADF target is reported to be ¥ 2-3 billion per annum.

54.   The previous trend of declining nominal public sector spending for agricultural has been reversed since 1985, but as a proportion of total state expenditure, agriculture's share has continued to follow a declining trend during the last ten years (World Bank [1990h], Table 1). Total social investment 18/ in capital construction for agriculture has increased in nominal terms during the same period (World Bank [1990h], Tables 1 and 2) but capital investment in other sectors of the economy has expanded far more rapidly, so that agriculture's share of public sector investment has fallen considerably from 7.0% during 1980-83 to 3.2% during 1985-88 (World Bank [1990h], Table 2). In real terms, the decline in the trend of State capital investment in agriculture over the reform period has been dramatic (World Bank [1990h], Table 3). Investment in "water conservation" (i.e., irrigation and drainage) which takes the lion's share of agricultural capital construction

---

16/ Thus the central government claws back from local governments an amount equivalent to part of the increase in their off-budget spending (e.g., on hotel construction).

17/ This tax is levied by the finance bureaux at all stages in the grain distribution chain from processing to final consumption, and is remitted by the processing/ handling enterprises, not by farmers.

18/ "Total social" investment includes "State" investment and estimates of investment by subprovincial units. The two series often are inconsistent.

investment dropped for four successive years (1983 through 1986) and the increase in the last two years will not have restored it to much more than two thirds of its nominal level in 1979 (World Bank [1990h], Table 3).

55.   With an increasing proportion of output coming from TVEs, 19/ and with the decentralization of financial controls to the lower levels of administration, central government's monopoly over enterprise revenue and investment has been relinquished. While agricultural taxes have remained fixed at very low levels and generate uncertain yields, investment in commercial and industrial development has represented a much more attractive use of funds for local governments. There has also been a sharp reduction in investment funds accumulated by the collectives. 20/ The introduction of the PRS denied collectives the ability to extract economic surpluses through the work point system. Similarly, with most rural labor now under household management it is much less easy to mobilize work forces on a large scale to maintain and develop agriculture infrastructure. Capital investment represented by labor "accumulation" is thus now at a much lower level than previously, one estimate putting it at only a quarter of what it used to be before the reforms (Watson 1989).

56.   Present Government Policy. Government has recently taken steps to ensure a greater allocation of investment resources to the agricultural sector, particularly for grain production. In October 1988, the State Council publicized its resolution to secure an increased level of agricultural output, especially, grain production, in 1989 and stressed its commitment to higher capital investment for the sector. Three main initiatives were announced which remain in force:

(a)   agriculture's share of the on-budget fixed capital investment would be gradually increased;

(b)   support for agricultural development programs in general and the state's grain sector initiatives in particular would be increased in terms of the proportion of the national government's total outlay so allocated; and

(c)   local governments (provincial and below) would be requested to increase the proportion of their total expenditure allocated to agriculture.

57.   Through the establishment of the various special funds, which effectively transfer off-budget resources onto the budget to finance agricultural investment, and directives to funding agencies, the Government appears to be strengthening centralized control over investment planning for agriculture.

19/ As compared to state-owned enterprises.

20/ In Chinese parlance, the "collective" is a generic term for units of local administration and their service agencies.

(Local branches of banks have hitherto been more accustomed to being given financing priorities by local governments, and the latter have not put agriculture high enough up the list). Central Government also appears to be concentrating mostly on investment to support grain production. It is unclear how much priority is being given to investment in grain handling, storage and distribution, but the indications are that this is considered to be of secondary importance compared with maintaining and increasing primary production capacity. There are also signs that the concept of regional self-sufficiency in grain is being resurrected as an essential component of agricultural strategy.

58. <u>Agricultural Credit</u>. Lending to the rural sector from the state banks and credit cooperatives has expanded rapidly in recent years, and is now one of the main sources of capital for grain sector investment. Much is in the form of directed credits, though local branches also are allowed to intermediate deposits and other non-governmental resources within the credit priorities established by Government. The biggest single source of deposits is individual households and the proportion of funds from this source in total deposits has also increased very rapidly in the last few years (World Bank [1990h], Tables 5 and 6). However the great bulk of lending by ABC goes to commerce and industry: 65% of outstanding loans as of the end of 1988. Lending for agricultural purposes represented 11.5% of ABC's outstanding loans (excluding loans to Rural Credit Cooperatives) in 1988. In contrast, 41% of outstanding loans as of the end of 1988 from the Rural Credit Cooperatives (RCC) were with farmers, but because of the much greater resources controlled by the ABC total lending to farmers through RCC (¥ 37.3 billion) was smaller than through the ABC (¥ 86.8 billion). Between them the ABC and RCCs account for virtually all formal sector direct lending to China's agriculturalists.

59.   Details of the term structure of ABC's lending indicate that 89.1% of its portfolio at end-1988 was in short-term loans (World Bank [1990h], Table 7). Roughly the same figure obtained for direct lending to individuals, most of whom presumably are farmers. Details for the RCCs are not available, though various Bank missions have been advised that nearly all of the RCCs' lending matures within one year or less. Though the percentages approved for medium and longer term (MLT) maturities are small, the figures are somewhat misleading in that ABC and the RCC are very conservative--farmer's reportedly feel compelled to use short maturities to finance purchases of machinery and other agricultural assets that are normally considered to be investment items. In spite of this the total increase in the volume of MLT loans being serviced by ABC during 1988 (¥ 3.91 billion--net of the increase in outstanding MLT loans to TVEs) is nearly equivalent to State financial expenditure for capital construction in agriculture. Since ABC's short-term assets account for only about 78% of its total assets (World Bank [1990h], Table 7) and longer-term resources exceed outstanding MLT loans by more than twice, ABC could comfortably double its current total volume of MLT loans (¥ 28.7 billion at end-1988) so long as its liquidity is maintained, maturities are kept aligned with the structure of longer term resources, and current credit restrictions

are not violated. **21/**   World Bank (1990h), paras 3.05-3.12 reviews the determinants of credit demand.

21/ ABC also provides preproduction crop financing to farmers to 20% of the value of contracted production (World Bank [1990h], Table 8).

Agricultural Sector Performance Projections

CHINA

OPTIONS FOR REFORM IN THE GRAIN SECTOR

Agricultural Sector Performance Projections

Table of Contents

AGRICULTURAL SECTOR PERFORMANCE PROJECTIONS

I. INTRODUCTION

1.   In consideration of the growing influence of market forces in
agriculture, even in the grain sector; of the increasing exposure of
agriculture to international price trends; the changing structure of demand in
China; and the partially "suppressed" pressures on the supply side to
reallocate land and other productive resources to higher-valued production
activities, a projections model (referred to below as the "MAT-1 model") was
developed by staff to show the effects of bifurcation in China's internal
grain markets when estimating the level and composition of both future demand
and future supply and to present more robust projections of production and
grain-based feed requirements in the livestock sector. Crude projections also
were made of subsidies and agricultural investment requirements.

2.   An adaptation of an agricultural sector simulation model developed by
staff during appraisal of the Rural Sector Adjustment Loan (RSAL: Ln. 2967-
CHA/Cr. 1932-CHA), [1] the MAT-1 model features relationships for production,
consumption and foreign trade in 17 agricultural commodities, and is driven by
own- and cross-price elasticities and various demand and supply shifters
(income and population growth, productivity increases). It solves for
quantities produced, consumed and traded, and domestic producer and consumer
prices. Border prices, transmission effects and price wedges, and exchange
rates are inputted exogenously. The model was improved for this study's
projections by mapping the operation of China's fragmented grain markets on
both the supply and demand side for major grains, by introducing intermediate
feed conversion activities to link final demand for livestock products with
the production and availability of feed grains, and by revalidation using
updated (1985-1987) input data. Projections to 1995 were made under several
assumptions concerning grain pricing policies, foreign trade policies,
productivity improvement and general macroeconomic growth. Performance during
the base period (1985-87) and summary indicators of projected sectoral
performance are shown in Table 1. Being elasticity driven, [2] its results are
subject to the usual estimation errors, which are probably magnified for an
agricultural sector that is as large and diverse as China's. For these
reasons, projections are made only until 1995, perhaps sufficient for this
report but clearly inadequate for an administration used to thinking in terms
of decades. Other features of this projection framework are discussed below.

II. DEMAND OUTLOOK AND DOMESTIC CONSUMPTION PROSPECTS

-Income Elasticities

3.   Direct Demand. Household income and expenditure data from large scale
SSB surveys of the urban and rural populations indicate that national average

---

[1] The model and its formulation are described in World Bank (1988), Annex 3.

[2] cf. Appendix for supply and demand elasticities employed by the model.

direct consumption of table grain peaked in 1984 at 257 kg per capita and then declined by about 3% to 249 kg per capita in 1988 (in unprocessed grain equivalent, cf. World Bank [1990a], Table 1). The decline in urban direct per capita consumption of grain has been sustained and pronounced, having fallen a total of 18% from 167 kg (in trade grain equivalent) in 1957 to 145 kg in 1981 to 137 kg in 1988 according to the State Statistical Bureau (SSB) data. Using the direct per capita grain consumption data shown in Table 2 of World Bank (1990a) for the period 1981-88 and urban per capita income from the same SSB surveys (expressed in constant 1980 yuan), simple regression analysis indicates that the urban income elasticity of direct consumption of grain (quantity, not expenditure) is about -0.2 (R^2 of 0.75). The regression analysis also suggests that trends in the retail price of grain explained very little of the decline in urban direct per capita grain consumption. [3]

4.   The trend in rural direct per capita consumption of grain is, by comparison, more difficult to discern. Rural direct consumption appears to have increased by 8% from 248 kg per capita (unprocessed grain equivalent) in 1978 to a peak of 267 kg in 1984 and then declined by 3% to 260 kg in 1988. As suggested by the figures below, the decline in direct per capita grain consumption has been more pronounced and has extended over a longer period of time in higher income rural areas relative to less well-off areas:

	Direct Consumption of Unprocessed Grain (kg/capita)			Average per Capita Income as percent of 1988 National Average
	1980	1984	1988	
Beijing (high income)	272	229	221	195%
Gansu (low income)	232	237	232	62%
Guangxi (low income)	256	277	244	78%

Source: SSB (1989), SSB (1987), Gansu Statistical Bureau (1987) and
          Guangxi Statistical Bureau (1989).

Using SSB household survey data for direct per capita grain consumption and per capita income (expressed in constant 1980 yuan) for 1978-88, simple regression analysis indicates that the rural income elasticity of direct consumption of grain (quantity, not expenditure) is about -0.06 at current levels of income (R^2 of 0.59). At the lower 1980 level of per capita income, on the other hand, the estimated income elasticity was 0.08. Also in rural areas, the regression analysis suggests that trends in the retail price of grain explained very little of the variation in direct grain consumption. [4]

---

[3]   Data and regression results are summarized in World Bank (1990a), Appendix 2.

[4]   cf. World Bank (1990a), Appendix 2.

5.   Income elasticities of direct demand for grain have also been estimated from cross sectional data from the SSB household surveys. Previous studies have mostly focused on the income elasticity of expenditure on grain; using expenditure data disaggregated by income group, van der Gaag (1984: 0.11 for Beijing in 1982) and World Bank (1987: 0.34 for Fuzhou and 0.45 for Tianjin in 1984) estimated positive income elasticities of expenditure on grain for urban populations. Since much of the increase in expenditure on grain as income rises is due to an increase in price paid for grain, [5]/ their estimated expenditure elasticities overstate the income elasticity of demand for grain measured in physical quantity terms. Urban and rural income elasticities of direct demand for grain (measured in physical quantity terms) have been reestimated for this study in World Bank (1990a) using cross sectional data from the 1988 SSB household surveys. Simple regression analysis of the cross sectional data grouped by absolute income indicates that the urban income elasticity of direct demand for grain is -0.33 at current levels of income (R^2 square of 0.77). Regression analysis of the data grouped by relative income indicates an income elasticity of direct demand of 0.15 (R^2 of 0.89). However, household expenditure data available for Xinxiang City (Henan) allow for correction of the confounding influence of household size, number of employed family members, and the number of non-family members who regularly eat meals at the family's home. Regression analysis of the Xinxiang data (grouped by relative income) indicates an income elasticity of demand for grain of -0.33 (adjusted R^2 of 0.86).

6.   Unfortunately, the SSB does not report rural income and consumption data disaggregated by income groups. Instead, rural income elasticities of demand have been derived from the SSB's provincial disaggregation of rural income and consumption data summarized in World Bank (1990a), Table 5. In contrast to a moderately negative elasticity (-0.06) estimated from time series data, simple regression analysis of the cross sectional data generates a moderately positive rural income elasticity of direct demand for grain of 0.13 at current levels of income (R^2 of 0.33).

7.   Indirect Demand. Indirect consumption of grain as animal feed is estimated to have tripled from 28 kg per capita in 1970 to 95 kg per capita in 1988. In sharp contrast to the expected continued decline in direct per capita consumption of grain, expected strong demand for animal products will continue to push up indirect demand for feed grain. The SSB time series and cross section sample survey data have been used to estimate the following income elasticities of demand for animal products for the urban and rural populations:

---

[5]/ SSB household survey data for 1988 indicate that consumers with the highest incomes paid about 20% more per kg of grain than did consumers with the lowest incomes (¥ 0.59/kg and ¥ 0.50 respectively).

	Urban		Rural	
	Time Series	Cross Section	Time Series	Cross Section
Pork	0.19	0.54	na	na
Beef & Mutton	1.50	0.72	na	na
Pork, Beef & Mutton	0.34	0.57	0.73	0.26
Poultry	1.66	0.93	1.48	2.16
Eggs	0.52	0.58	1.06	1.66
Fish	0.04	0.59	0.89	4.54

Source: Estimated from SSB (1989) household income and expenditure data.

As a function of the feed conversion ratios (FCRs) reported in Table 3 of World Bank (1990a) and expected growth in per capita income, these strongly positive estimated income elasticities of demand suggest continued rapid growth in demand for feed grain.

-Price Elasticities

8.   Price changes moderate differences between the supply and demand of grain as a function of own and cross price elasticities of both supply and demand. However, the state imposes restrictions on free market trade in grain, administers prices for a large share of commercial grain trade, and enforces mandatory grain procurement quotas. [6/] These practices affect the smooth functioning of the price mechanism, and it is difficult to predict the impact of price changes and reforms with certainty. In her theoretical analysis of the interaction between agricultural markets and state commercial planning, Sicular (1988a; pp. 285-286) concludes that "in the presence of markets, producers and consumers will look at market prices, not state prices and quotas, in allocating their resources" and "although state prices and quotas do not affect production and consumption directly, they nevertheless influence them indirectly through their effects on the distribution of income and equilibrium market prices." In the rural sector, more than half of the grain procured by the government is purchased at below market planned prices. The government's intervention in rural sales of grain is, by comparison, moderate. Sicular's analysis suggests that future changes in the rural free market price of grain and reforms of the volume and price of planned grain procurement will affect rural grain supply and demand both directly, since the free market price is the effective marginal price for most surplus grain producers and most rural consumers, and indirectly, since the government planned procurement price affects rural income and, hence, investment (in productive capacity) and consumption (as a function of the income elasticity of demand).

[6/] Grain marketing and prices are discussed in World Bank (1990g).

163

9.   In the urban sector, the government supplies more than 90% of the grain consumed by the registered urban population at planned "ration" prices which are only one-third to one-quarter of the urban free market price. It is the contention of this paper that the urban free market retail price of grain is the effective marginal price to urban consumers, and that changes to the free market price will directly affect urban demand for grain. Reform of the urban ration price of grain will affect urban demand only indirectly, through consequent changes in real income. [7/] Urban household income and expenditure survey data from Guangdong and Fujian for 1987 and 1988 strongly support the hypotheses that the subsidy element of grain ration coupons is now fully monetized and that substantial increases in ration prices (particularly when offset with compensating income transfers) will have negligible effects on grain consumption. Both provinces doubled the ration price of grain to urban consumers (ration recipients were compensated with offsetting wage payments) in early-1988. The urban household survey data indicate that, despite the sharp increase in ration prices, per capita grain consumption increased in Guangdong from 115.6 kg in 1987 to 117.7 kg in 1988 and in Fujian from 139.2 kg in 1987 to 139.7 kg in 1988 (Guangdong Statistical Bureau, 1989, and Fujian Statistical Bureau, 1989).

10.   In both the rural and urban sectors, changes in prices of animal products and other nongrain foods will affect the supply and demand of grain through cross price elasticities of demand and through demand for animal feed.

-Total Demand for Grain

11.   The MAT-1 simulation model projects total demand for grain from the base period of 1985/87 to 1995 as a function of expected growth in per capita income (up 42%) and population (up 11%), [8/] expected changes in the urban and rural distribution of total population (from 28% urban and 72% rural in the base period to 35% urban and 65% rural in 1995), estimated income elasticities of demand and FCRs, and endogenous real price movements. [9/] The base run assumes moderate growth in agricultural productivity and per capita incomes (notes to Table 1), essentially free international trade in non-grain products (but maintenance of China's overvalued exchange rate), a partial liberalization of China's foreign trade in grains, and maintenance of China's bifurcated internal grain markets with real prices for contract procurement and rationed sales (the administered segment of these markets) maintained at their real 1986 levels. The other scenarios are based on several modifications to base run assumptions as indicated in the notes to Table 1. At constant 1986 prices, the model's base run solution projects total demand for grain to increase by 19% to 482 million tons in 1995, including an 11% increase in

---

7/   Consumer food subsidies and their impact on urban welfare and income are discussed in Annex 3.

8/   National figures comprise expected increases in urban and rural per capita income of 38% and 30% respectively and increases in urban and rural population of 39% and 0.3% respectively.

9/   The income elasticities of demand used in the model are compared with estimates derived by Wiens (1987) and from Taiwan in World Bank (1990a), Table 7. The feed conversion ratios used in the model are compared with USDA (1987) estimated FCRs in World Bank (1990a), Appendix 1.

direct demand for table grain and a 55% increase in indirect demand as animal feed. The revealed composite per capita income elasticity of total demand for grain is 0.17, comprising income elasticities of direct demand for grain of 0.01 and indirect demand as animal feed of 0.94. Total utilization of grain in 1995, after equilibrating supply and demand of grain through a combination of international trade and price changes in the base run of the model, is projected to be 471 million tons (Table 2).

-Per Capita Direct Consumption and Nutrition

12.   Several variants were run to estimate the effects of different configurations in sectoral policy and general economic performance on per capita consumption balances. The results are shown in Table 3.

13.   Comparing both the base run and other projection scenarios with base period values (actual 1985-1987 performance), the most striking result is the projected general constancy in the direct per capita consumption of grains once more rational pricing policies are introduced, and the strong stimulus given to consumption of animal products. This occurs in both the rural areas, where the direct consumption of grains continues to be higher than in urban areas, and in urban areas (where consumption of meats and fish continues to be higher). A doubling of the administered prices for grains in the absence of other policy changes (second scenario) would have strikingly little effect on performance in the real sector, [10]/ no doubt because about only 1/8 of total grain consumed and produced in China passes through the official channels at the ration sales and contract procurement prices). However, the conjoint influence of per capita income growth and the productivity assumptions on the intake of livestock products is profound (contrast scenarios 3 and 4 with the base run).

14.   In all of the scenarios, the projected small decline in direct consumption of rice remains basically invariant to the policy and technical assumptions made. This confirms the findings in Annex 2, that as a result of China's already successful production policies, China's consumers have become awash in rice, and if given an opportunity, would simply reduce their overall intake. Demand for wheat, on the other hand, would increase. Under all of the scenarios, further improvements in China's already remarkable standards of nutrition could be expected to occur, with the least improvement being associated with a prolonged economic recession (Table 4). Mapping present (1986) patterns, the urban diet would be better furnished with proteins and fats than would diets of rural people, whereas the latter would continue to consume more calories per capita than urban residents. This no doubt is a reflection of higher per capita incomes in urban areas and the workings of China's income elasticities of demand for agricultural products.

10/ Though it could have fairly profound financial implications (para 23).

III. AGGREGATE SUPPLY PROSPECTS

15.   Projected grain demand would be met from three sources: domestic production, net imports and stocks. China will have to depend on all three sources but their relative importance will be dictated by economic conditions in China and on the world grain markets, and by the political and food security concerns of national leaders. [11]   Based on projected demand of 471 million tons in 1995 and current (1989) production of about 407 million tons, China would have to expand grain production by about 65 million tons between 1990 and 1995 to fully meet the projected consumption requirement from domestic production. Considering the volume of investment and expenditure required, this doesn't appear feasible, although on strictly technical grounds, it could possibly be achieved by the Year 2000. [12]

16.   An analysis of technical production possibilities provides an important dimension to analysis of the supply problem, but does not address opportunity costs and therefore can't address issues of economic feasibility and sustainability. Runs of the MAT-1 model are therefore employed for this purpose. The array of production projections corresponding with the study's policy scenarios are set forth in Table 5. In all but the recession scenarios, a considerable expansion of grain production is projected, corresponding with growth rates in output value of between 1.9 and 2.1% p.a. Indeed, under the most optimistic of the "recovery" scenarios, grain production is projected to reach 472.8 million tons (perhaps because the MAT-1 framework is not resource constrained.) In all of the scenarios, however, the results appear to be driven about equally by demand and the assumed productivity increases. This is shown by the similar results of the two "recovery/trade reform" scenarios, where the first one assumes higher productivity growth than the second, but the latter contains higher income growth, devaluation and unrestricted free trade in agricultural products. [13]

17.   The scenarios most closely resembling the grain policy situation during the base period are the "recession" scenarios in Table 5, especially the second one: "general economic recession" (one can admittedly quibble with the terminology). This scenario features productivity growth that is marginally lower than the average of the past two decades, a moderate devaluation (which occurred *de facto* after 60 or so regional exchange adjustment centers were established in 1986-88), but maintenance of import restrictions. Here, total grain production by Chinese reckoning of 449.0 million tons represents annual grain production growth of "only" 1.53% p.a. between 1986-95, which admittedly compares well with international trends, but is considerably less than the 5.0% p.a. average annual increase realized by China during the first half of

---

11/ Grain stocks were rather low in 1986-88 by Chinese standards (though quite high by international standards), but the procurement and storage system reportedly has again been overwhelmed by the record harvest in 1989, with a considerable volume of surplus grain being kept on-farm in makeshift stores as it was after the previous record harvest in 1984.

12/ Technical production possibilities are reviewed in World Bank (1990c).

13/ Though not shown in Table 5, increased exports account for the fillip given to rice production, while the decreased production of animal feeds is made up through an expansion of feed imports and an attenuation of livestock exports to service strong internal demand.

the 1980s. There would be, however, an expansion of vegetable production by almost 20 million tons, partially in response to foreign demand, but mainly in response to the assumed low growth in per capita incomes, whose production would be availed by an increase in the multiple cropping index from 146 in 1986 to 154 in 1995.

18.   The implications of this comparison are sobering. Were China to maintain basically current restrictions on grain marketing and foreign trade in grains, the likely result will be a continued frustration of its longer-term grain and livestock sectoral production objectives. To the extent that yield increases at the farm level also reflect market forces, through the link between the uptake of superior technologies and "revealed" profitability, the productivity growth assumptions in this scenario may not be too far off the mark under the current policy environment. Further, as shown below in Section IV, these disappointing results would likely occur in an environment of escalating market prices. Implications from the "recovery" scenarios are equally sobering: being essentially "market" or demand driven, it will not be enough for China's agricultural sector to produce only what can be produced. For example, the expansion of rice exports and comparatively limited importation of other agricultural commodities to satisfy an increasingly powerful internal market, will require upgrades in quality on a broad scale. In rice, for example, China has proved its ability to secure very high yields, but the bulk of production is low quality, a result of breeding deficiencies (especially hybrids) and poor post-harvest care. In the face of strong competition from the USA, Thailand, most recently from Vietnam and quite likely from Burma in the future, it may prove very difficult for China to regain entry in international rice markets on a broad scale using its current varieties, post-harvest and grading procedures.

IV. DOMESTIC PRICE PROSPECTS

19.   Projections of domestic agricultural prices were made using the MAT-1 model. Summary trends under various policy scenarios, in constant 1986 prices, are shown on the left hand side of Table 6. A comparison of these trends with projected movements in international prices is shown on the right hand side of the table for the base run. Not surprisingly, the projections mirror the results of the volumetric projections discussed above, for consumption, production and China's foreign grain trade.

20.   In all of the scenarios, the domestic prices of wheat and coarse grain prices, and especially the prices of livestock products are projected to increase in real terms. Livestock and feed grain (i.e. coarse grain) prices are sensitive to a slow down in per capita income growth and productivity growth (the two "recession" scenarios). Domestic rice prices, on the other hand, are projected to decline under all scenarios, a reflection of the currently saturated rice market in China and limited export opportunities for China's low quality rice. The results also show that if constrained growth in trend prices is an important objective of grain sector policy, the least disruptive scenario would be to raise contract procurement and urban ration prices (scenario 2) without further adjustments to the trade regime for grains

and the real exchange rate. __14/__ Though there would be an opportunity cost: about 9.6 million tons annually in foregone grain production, more than 20 million tons in foregone consumption, and 5.8 million tons/year in foregone intake of livestock products (Table 5 - compare scenario 2 with the "recovery and trade policy reform" scenario). All of the projections suggest, however, that it is the consumption of animal products which will drive both the prices of feed _and_ food grains in the coming years, since the volumes of urban and rural per capita direct consumption are basically invariant across scenarios (Table 3) while the consumption of animal products and feedgrains are quite volatile. Further, the level of increased animal products consumption will largely determine (together with productivity growth) the size and composition of future increments in Chinese grain production.

21.   The ratios of projected trends in domestic wholesale prices to the Bank's international price projections (Table 6) again show that only marginal gains in the export market could be expected should China continue to stimulate the production of low quality rice. Expansion of wheat production, in the face of competing demands for agricultural land from maize, soybean and industrial crops, again is a high cost production strategy. Future demand increments, _ceteris paribus_, should continue to met by importations. These indices also reinforce the conclusion drawn above that China would be ill-advised to concentrate in the future as it has in the past on maize exportation as a policy objective, rather than using domestically produced maize to satisfy the growing internal demand for feedgrains, while meeting unfulfilled demand through lower cost imports. The comparisons suggest that the same may be said for soybeans should international prices continue to stiffen.

V. PROJECTED SUBSIDIES AND INVESTMENT REQUIREMENTS

22.   The total value of hidden consumer **subsidies** in 1985/87 ("1986"), measured with reference to domestic free market prices, was estimated to be ¥ 40.7 billion, nearly ¼ of the total value of agricultural output in that year (Table 7). This was partially offset by the indirect producer tax, implicit in the low contract procurement prices, which was estimated to be ¥ 19 billion or nearly ½ the value of hidden subsidies. __15/__ The associated opportunity cost to the economy in 1986, computed with reference to price differentials only, roughly made up the difference between the hidden subsidies and indirect tax (Table 7). __16/__

__14/__ Assuming that the moderate trends in agricultural productivity can be maintained and that growth of urban and rural per capita incomes won't diverge much from recent levels.

__15/__ Conceptually, these measures correspond roughly to total values of PSEs and CSEs estimated in World Bank (1990g), with market prices being used in place of border prices.

__16/__ It should be noted that this is an incomplete measure of the total cost of consumer subsidization borne by government. Omitted items include the coverage of grain bureaux' operating losses and foreign trade subsidies. The more comprehensive definition, encompassing total financial outlays of between   to ⅓ greater than the values shown in Table 7, is used in the discussion of subsidies in the main text and Annex 3.

23.   Real values of both the hidden subsidies and indirect producer taxes decline considerably when projections are made under the MAT-1 policy assumptions, as does the estimated opportunity cost to the economy. Not surprisingly, the biggest bite occurs through the simple expedient of doubling the administered prices associated with grain procurements and ration sales (though not the largest projected increase in GVAO): projection scenario 2 in Table 7. Even under the other scenarios, however, the projected opportunity cost to the economy declines somewhat, while the farming population would be the main beneficiaries--who respond to higher real incomes by increasing production, and urban consumers would be the main losers--due mainly to reduced subsidization and shifts in the commodity composition of consumption towards unsubsidized, higher valued products (Table 3).

24.   The average annual **investment** (between 1986-1995) needed to achieve the agricultural sector growth projections shown above, was computed using crude incremental capital-output ratios, that were constructed from a review of staff appraisal reports for agricultural projects in China and an assumed gestation period of 5 years. Thus the relative values shown in the last column of Table 7 may be a more reliable indicator than the value of the estimates per sé. There are two striking features in these estimates. First, a doubling of annual investment may be required to secure the additional GVAO shown between the agricultural recession scenario and the sustained recovery scenario, whereas more than half of the increment between these two scenarios could be achieved under base run assumptions (first scenario) with only slightly more than a 50% increase in annual investment outlays. From the vantage point of the MAT-1 projections, which implicitly is a "partial equilibrium" approach, being focussed on and solving for only relationships in the agricultural sector, it is tempting to suggest that the gains from a full scale agricultural liberalization may not be sufficient to justify the increased investments associated with the production possibilities thereby availed. Of course, a much more detailed (and intersectoral) analysis is required to answer the question: "how much agricultural investment is enough ?".

25.   Related, of course, would be the degree of agricultural liberalization to be encouraged as a matter of sectoral policy and expected trends in the associated agricultural performance indicators. Given the likely continued decline in the overall contribution from agricultural to GDP growth and foreign trade, [17] it could be argued that there is less urgency in completely liberalizing agriculture *vis-a-vis* other productive sectors in order to induce more efficient overall economic performance, since liberalization in agriculture already is much more pronounced, while the sheer numbers that would be affected directly by the shocks associated with a complete liberalization vastly exceed those who would be affected by comprehensive reform of urban-based activities.

---

[17] The latter being mitigated somewhat were China to unilaterally liberalize its foreign trade in grains.

Annex 4 Table 1. **Grains and Livestock Products: Projected Trends In Real Indicators to 1995**

(base year = 1986)

	Grain Production /a		Consumption				
			Total /a		Per Capita		
	Rate of Growth	Total Production	Grain	of which: Feeds	Grain (Direct)/b urban	rural	Livestock Products
	(% p.a.)	--(mil. tons)--			--------(kg/cap)--------		
Base Period (1986) /c	--	391.7	406.2	71.5	179.7	235.8	28.9
Projection Scenarios (1995)							
1. Base Run: /d	1.87	462.8	471.1	101.0	181.5	240.7	39.3
2. Grain Ration and Contract Procurement Prices Doubled: /e	1.88	463.1	470.8	100.7	181.4	240.9	39.2
3. Prolonged Agricultural Recession: /f	1.53	449.0	446.9	84.4	179.5	234.2	30.6
4. Sustained Agricultural Recovery: /g	2.11	472.8	484.3	111.1	182.5	243.6	44.8

Source: MAT-1 Model Projection Runs

Notes:

1. Productivity Growth Assumptions

	crop yields	feed conversion efficiencies
	(% p.a., 1986-1995)	
low =	1.0	0.9
moderate =	1.5	1.0
high =	1.75	1.05

2. Assumed Growth in Real Per Capita Incomes

	urban	rural
	(% p.a., 1986-1995)	
base run =	3.6	3.0
recession =	2.5	2.1
recovery: 3(a) =	5.1	4.3
3(b) =	6.4	5.4

/a based on Chinese definition: includes fine and coarse grains, some tubers and soybeans at unmilled weights.
/b milled equivalents
/c 1985-87 (= "1986").
/d moderate productivity increases, base run per capita income growth assumptions, essentially free trade in agricultural products.
/e other assumptions same as base run.
/f devaluation, but with restricted grain imports, low productivity growth and recession assumptions.
/g high productivity growth, income growth assumptions: "recovery 3(a)", others as in base run.

Annex 4 Table 2. **Comparison of Base Year Consumption With Base Run Projections**

	Base Year (1985-87)		Base Run Projection (1995)	
	million mt	% share	million mt	% share
CROPS				
TOTAL GRAINS	406.2	100	471.1	100
Table Grains:				
-Rice	177.6	44	190.3	40
-Wheat	93.3	23	113.9	24
-Coarse Grains	40.6	10	40.2	8
-Soybean	8.6	2	11.8	3
-Tubers	14.5	3	13.8	3
Animal Feeds:				
-Feedgrains	56.8	14	82.6	18
-Tubers	14.7	4	18.4	4
HORTICULTURE	175.4	100	208.0	100
Fruits	11.4	6	19.1	9
Vegetables	163.9	94	188.9	91
OTHER CROPS	22.9	100	34.1	100
Oilseeds	13.6	59	19.5	57
Cotton	3.7	16	4.9	14
Sugar	5.6	24	9.8	29
ANIMAL PRODUCTS	31.6	100	48.4	100
Pork	15.9	50	22.4	46
Poultry	1.5	5	2.4	5
Mutton	0.7	2	0.7	1
Beef	0.4	1	0.7	1
Milk	2.4	8	4.4	9
Eggs	4.5	14	7.6	16
Fish	6.2	20	10.3	22

Source: MAT-1 Projections

Annex 4 Table 3. Projected Changes in Direct Per Capita Consumption of Grains and Livestock Products (1985-1995)
(kg per capita per year)

| | GRAINS | | | | | | LIVESTOCK PRODUCTS | | | | | | |
	TOTAL GRAINS /a	Rice	Wheat	Coarse Grains	Soybeans	Tubers	TOTAL MEAT & FISH	White Meat Pork	White Meat Poultry	Red Meats	Milk	Eggs	Fish
Base Period (1985-1987)	220.1 (313.5)	105.0	68.8	30.3	5.7	10.4	22.3	14.4	1.3	1.0	2.3	4.3	5.6
Projection Scenarios (1995)													
1. Base Run /b	220.0 (312.5)	101.5	75.5	27.0	7.0	8.9	29.7	18.3	1.9	1.1	3.5	6.1	8.3
2. Ration and Contract Prices Doubled: /c	220.1 (312.6)	101.6	75.5	27.0	7.0	8.9	29.6	18.3	1.9	1.1	3.5	6.1	8.2
3. Prolonged Agricultural Recession /d	215.0 (306.1)	101.7	71.6	26.4	6.7	8.6	23.3	14.5	1.4	0.9	2.4	4.9	6.5
4. Sustained Agricultural Recovery /e	222.2 (315.2)	101.0	78.6	26.3	7.5	8.8	33.5	20.6	2.2	1.2	4.2	7.1	9.5

Rural/Urban Comparison

| | BASE PERIOD | | | BASE RUN | | | ADMINISTERED PRICES DOUBLED | | | RECESSION | | | RECOVERY | | |
	Rural	Urban	National Average	Rural	Urban	National Average	Rural	Urban	National Average	Rural	Urban	National Average	Rural	Urban	National Average
TOTAL GRAINS	235.8	179.7	220.1	240.7	181.5	220.0	240.9	181.4	220.1	234.2	179.5	215.0	243.6	182.5	222.2
Rice	115.9	76.9	105.0	116.7	73.5	101.5	116.6	73.8	101.6	116.3	74.6	101.7	116.9	71.7	101.0
Wheat	65.3	77.6	68.8	71.4	83.3	75.5	71.6	82.8	75.5	66.7	80.6	74.5	74.5	86.1	78.6
Coarse Grains	36.9	13.3	30.3	34.9	12.1	27.0	34.9	12.2	27.0	34.0	12.2	26.4	34.2	11.6	26.3
Soybeans	4.8	8.1	5.7	5.8	9.3	7.0	5.8	9.2	7.0	5.5	9.0	6.7	6.2	9.9	7.5
Tubers	12.9	8.9	10.4	11.9	3.3	8.9	11.9	3.3	8.9	11.6	3.2	8.6	11.8	3.2	8.8
TOTAL MEAT & FISH	16.9	36.4	22.3	24.3	39.5	29.7	24.5	39.0	29.6	19.0	31.4	23.3	27.4	44.8	33.5
Pork	12.0	20.6	14.4	16.1	22.5	18.3	16.2	22.2	18.3	12.5	18.1	14.5	18.0	25.3	20.6
Poultry	0.8	2.6	1.3	1.5	2.8	1.9	1.5	2.8	1.9	1.1	2.1	1.4	1.7	3.2	2.2
Red Meats	1.1	0.9	1.0	1.2	1.0	1.1	1.2	1.1	1.1	1.0	0.8	0.9	1.3	1.1	1.2
Fish	2.9	12.4	5.6	5.6	13.3	8.3	5.7	13.0	8.2	4.4	10.3	6.5	6.4	15.2	9.5

Source: MAT-1 Model Projection Runs

Notes: (see notes to Table 1)

/a milled equivalents (based on Chinese definition: includes fine and coarse grains, some tubers and soybeans). Totals in parentheses at unmilled weights.
/b moderate productivity increases, base run per capita income growth assumptions, essentially free trade in agric. products.
/c other assumptions same as base run.
/d devaluation, but with restricted grain imports, low productivity growth and recession assumptions.
/e high productivity growth, income growth assumptions; "recovery 3(a)", others as in base run.

Annex 4 Table 4. Projected Changes In Nutrition Levels (1986-1995)

Projection Scenarios

| | Daily Per Capita Intake of: | | | | | | | | |
| | CALORIES (Kcal) | | | PROTEIN (grams) | | | FATS (grams) | | |
	Rural	Urban	Total	Rural	Urban	Total	Rural	Urban	Total
1. Base Run /a	2880	2520	2754	76	81	78	40	56	46
2. Grain Ration and Contract Procurement Prices Doubled: /b	2885	2506	2753	76	81	78	40	56	46
3. Prolonged Agric. Recession /c	2768	2433	2651	73	78	75	37	53	43
4. Sustained Agric. Recovery /d	2952	2599	2828	79	85	81	43	61	49

Source: MAT-1 Model Projection Runs

Notes: (see notes to Table 1)

/a moderate productivity increases, base run per capita income growth assumptions (Table 1), essentially free trade in agric. products.
/b other assumptions same as base run.
/c devaluation, but with restricted grain imports, low productivity growth and recession assumptions.
/d high productivity and income growth assumptions, others as in base run.

Annex 4 Table 5. Projected Changes in the Composition of Agricultural Production (1986-1995)

(million metric tons)

	TOTAL GRAINS /a	TABLE GRAINS Rice	Wheat	Coarse Grains	Soybean	Tubers	ANIMAL FEEDS Grains /b	Tubers	OTHER OILS/INDUSTRIAL CROPS Oilseeds	Cotton	Sugar	MULTIPLE CROPPING INDEX
Base Period (1985-1987)	391.7	171.7	87.9	37.5	11.4	13.3	56.7	13.3	15.3	4.0	4.9	146
Projection Scenarios (1995)												
1. Base Run /c	462.8	193.5	111.4	42.7	12.9	13.8	73.9	14.6	19.0	5.1	7.5	151
2. Ration and Contract Prices Doubled: /d	463.1	193.6	111.4	42.7	12.9	13.8	74.0	14.7	19.0	5.1	7.4	151
3. Recession Scenarios:												
-low productivity growth /g	446.2	190.2	106.0	40.6	12.4	13.7	69.1	14.1	18.3	4.8	6.9	153
-general agric. recession /f	449.0	190.8	107.9	40.2	12.3	13.4	70.0	14.4	18.0	4.7	7.4	154
4. Recovery/Trade Reform Scenarios:												
-agricultural "recovery" /g	472.8	194.4	115.5	42.8	13.3	13.6	78.1	15.2	20.2	5.3	8.0	151
-recovery and trade policy reform /h	472.7	200.2	112.8	43.0	13.3	13.5	75.0	15.0	20.2	5.3	7.7	154

	HORTICULTURE Fruits	Vegetables	TOTAL MEATS & FISH	LIVESTOCK PRODUCTS White Meats Pork	Poultry	Red Meats	Milk	Others Eggs	Fish
Base Period (1985-1987)	14.1	167.9	29.1	17.6	1.9	1.3	3.3	5.6	8.3
Projection Scenarios (1995)									
1. Base Run /c	18.1	189.3	33.3	20.5	2.1	1.3	3.5	7.0	9.4
2. Ration and Contract Prices Doubled: /d	18.1	189.4	33.2	20.5	2.1	1.3	3.5	7.0	9.4
3. Recession Scenarios:									
-low productivity growth /g	16.9	187.3	28.3	17.5	1.8	1.1	2.9	6.0	8.0
-general agricultural recession /f	16.7	186.4	28.6	17.7	1.8	1.1	2.9	6.1	8.1
4. Recovery/Trade Reform Scenarios:									
-general agric. "recovery" /g	19.1	192.0	31.5	19.5	1.9	1.3	2.4	6.8	8.8
-recovery and trade policy reform /h	18.0	192.1	26.3	16.2	1.6	1.3	1.7	5.8	7.2

Source: MAT-1 Model Projection Runs

Notes: (see notes to Table 1)

/a based on Chinese definition: includes fine and coarse grains, some tubers and soybeans at unmilled weights.
/b mainly coarse grains.
/c moderate productivity increases, base run per capita income growth assumptions, essentially free trade in agric. products.
/d other assumptions same as base run.
/e low productivity growth plus base run assumptions.
/f devaluation, but with restricted grain imports, low productivity growth and recession assumptions.
/g high productivity growth, income growth assumptions: "recovery 3(a)", others as in base run.
/h moderate productivity growth, "recovery 3(b)" assumptions, devaluation and free trade in agricultural products.

174

Annex 4 Table 6. Projected Price Trends to 1995 Grains and Livestock Products

(base year = 1986)

Scenario	Domestic Price Trends ——(total % change: 1986-95)——					
	All Crops	Rice	Wheat	Coarse Grains	Soybeans	Livestock Products
1. Base Run /a	0.1	-6.9	3.4	11.3	-6.7	15.6
2. Grain Ration and Contract Procurement Prices Doubled: /b	0.1	-6.8	3.3	10.9	-6.8	15.3
3. Recession Scenarios:						
-low productivity growth /c	6.0	-1.3	11.4	18.5	-6.1	20.6
-general agric. recession /d	8.0	-0.5	17.4	28.9	-8.1	30.5
4. Recovery/Trade Reform Scenarios:						
-general agric. "recovery" /e	0.5	-10.4	4.0	13.8	-4.7	18.9
-recovery and trade policy reform /f	5.0	-0.6	6.0	26.8	0.0	23.9

Domestic/International Price Ratio

(constant 1985 prices, 1986=100)

Year	Rice	Wheat	Maize	Soybeans
1986-	100	100	100	100
1995-	99	137	129	92

Source: MAT-1 Projections

Notes: (see notes to Table 1)

Footnotes /a - /f: (see ff /g - /h, bottom of Table 5)

Annex 4 Table 7. Projected Changes GVAO and Sector Financing Requirements (1986-1995)

| | GROSS VALUE OF AGRICULTURAL OUTPUT | NET SUBSIDIES | | | ANNUAL INVESTMENT REQUIREMENT (1986-1995) |
		Hidden Consumer Subsidies	Indirect Producer Tax	Opportunity Cost to the Economy /a	
	------------------------------(1986 Yuan Billions)------------------------------				
Base Period (1985-1987)	156.2	40.7	19.0	21.6	--
Projection Scenarios (1995)					
1. Base Run /b	184.2	24.6	5.7	18.9	16.1
2. Grain Ration and Contract Procurement Prices Doubled: /c	184.1	13.9	2.9	11.0	16.1
3. Prolonged Agric. Recession /d	173.8	28.1	8.1	19.9	10.1
4. Sustained Agric. Recovery /e	191.7	24.2	5.5	18.8	20.4

Source: MAT-1 Model Projection Runs

/a excludes import subsidies and taxes, and coverage of grain bureaux' operating losses.
/b moderate productivity increases, base run per capita income growth assumptions (notes to Table 1), essentially free trade in agricultural products.
/c other assumptions same as base run.
/d devaluation, but with restricted grain imports, low productivity and income growth assumptions.
/e high productivity growth and income growth, other assumptions as in base run.

ELASTICITIES OF DEMAND AND SUPPLY EMPLOYED IN THE MAT-1 MODEL

A. Income Elasticities of Demand

	Code	Urban	Rural
Food Grains (direct demand)			
Rice	RIC	-0.1	0.0
Wheat	WHE	+0.15	+0.25
Coarse Grains	COG	-0.2	-0.1
Tubers	TUB	-0.2	-0.1
Soybeans	SOY	+0.3	+0.45
Feed Grains (indirect demand)			
Grains:			
-pork	GPK	+0.5	+0.75
-poultry	GPL	+1.0	+2.0
-beef	GBF	+0.75	+1.0
-mutton	GMU	-0.4	-0.2
-milk	GMI	+1.5	+2.5
-eggs	GEG	+0.8	+1.2
-fish	GFI	+0.75	+1.5
Tubers:			
-pork	TPK	+0.5	+0.75
-beef	TBF	+0.75	+1.0
-mutton	TMU	-0.4	-0.2
-milk	TMI	+1.5	+2.5
Other Commodities			
Oilseed	OIL	+0.5	+0.65
Sugar	SUG	+1.5	+0.2
Vegetables	VEG	0.0	+0.1
Fruit	FRU	+2.0	+2.5
Cotton	COT	+0.3	+0.4
Pork	PRK	+0.5	+0.75
Poultry	PLT	+1.3	+2.2
Beef	BEF	+0.75	+1.0
Mutton	MUT	-0.4	-0.2
Milk	MIL	+1.5	+2.5
Egg	EGG	+0.8	+1.2
Fish	FIS	+0.75	+1.5

177

B. Price Elasticities of Demand

	Code	Urban	Rural
Food Grains (direct demand)			
Rice	RIC	-0.1	-0.05
Wheat	WHE	-0.2	-0.25
Coarse Grains	COG	-0.3	-0.2
Tubers	TUB	-0.3	-0.2
Soybeans	SOY	-0.4	-0.45
Feed Grains (indirect demand)			
Grains:			
-pork	GPK	-0.5	-0.6
-poultry	GPL	-0.9	-1.2
-beef	GBF	-0.8	-0.85
-mutton	GMU	-0.6	-0.7
-milk	GMI	-0.9	-1.1
-eggs	GEG	-0.5	-0.6
-fish	GFI	-0.5	-0.7
Tubers:			
-pork	TPK	-0.5	-0.6
-beef	TBF	-0.8	-0.85
-mutton	TMU	-0.6	-0.7
-milk	TMI	-0.9	-1.1
Other Commodities			
Oilseed	OIL	-0.3	-0.35
Sugar	SUG	-0.2	-0.3
Vegetables	VEG	-0.3	-0.2
Fruit	FRU	-0.6	-0.7
Cotton	COT	-0.1	-0.15
Pork	PRK	-0.5	-0.6
Poultry	PLT	-0.9	-1.2
Beef	BEF	-0.8	-0.85
Mutton	MUT	-0.6	-0.7
Milk	MIL	-0.9	-1.1
Egg	EGG	-0.5	-0.6
Fish	FIS	-0.5	-1.2

C. Price Elasticities of Supply

Table 1

	RIC	WHE	COG	TUB	SOY	GPK	GPL	GBF	GMU	GMT	GEG	GFI	TRK	TBF	TMU	TMI
RIC	0.2															
WHE		0.2				0.3										
COG			0.3				0.3	0.2								
TUB				0.3									0.3			
SOY					0.2											
GPK			-0.2			-0.31										
GPL			-0.2				-0.03									
GBF			-0.2					-0.02								
GMU			-0.2						0.3			0.4				
GMT			-0.2							0.2	1.0					
GEG											-0.06					
GFI												-0.03				
TRK				-0.3									-0.27	0.3		
TBF				-0.3										-0.02	0.3	
TMU				-0.3											-0.01	0.3
TMI																-0.01

Table 2

	OIL	SUG	VEG	FRU	COT	PRK	PLT	BEF	MUT	MIL	EGG	FIS
OIL	0.4											
SUG		0.2										
VEG			0.5									
FRU				0.05								
COT					0.3							
PRK						1.0						
PLT							1.0					
BEF								0.2				
MUT									0.3			
MIL										0.2		
EGG											1.0	
FIS												0.4

Distributors of World Bank Publications

ARGENTINA
Carlos Hirsch, SRL
Galeria Guemes
Florida 165, 4th Floor-Ofc. 453/465
1333 Buenos Aires

AUSTRALIA, PAPUA NEW GUINEA, FIJI, SOLOMON ISLANDS, VANUATU, AND WESTERN SAMOA
D.A. Books & Journals
648 Whitehorse Road
Mitcham 3132
Victoria

AUSTRIA
Gerold and Co.
Graben 31
A-1011 Wien

BAHRAIN
Bahrain Research and Consultancy
Associates Ltd.
P.O. Box 22103
Manama Town 317

BANGLADESH
Micro Industries Development
Assistance Society (MIDAS)
House 5, Road 16
Dhanmondi R/Area
Dhaka 1209

Branch offices:
Main Road
Maijdee Court
Noakhali - 3800

76, K.D.A. Avenue
Kulna

BELGIUM
Jean De Lannoy
Av. du Roi 202
1060 Brussels

CANADA
Le Diffuseur
C.P. 85, 1501B rue Ampère
Boucherville, Québec
J4B 5E6

CHINA
China Financial & Economic
Publishing House
8, Da Fo Si Dong Jie
Beijing

COLOMBIA
Infoenlace Ltda.
Apartado Aereo 34270
Bogota D.E.

COTE D'IVOIRE
Centre d'Edition et de Diffusion
Africaines (CEDA)
04 B.P. 541
Abidjan 04 Plateau

CYPRUS
MEMRB Information Services
P.O. Box 2098
Nicosia

DENMARK
SamfundsLitteratur
Rosenoerns Allé 11
DK-1970 Frederiksberg C

DOMINICAN REPUBLIC
Editora Taller, C. por A.
Restauración e Isabel la Católica 309
Apartado Postal 2190
Santo Domingo

EL SALVADOR
Fusades
Avenida Manuel Enrique Araujo #3530
Edificio SISA, 1er. Piso
San Salvador

EGYPT, ARAB REPUBLIC OF
Al Ahram
Al Galaa Street
Cairo

The Middle East Observer
8 Chawarbi Street
Cairo

FINLAND
Akateeminen Kirjakauppa
P.O. Box 128
SF-00101
Helsinki 10

FRANCE
World Bank Publications
66, avenue d'Iéna
75116 Paris

GERMANY
UNO-Verlag
Poppelsdorfer Allee 55
D-5300 Bonn 1

GREECE
KEME
24, Ippodamou Street Platia Plastiras
Athens-11635

GUATEMALA
Librerias Piedra Santa
5a. Calle 7-55
Zona 1
Guatemala City

HONG KONG, MACAO
Asia 2000 Ltd.
6 Fl., 146 Prince Edward
Road, W.
Kowloon
Hong Kong

INDIA
Allied Publishers Private Ltd.
751 Mount Road
Madras - 600 002

Branch offices:
15 J.N. Heredia Marg
Ballard Estate
Bombay - 400 038

13/14 Asaf Ali Road
New Delhi - 110 002

17 Chittaranjan Avenue
Calcutta - 700 072

Jayadeva Hostel Building
5th Main Road Gandhinagar
Bangalore - 560 009

3-5-1129 Kachiguda Cross Road
Hyderabad - 500 027

Prarthana Flats, 2nd Floor
Near Thakore Baug, Navrangpura
Ahmedabad - 380 009

Patiala House
16-A Ashok Marg
Lucknow - 226 001

INDONESIA
Pt. Indira Limited
Jl. Sam Ratulangi 37
P.O. Box 181
Jakarta Pusat

ITALY
Licosa Commissionaria Sansoni SPA
Via Benedetto Fortini, 120/10
Casella Postale 552
50125 Florence

JAPAN
Eastern Book Service
37-3, Hongo 3-Chome, Bunkyo-ku 113
Tokyo

KENYA
Africa Book Service (E.A.) Ltd.
P.O. Box 45245
Nairobi

KOREA, REPUBLIC OF
Pan Korea Book Corporation
P.O. Box 101, Kwangwhamun
Seoul

KUWAIT
MEMRB Information Services
P.O. Box 5465

MALAYSIA
University of Malaya Cooperative
Bookshop, Limited
P.O. Box 1127, Jalan Pantai Baru
Kuala Lumpur

MEXICO
INFOTEC
Apartado Postal 22-860
14060 Tlalpan, Mexico D.F.

MOROCCO
Société d'Etudes Marketing Marocaine
12 rue Mozart, Bd. d'Anfa
Casablanca

NETHERLANDS
InOr-Publikaties b.v.
P.O. Box 14
7240 BA Lochem

NEW ZEALAND
Hills Library and Information Service
Private Bag
New Market
Auckland

NIGERIA
University Press Limited
Three Crowns Building Jericho
Private Mail Bag 5095
Ibadan

NORWAY
Narvesen Information Center
Book Department
P.O. Box 6125 Etterstad
N-0602 Oslo 6

OMAN
MEMRB Information Services
P.O. Box 1613, Seeb Airport
Muscat

PAKISTAN
Mirza Book Agency
65, Shahrah-e-Quaid-e-Azam
P.O. Box No. 729
Lahore 3

PERU
Editorial Desarrollo SA
Apartado 3824
Lima

PHILIPPINES
International Book Center
Fifth Floor, Filipinas Life Building
Ayala Avenue, Makati
Metro Manila

POLAND
ORPAN
Palac Kultury i Nauki
00-901 Warszawa

PORTUGAL
Livraria Portugal
Rua Do Carmo 70-74
1200 Lisbon

SAUDI ARABIA, QATAR
Jarir Book Store
P.O. Box 3196
Riyadh 11471

MEMRB Information Services
Branch offices:
Al Alsa Street
Al Dahna Center
First Floor
P.O. Box 7188
Riyadh

Haji Abdullah Alireza Building
King Khaled Street
P.O. Box 3969
Damman

33, Mohammed Hassan Awad Street
P.O. Box 5978
Jeddah

SINGAPORE, TAIWAN, MYANMAR, BRUNEI
Information Publications
Private, Ltd.
02-06 1st Fl., Pei-Fu Industrial
Bldg.
24 New Industrial Road
Singapore 1953

SOUTH AFRICA, BOTSWANA
For single titles:
Oxford University Press
Southern Africa
P.O. Box 1141
Cape Town 8000

For subscription orders:
International Subscription Service
P.O. Box 41095
Craighall
Johannesburg 2024

SPAIN
Mundi-Prensa Libros, S.A.
Castello 37
28001 Madrid

Librería Internacional AEDOS
Consell de Cent, 391
08009 Barcelona

SRI LANKA AND THE MALDIVES
Lake House Bookshop
P.O. Box 244
100, Sir Chittampalam A.
Gardiner Mawatha
Colombo 2

SWEDEN
For single titles:
Fritzes Fackboksforetaget
Regeringsgatan 12, Box 16356
S-103 27 Stockholm

For subscription orders:
Wennergren-Williams AB
Box 30004
S-104 25 Stockholm

SWITZERLAND
For single titles:
Librairie Payot
6, rue Grenus
Case postale 381
CH 1211 Geneva 11

For subscription orders:
Librairie Payot
Service des Abonnements
Case postale 3312
CH 1002 Lausanne

TANZANIA
Oxford University Press
P.O. Box 5299
Dar es Salaam

THAILAND
Central Department Store
306 Silom Road
Bangkok

TRINIDAD & TOBAGO, ANTIGUA BARBUDA, BARBADOS, DOMINICA, GRENADA, GUYANA, JAMAICA, MONTSERRAT, ST. KITTS & NEVIS, ST. LUCIA, ST. VINCENT & GRENADINES
Systematics Studies Unit
#9 Watts Street
Curepe
Trinidad, West Indies

UNITED ARAB EMIRATES
MEMRB Gulf Co.
P.O. Box 6097
Sharjah

UNITED KINGDOM
Microinfo Ltd.
P.O. Box 3
Alton, Hampshire GU34 2PG
England

VENEZUELA
Libreria del Este
Aptdo. 60.337
Caracas 1060-A

YUGOSLAVIA
Jugoslovenska Knjiga
P.O. Box 36
Trg Republike
YU-11000 Belgrade

Prices and credit terms vary from country to country. Consult your local distributor before placing an order.

U.S.S.R.

JAPAN

Sea of Japan

REP. OF KOREA

D.P.R. OF KOREA

PACIFIC OCEAN

HEILONGJIANG

Harbin

1

Changchun

JILIN

Shenyang

LIAONING

Yellow Sea

East China Sea

Shanghai

SHANGHAI

Nanjing

JIANGSU

ZHEJIANG

Hangzhou

Fuzhou

FUJIAN

TAIWAN

PHILIPPINES

Jinan

SHANDONG

Tianjin

TIANJIN

BEIJING

BEIJING

Shijiazhuang

HEBEI

Hefei

ANHUI

4

Nanchang

JIANGXI

Wuhan

HUBEI

Zhengzhou

HENAN

Taiyuan

SHANXI

Hohhot

NEI MONGOL

Xi'an

SHAANXI

Yinchuan

NINGXIA

Lanzhou

GANSU

Xining

QINGHAI

3

Urumqi

XINJIANG

XIZANG

Lhasa

NEPAL

AFGHANISTAN

MONGOLIA

U.S.S.R.

Chengdu

SICHUAN

5

Kunming

YUNNAN

Guiyang

GUIZHOU

HUNAN

Chengdu

Nanning

GUANGXI

GUANGDONG

Guangzhou

HONG KONG, U.K.

Macao, Port.

HAINAN

Haikou

South China Sea

6

VIET NAM

LAO PEOPLE'S DEM. REP.

THAILAND

MYANMAR

Yangtze

GRAIN PRODUCTION REGIONS

1 North-east
2 North
3 North-west
4 Middle and Lower Reaches of Yangtze
5 South-west
6 South

CHINA

GRAIN PRODUCTION GROWTH RATES BY PROVINCE, 1983-1987

Grain Production Region Boundaries (Administrative and Planning)

Percent Per Annum

>4.0
2.1 - 4.0
0.0 - 2.0
<0.0

Grand Canal
Selected Towns
Province Capitals
National Capital
Province Boundaries
International Boundaries

KILOMETERS   0   100   200   300   400   500   600   700   800
MILES   0   100   200   300   400   500

JUNE 1991